Cattle Droving, Cotton and Landownership:
a Cumbrian Family Saga

Cattle Droving, Cotton and Landownership:
a Cumbrian Family Saga

Peter Roebuck

Emeritus Professor of History,
University of Ulster

CUMBERLAND AND WESTMORLAND
ANTIQUARIAN AND ARCHAEOLOGICAL SOCIETY
2014

Cumberland and Westmorland
Antiquarian and Archaeological Society
Hon. General Editor
Professor Colin Richards

Cattle Droving, Cotton and Landownership:
a Cumbrian Family Saga

For
Fiona, Thomas and James

EXTRA SERIES NO. XLIII

ISBN 978 1 873124 66 6

Printed by
Titus Wilson & Son, Kendal
2014

Contents

List of Maps, Illustrations and Pedigrees

Preface

Although a regular visitor for over 40 years, I came to live in Cumbria only in 2007. Fiona and I then bought Old Town House, off the A6 just south of High Hesket and half way between Carlisle and Penrith. Recently retired from Northern Ireland, we wanted to retain a base there, but also to re-establish roots in the north of England where both of us had spent formative years. We bought the house because we liked it, knowing nothing about its origins beyond the estate agent's blurb, which described it as 'early eighteenth-century'. Within a week Fiona met the late Rita Blake, then chairman of the Hesket Local History Group, who told her that she had information about the house which would interest us. Rita shared with us her correspondence of the early 1990s with a Robert Parker of Morecambe[1]. This referred to the will of March 1686 of a Christopher Parker, which mentioned 'my new dwelling house at Hesket' – Old Town House. Having found the will and its associated inventory on my first visit to the Cumbria Archives Service in Carlisle, I determined to research the history of the property and the family who built it. This book records what I found.

It is a remarkable story, a family saga. The Parkers originated as Cumbrian yeomen farmers at Wreay, a village just south of Carlisle. Before Old Town House was built c.1680, and for a century afterwards, the family prospered by servicing the expanding cattle-droving trade and through success in the marriage market. Then, during the later eighteenth century, a group of them went south to Lancashire to seek their fortune in the cotton industry. Over the next three decades they were extremely enterprising and amassed considerable wealth - manufacturing cloth, marketing it widely, and later developing a chain of warehouses for let in central Manchester. In the early 1820s, while still developing their businesses, they returned to Cumbria after purchasing estates at Warwick Hall near Carlisle and at Skirwith Abbey near Penrith. Descended from generations of yeomen farmers and then having been industrialists and merchants, they were granted arms and became members of the Cumbrian landed gentry. Old Town House was retained throughout and passed out of their possession only when, along with Warwick Hall, it was sold at the turn of the nineteenth century. An indirect male heir, who had insufficient means or will to sustain his position, chose to live in the south of England and sold all his property in Cumberland.

Like most families the Parkers had their share of triumphs and tragedies. There are vibrant human elements in their story, but much more. Their

---

1   Copies of letters, in the author's possession, from Robert Parker to Rita Blake of 31 July & 3 Nov. 1992, and 29 Jan. 1993.

ancestors witnessed the mayhem in the borders during the closing years of Elizabeth I's reign and, later, the successful efforts of James I to bring order to the area. They played an active role in the subsequent growth of the cattle-droving trade, the extent of whose impact on the regional economy is largely hidden because, unlike all other heavy goods, cattle moved themselves to market: but there is much more than a glimpse of it here. Servicing the droving trade – accommodating and feeding the cattle and their drovers – was the chief source of the Parkers' income for 150 years. It was a landless youngest son, Robert Parker, who first became involved in the cotton trade just when it was leading the process of industrialisation in England. He was financed by a mortgage on the property at Old Town, and was eventually joined in business in Stockport and Manchester by his eldest brother, Thomas, who owned the ancestral home; by the latter's three sons, Thomas, Robert junior and William; and by their cousin, Christopher Parker of Petteril Green. Together, all six men became manufacturers, merchants and philanthropists, exported cotton goods all over the world, and contributed substantially to the urban development of central Manchester. On returning to Cumbria they were energetically engaged in improvements at, and around, both Warwick Hall and Skirwith Abbey, though they were obliged to make drastic adjustments to their operations following the sudden mental incapacity of Robert junior. By the mid-1820s they were respected senior members of the county community. Decline when it came was due primarily to the division of their property following failure in the direct male line, the one area of their lives over which they had least control. The estate having been split from 1856, the fortunes of the various branches of the family declined and, along with Warwick Hall, the Old Town property was sold to clear mounting debts. In all its variety over this very long period the experience of the Parkers casts considerable light on the economic and social history of north-west England, and of links between Cumbria and Lancashire in particular[2].

Although I have received a great deal of assistance with my work, gratefully acknowledged, I alone am responsible for the views expressed here. Not to have recorded them would have been ungenerous to the good fortune which brought me to Old Town. This has been a labour of love for a place.

Old Town House,
June 2014

---

[2]   In addition to other material, this study draws on a number of collections of manuscripts – see Bibliography. Two in particular are so extensive that, if undue length and repetition are to be avoided, special treatment is required. So, although all other references adhere to the standard CWAAS usage, abbreviations have been adopted for citations from these two collections, as follows: Pkr A for the manuscripts drawn from the seven large boxes of papers in the Newbiggin Hall Collection, held at CAS (C), WDX/Pkr/1/1-7; and Pkr B for the 50 volumes/files of copy documents and other papers collected by Robert Parker of Morecambe (d. 1994), held at CAS (C), WDX/Pkr/2/1-50.

Acknowledgements

In the course of researching and writing this book I have received much help. The late Rita Blake, then chairman of the Hesket Local History Group, set me on my way by sharing her correspondence with the late Robert Parker of Morecambe, who had devoted over two decades of his retirement to collecting material and compiling comprehensive, annotated pedigrees of the various branches of the Parker family. She also gave me copies of material relating to High Hesket and, above all, directed me to the two extensive collections of Parker documents then held at the Kendal office of the Cumbria Archives Service. My earliest searches were facilitated by the staff at Kendal. Later, through the intervention of David Bowcock, until recently senior archivist at Carlisle, without whose help in this regard I could not have embarked on a book-length study, these collections were re-located to Carlisle. In so far as they relate to Cumbria they are concerned almost exclusively with the north-east of the county; and, indeed, the new archival facilities at Petteril Bank Road are attached to one of the several houses which the Parkers bought, and sold, during the nineteenth and twentieth centuries. The splendid facilities there are only exceeded by the quality of the service delivered by the staff and I owe a special debt to all those who helped me, particularly David Bowcock, Tom Robson, Louise Smith, Simone Rouse, Lynda Collin, Chris Brader and Francesca Halfacree. I also extend warm thanks for their assistance to Bronwen Simpson of Stockport Heritage Services and to Andrew Lucas of the Stockport Local Heritage Library. I am grateful to James Peters, archivist at the University of Manchester Library, for permission to incorporate material from the on-line edition of the Oldknow Papers.

All historical research is conducted against the background of earlier published work and so libraries are as important as record offices. I am grateful for assistance from the staff of the library of the University of Lancaster; of the local studies collection of the central library in Carlisle (particularly Stephen White); and of Penrith Library. Special thanks are extended to Janet Peden and her colleagues in the Coleraine library of the University of Ulster, my former employer, who repeatedly went out of their way to help me. I have also been able to draw freely on the unrivalled knowledge of the local history of north Cumbria of Denis Perriam, who could not have been more generous in anticipating and responding to my queries. I am indebted to the following for helping me to illustrate this book: Tom Ritchie for illustrations 1, 4, 5, 7 and 20; the Cumbria Archives Service at Carlisle for 9, 10, 11, 13 and 14; James Heald for 15; Denis Perriam for 16; Stephen White for 17 and 19; and Carlisle City Council for 18. The maps at 3, 8 and 12 were made by

Bryan Harper. The pedigrees at 2 and 21 were compiled by the late Robert Parker of Morecambe and are at Pkr B, 5. The photograph at 6 is in my possession.

I am deeply grateful to Bryan Harper of Titus Wilson and Son for the care with which he took my manuscript through the press. I also take pleasure in testifying to the excellence of the guidance and assistance with the entire work which I have received from the series editor, Professor Colin Richards.

I pay high tribute to my close friends at Old Town, Harry King and Mark Lambert, both splendid neighbours, who have endured innumerable discussions about the Parkers and been a constant source of advice, encouragement and good fellowship. In High Hesket Mr. & Mrs. Robert Ferguson gave me numerous records relating to the property at Old Town as well as personal testimony of their experience when resident here; and Mr.& Mrs. Arthur Graves kindly showed me material in their possession relating to its eventual sale.

I am greatly indebted to a number of fellow historians for comments on drafts of this work as it has progressed - Professor Michael Mullett, Dr. Gerry O'Brien, Adrian Allen, Steve Ickringill and Trevor Parkhill. All have willingly supported my endeavours and made numerous helpful suggestions. While they must not be held responsible for this final version, I thank them warmly.

During the later stages of my work I enjoyed an unexpected bonus, meeting several members of the Parker family. Simon and Kate Parker, who recently came north to live permanently in Cumbria, were full of enthusiasm for my task; and it was they who tracked down the portrait of Thomas Parker (1784-1828). With great generosity Cathie Parker of Maughold, Isle of Man, gave me unfettered access at Old Town to the surviving papers of her late father, Oliver Parker; and seeing Old Town for the first time, her brother, another Simon, subsequently retrieved them.

For many years my two sons, Tom and James, have not only tolerated my intoxication with the past but have sustained it in ways of which they (but certainly not I) may be only dimly aware: any historian of a family's history inevitably reflects on their own experience, and I do so entirely benignly. My greatest debt, beyond a shadow of a doubt, is to my wife, Fiona, who, in addition to her personal support throughout my work, has masterminded the refurbishment of the house and garden at Old Town and in doing so has brought both back to vibrant life. The dedication of this book registers my deep gratitude to all three of them for their assistance with this book and, indeed, with so very much more.

Figure 1. Old Town House today.

Introduction

The twin threats of disease and death stalked the land in pre-industrial times. Infant mortality was so high as to be commonplace, with up to half of those born dying before the age of five. Beyond five, life expectancy rose steadily. Even so, local communities were periodically devastated by waves of infection for which there was no sure remedy and to which they had little resistance. This is what happened in England during the period 1680-86, when mortality rates reached crisis levels in all but 1683-84. In the parish of St. Mary's, Hesket-in-the-Forest in north-east Cumberland, burials were more numerous during the 1680s than during either the 1670s or the 1690s[1]. It was a grim decade.

Towards the end of the winter of 1685-86 one of those cut down as a relatively young man was Christopher Parker, a yeoman farmer. He probably spent his last days in the older and larger of the two houses which he owned in the district: that at Carleton, just south-east of the city of Carlisle, and two miles north of the village of Wreay where previous generations of the family had lived. His father had died in 1683 and was perhaps another casualty of the wave of local sickness. No doubt helped by his solicitor, Christopher executed a will on 25 March 1686. He died soon afterwards, for the will was proved on 10 April. We do not know when he was born: but having married in 1669 and been without children for almost a decade, he and his wife, Jane, then produced four – a son and three daughters – in quick succession. At his death Christopher was probably in his mid-to-late-30s[2].

The will began with the customary invocations. 'Sick and weak in body', Christopher thanked God that he was 'of good and perfect memory' and committed his 'soul into the hands of...my Creator'. He went on to bequeath to his only son and heir, Thomas, his prized items of furniture - two 'arkes' [large wooden chests] and two tables, a pair in each of his houses at Carleton and Old Town. There were five small bequests, mainly to younger relations: two, each for ten shillings; and three, each for five shillings. Beyond these, the rest of his personal estate, valued at £90.3s.0d., was left in equal parts to his three daughters, Anne, Dorothy and Margaret. When this was divided three

---

1   E.A. Wrigley & R.S. Schofield, *The Population History of England 1541-1871: A Reconstruction* (London, 1981), 249-252, 295, 341, 363; R.A. Houston, *The Population History of Britain and Ireland 1500-1750* (London, 1992), 47-57; CAS (C), PR 35/31, Parish Registers (typescript transcripts at 35/131).

2   Pkr B, 28, Christopher's Will of 25 Mar. and Inventory of 31 Apr. 1686. Throughout this study all names and dates of births, marriages and deaths, and details of all descents and demographic outcomes, are drawn from the annotated pedigrees of the nine branches of the Parker family compiled by Robert Parker at Pkr B, 5 (Figure 2).

Figure 2. Pedigree of the Old Town branch of the Parker Family.

THOMAS (c.1630-1683), yeoman farmer of Greane Head, Wreay, had issue:

1. CHRISTOPHER of whom presently.
2. WILLIAM m. 1672 Mary Hodgson and d. 1715, having issue Margaret (b. 1686) and Mary (m. 1703 John Scott).
3. THOMAS m. 1679 Frances Ollivant and d. 1701, having issue Jane (b. 1681, m. 1704 John Wilson and d. 1709).
4. ROBERT m. 1683 Mary Barrow and d. 1705, having issue Richard (1684-94), Robert (b. 1696) and Sara (b. 1697).

CHRISTOPHER (? – 1686), yeoman farmer of Carleton and Old Town, m. Jane Holme (d. 1715) and had issue:

1. THOMAS of whom presently.
2. ANNE m. 1698 John Hesket.
3. DOROTHY m. 1702 Bernard Barton.
4. MARGARET m. 1716 George Graham.

THOMAS (1678-1760), yeoman farmer of Old Town, m. 1696 Mary Nicolson of Park Broom, Linstock (d. 1747), and had issue:

1. CHRISTOPHER of whom presently.
2. BARBARA b. 1698, m. 1724 Thomas Nicolson of Park Broom
3. THOMAS b. 1701 and d. 1755 unmarried.
4. JOSEPH b. 1705, Curate of Wreay (1738-1783).
5. JOHN b. 1706, Curate of Wreay (1733-1735).
6. ELIZABETH b. 1710, m. 1731 William Coulthard.
7. ISAAC b. 1712, d. 1733.
8. MARY b. 1717, m. 1738 William Nelson.
9. CHARLES b. 1723.
10. BEATRICE m. Joseph James.

CHRISTOPHER (1696-1776), yeoman farmer of Old Town and of Orton and Gilse, Westmorland, m. 1731 Agnes, 3rd d. of Anthony Holme of Dillicar Park, Westmorland (1702-1788), and had issue:

1. THOMAS of whom presently.
2. ANTHONY of Carleton (1735-1820).
3. JOHN (1737-1779), Curate of Orton and then of Selside.
4. ROBERT (1744-1815) of Heaton Norris, Stockport, m. 1808 Sarah Pollitt (d. 1856).

THOMAS (1732-1807), yeoman farmer of Old Town and of Stockport, m. firstly 1765 Margaret Wray of Gowborough Hall (d. 1782 without issue), and secondly 1783 Jane Faulder of Beaumont Hall (d. 1810), having issue:

1. THOMAS (1784-1828), merchant and then gentleman of Old Town, Stockport and Warwick Hall, m. 1809 Mary Heald of Portwood, near Stockport (d. 1857), without issue.
2. ROBERT (1787-1850), merchant and then gentleman of Stockport, Warwick Hall and Skirwith Abbey, d. unmarried.
3. WILLIAM (1789-1856), merchant and then gentleman of Old Town, Stockport, Warwick Hall and Skirwith Abbey, d. unmarried.

ways the individual bequests to the young girls were moderate. Nevertheless, the gross value of Christopher's personal estate placed him among the more substantial of the region's yeomen farmers; and, noticeably, nothing other than the 'arkes' and tables went to his heir, Thomas, who he clearly felt was well provided for by his inheritance. At that point all four of Christopher's children were very young, the eldest, Thomas, being only seven or eight years old. A key clause in his will came last: the appointment of his three brothers – William, Thomas and Robert – as his executors and the guardians of his children until they came of age.

There are three significant features of this will. Firstly, it was much more detailed and precise than that made by his father three years earlier and, indeed, than those left by the next two generations of the family. Christopher's executors and the guardians of his children were urged to 'educate and bring them up according to their quality and degree'; and in particular, and somewhat anachronistically (for the abolition of the Court of Wards during the Interregnum had not been reversed at the restoration of Charles II in 1660), they were vested with responsibility for 'the wardship of the said Thomas and of all of his lands and tenements'[3]. Here was a man who, though distressed by the prospect of his early demise, felt that he had bettered his fortunes and done well for himself and his family. Few contemporary yeomen farmers addressed their executors so formally or possessed two houses and adjacent properties some six miles apart.

Yet, secondly, what grounds were there for this conviction? Why, and how, did Christopher feel that he had moved the family on? The answer to these questions is two-fold. Thomas, his heir, inherited 'lands and tenements' which were more substantial than Christopher had come into. The location of his property was also significant. That near Carleton was next to one of the main southern cattle-droving routes out of Carlisle; while that at Old Town lay further south on the same route, just beyond the village of High Hesket[4] and opposite the junction with another drove road. The latter came from the north-east, from Bewcastle or Longtown via Brampton, proceeded down the east bank of the River Eden, passed through Armathwaite with its bridge over the river, and then linked with the other route at Old Town some two-and-a-half miles away[5]. Near Old Town, on land to the north of the road from Armathwaite, was a small lake, Tarn Wadling, where the cattle could be watered towards the end of their day's journey. Sited a little further on at the

3   Following confirmation of the Court's abolition at the Restoration, responsibility for the oversight of the affairs of minors passed to the Court of Chancery – P. Roebuck, 'Post-Restoration Landownership: The Impact of the Abolition of Wardship', *Journal of British Studies*, xviii, 1 (Fall, 1978).

4   Until the later 18th century High Hesket and Low Hesket were known respectively as Upper Hesket and Nether Hesket. The modern names are used here throughout.

5   J.D. Marshall, 'Drovers, Fairs and Cattle Routes' in *Old Lakeland: Some Cumbrian Social History* (Newton Abbot, 1971), 77, 93.

Figure 3. Map showing locations mentioned in the text: Cumbria.

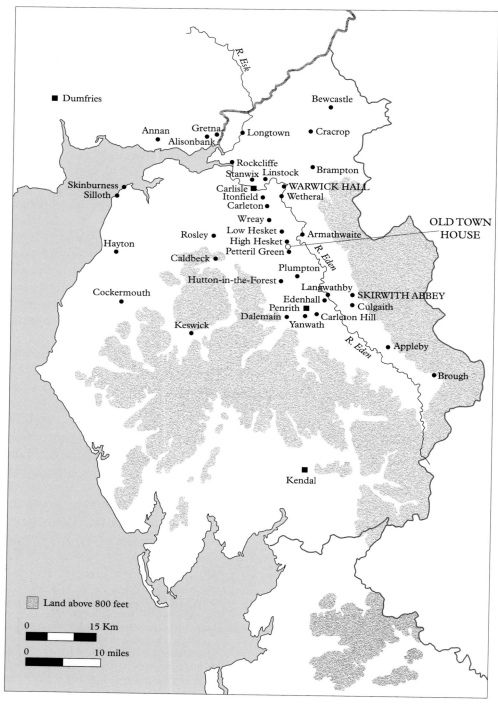

junction with the major route out of Carlisle, Christopher Parker's property offered opportunities for enterprise which were beyond the reach of most yeomen farmers.

By the mid-seventeenth century Cumbria had an intricate network of drove roads bringing cattle south from Scotland; and from Ireland too, until this branch of the trade was restricted to certain months of the year in 1664; and then banned, temporarily from 1667, and permanently from 1681[6]. Although cattle crossed at various points along the border, the west coast routes through Cumberland were used much more extensively than those on the east through Northumberland. Besides being the natural route for cattle from Ulster via the short sea-crossing from Donaghadee on the Co. Down coast to Portpatrick in Wigtownshire, the western drove roads were developed by the movement of cattle from the great breeding grounds of Wigtownshire, Galloway and Dumfriesshire[7]. Droving down the east coast was much slower to grow and initially those routes were used primarily by sheep. Then, as now, the east coast was largely devoted to arable farming rather than pasture, and the passage due south from Jedburgh was via very steep inclines which led to largely uninhabited moorland, where there were few attractive overnight stances for cattle. Longer-distance cattle droving from the Scottish Highlands got underway only once the movement of Irish cattle to Britain had been prohibited during the 1660s: especially from Argyllshire, and then around the turn of the century from even further north[8]. In contrast, according to local customs officials, 18,364 Scottish cattle passed through Carlisle in 1662-63; and the total of Scottish and Irish cattle entering Cumberland was 26,440[9]. At a few strategic points in this network were extensive pasture grounds where the cattle paused and were fattened prior to sale at the fairground at Rosley (near and to the west of the Heskets), or further south in Penrith, Brough and beyond. The lands around High and Low Hesket and nearby Broadfield Common were 'much used' pasture areas[10]. Christopher Parker's property lay there, flanking the confluence of the two drove roads.

Christopher earned most of his income from fattening cattle and servicing the needs of the droving trade. At his death his own herd included 16 beasts with a combined value of almost £30; and, significantly, at the end of the

---

6   D. Woodward, 'The Anglo-Irish Livestock Trade in the 17th Century', *Irish Historical Studies*, xviii (1973), 499-504.

7   Marshall, 'Drovers, Fairs and Cattle Routes, 76-98; H. Allen, *Donaghadee: An Illustrated History* (Dundonald, 2006), 21-22, 32, 51-52; W. Thompson, 'Cattle Droving between Scotland and England', *Journal of the British Archaeological Association*, 37 (1932), 176-177; A.R.B. Haldane, *The Drove Roads of Scotland* (Newton Abbot, 1973), 161-167.

8   I.D. Whyte, *Agriculture and Society in 17th-Century Scotland* (Edinburgh, 1979), 240-241.

9   Woodward, 'Anglo-Irish Livestock Trade', 497. The former figure has commonly been cited as 18,574 but, according to Woodward, this derived from an arithmetical error in the manuscript concerned, which he corrected.

10 Marshall, 'Drovers, Fairs and Cattle Routes', 80.

winter of 1686 he still held stocks of oats, bigg, rye, hay and straw together worth over £20. Moreover, the debts owing to him (£53) and by him (£79) indicate that he was actively engaged in the local commercial economy. Many of the cattle fattened on his property belonged to others and were destined for market. Others were brought there on his or his neighbours' accounts, for Cumbrian farmers were increasingly involved in purchasing and overwintering young cattle for later re-sale[11]. Because of the seasonal nature of the droving trade (largely, though not exclusively, late spring to early autumn), such income would not have featured in the inventory accompanying his will of March 1686: if he had lived for a few more months the value of his personal estate would have been even larger.

The third significant feature of his will is its statement that one pair of his prized 'arkes' and tables was 'standing and being in my new dwelling house at Hesket', that at Old Town. Thus, contrary to estate agents' brochures of recent decades, which describe the property's origins as 'early eighteenth-century', the house was first built around 1680. Having acquired land at this strategic point (Figure 4), Christopher Parker built a house there in order to have a base on the property which provided a significant proportion of his income. It was primarily this property which was to provide his successors with a steady increase in their wealth and status over the next century; and then to act as a springboard to their further success.

Figure 4. The junction of the two drove roads, south of Old Town House.

11   J.V. Beckett, 'Landownership in Cumbria c.1680-c.1750', unpublished D.Phil. Thesis, Lancaster University, 1975, 48, 153; A.B. Appleby, *Famine in Tudor and Stuart England* (Liverpool, 1978), 43-44, 48-49, 93-94, 163; J. Thirsk, (ed.) *The Agrarian History of England and Wales, v 1640-1750* (Cambridge, 1984), 12-15.

Chapter 1:

Yeomen Farmers in the
17th and 18th Centuries

CATTLE DROVING

Cattle droving from the largely pastoral regions of Ireland, Scotland, Wales and northern England to the more populous markets in the midlands and south-east of England goes so far back in history as to be impossible to trace with any accuracy. Nevertheless, a broad pattern is evident from the sixteenth century, when the activity in Scotland was undergoing a 'gradual transition from lawless cattle-driving ['reiving'] to lawful cattle-droving'. Throughout the 1500s trade was spasmodic and at times severely disrupted, especially by reivers. Territorial disputes and general unrest along the border were as bad as they had ever been in the decades after 1550 and later became widespread, particularly in the west, the gateway to Cumbria. In the late 1590s many raids penetrated further south than before; both Low and High Hesket – some eight and nine miles respectively south of Carlisle - were twice attacked and plundered by a band of reivers led by Willie Armstrong of Kinmont[1]. There was feuding, general lawlessness and, above all, cattle and sheep rustling from both north and south of the border, all of which heightened insecurity and discouraged settled agriculture. Prompted by Elizabeth I, the joint endeavours of the English and Scottish governments led to the Treaty of Carlisle in 1597, which instituted swingeing penalties for a range of crimes – murder, raiding, theft and ransom – and which, in addition to inviting claims for damages, established arrangements for restitution[2]. Some years later, however, these measures, which had proved unavailing, were overtaken by dramatic events.

Earlier, it had sometimes suited James VI of Scotland, politically, to ignore these problems; but his attitude changed markedly as soon as it became clear that he would accede to the English throne as James I. By the time of Elizabeth I's death in 1603 James was acutely aware of the threat posed by the reivers, not least to public perceptions of his own performance, and he determined to stamp his authority on this aspect of affairs from the very outset of his reign in England. Scottish reivers played into James's hands in 1603 by embarking

---

1 Haldane, *Drove Roads of Scotland*, 2 (quotation); Pkr A, 24, p. 16. Armstrong's last foray, also 'probably on Low and High Hesket', was in 1602. – G. Macdonald Fraser, *The Steel Bonnets: the Story of the Anglo-Scottish Border Reivers* (London, 1971), 103.

2 Haldane, *Drove Roads of* Scotland, 13,15; J.B. Gavin, 'The Bishop of Durham, the West March Border Negotiations, and the Treaty of Carlisle, 1597', *CW2*, lxxiii, 120-142.

on a major cross-border foray as far south as Penrith, driving off over 1,000 cattle and nearly 4,000 sheep and goats; and, according to some historians, many more than this[3]. James heard the news while pausing at Berwick en route to London to claim the English throne. Even by the standards of the day, his reaction was fierce; it was also systematic and sustained. Some of the perpetrators were quickly apprehended and summarily executed; many more met the same fate in succeeding years; and certain notorious reiver families were forcibly exiled. James abolished the previous territorial divisions of the border area, the Marches, together with the associated posts of warden, changing the name of the border counties to the Middle Shires. The border laws were abolished and replaced by the common law of the realm, which throughout the region was presided over by a special commission of ten – five Scotsmen and five Englishmen, sitting in Carlisle[4]. Trouble did not disappear overnight, but was drastically reduced and steadily ebbed away. As late as the 1670s there were very occasional forays from marauding 'mosstroopers', as they were then called, but few, if any, of these proceeded beyond the immediate border area[5]. Against the background of previous mayhem, a wholly new order was firmly and successfully established within a decade of James I's accession.

The first detailed but isolated evidence of the droving trade dates from the period November 1617 to November 1618 when some 5,641 cattle, 3,752 sheep and a few score of horses were taken into Cumberland via the former West March. Simultaneously, the trade was further promoted by the Scottish Privy Council. It ordered a new drove road to be constructed between Annan and Gretna, which was completed in 1619. By 1626 there were complaints that cattle exports were causing shortages and price rises in the Scottish domestic market. At Alisonbank near Gretna 'droves of cattle from Galloway were an established trade' by 1632. In 1639 fairs at Rosley and Cockermouth were formally established by Algernon Percy, 10th earl of Northumberland and the former became one of the leading centres for cattle sales for decades to come[6]. Significantly, in 1653 Cromwell's plan for union between England and Scotland caused consternation in Carlisle, which faced the loss of its 'Scotland toll, being 1d. a beast payable by both English and Scottish for four-footed goods brought hence'. The mayor and 20 aldermen and citizens

---

3   J. Walker, *The History of Penrith* (Penrith, 1858), 59-60; A. Moffat, *The Borders* (Selkirk, 2002), 237-267.

4   G.P. Jones, 'King James I and the Western Border', *CW2*, lxix, 129-151.

5   Jones, 'James I and the Western Border', 149; F.H.M. Parker, 'The Parkers of Old Town: with Some Notes on the Branthwaites of Carlingill and the Birkbecks of Orton Hall', *CW1*, xvi, 105; G. Watson, *The Border Reivers* (Alnwick, 1988), 195; M.J.H. Robson, *Ride with the Moonlight: the Mosstroopers of the Border* (Newcastleton, 1987), 50.

6   Whyte, *Agriculture and Society*, 236; Haldane, *Drove Roads of Scotland*, 18, 31; W.A.J. Prevost, 'The Turnpike and Custom Post at Alisonbank', *CW2*, lxxiii, 293; *Calendar of State Papers, Domestic Series, 1638-39*, 510. For developments at Rosley, see J.D. Marshall 'Drovers, Fairs and Cattle Routes', 92-96 and *Portrait of Cumbria* (London, 1981), 56.

petitioned Parliament for 'immunity', but to no avail[7]. Though rescinded at the Restoration in 1660, union was promulgated under Cromwell and, completely unhindered for the first time, cross-border trade forged ahead. Thus, the figures reported by re-instated customs officials for the number of cattle driven through Carlisle and through Cumberland in the early 1660s – 18,364 Scottish, and 26,440 Scottish and Irish[8] – were recorded against a background of growth in the droving trade over several previous decades.

THE ORIGINS OF THE FAMILY

Successive generations of the Parker family viewed these developments from ringside seats. During the later sixteenth century they lived in the heartland of the most troubled area, the West March, just south of Carlisle – in Wreay (or Petterill Wreay as it was then called, after the river which flowed nearby). Owing to the lack of parish registers before 1660, their relationship to later Parkers cannot be tracked precisely but the evidence strongly suggests a direct male line. Wills exist for two Thomas Parkers, both of Petterill Wreay, in 1566 and 1594 respectively; and, as we shall see, Thomas was more often than not the Christian name of the family's eldest son. Since the first Thomas stated in his will that he had a son named Thomas, it is likely that the second was that son. Along with their neighbours, both men were expected to fight as well as to farm. Among the possessions of this second Thomas, valued at 20 shillings, were 'one Jacke, one steal cappe and his rydinge geare and his apperell'. A 'Jacke' was a leather fighting jacket which often had slabs of metal sewn into it. Along with the helmet, saddle and harness (and his horse), it was needed when the warden of the West March and/or the lord of the manor required customary tenants to turn out against marauding Scots, no doubt with 'apperell' sporting the lord's colours[9]. So, during the unrest which swept the borders in the late sixteenth century it was Thomas Parker's duty, when called upon, to leave his ringside seat and jump into the ring itself. And at no period was this more likely to have been necessary than during his lifetime.

Christopher Parker's father, another Thomas, was probably the grandson or great-grandson of the Parker who died in 1594 (whose son was yet another Thomas). Born in c. 1630, he spent all his life in Wreay. The village had a green and, though now bisected by a road, it still has; and Thomas lived on what remains one of the more prominent sites in the village, on rising ground to the north of the green – hence his address, 'of Greane Head, Wreay' (Figure 5).

7   *Calendar of State Papers, Domestic Series, 1653-54*, 255.
8   D. Woodward, 'The Anglo-Irish Livestock Trade of the Seventeenth Century', *Irish Historical Studies*, xviii (1973), 497, n. 35.
9   Pkr B, 28, Wills of 25 June 1566 and 26 March 1594 and their associated inventories; D. Uttley, 'The Decline of the Cumbrian Yeoman: Fact or Fiction', *CW3*, vii (2007), 123.

Figure 5. The site of the Parkers' house at 'Greane Head', Wreay.

During the decades from 1630, before the main southerly droving routes became firmly established, it is likely that droves of cattle passed Thomas's home, for one ancient trackway led south from Dumfries to Carlisle, and then went on to Penrith via Wreay[10]. Two of what were to become major routes ran close by – that to the west leading to Broadfield Common and Rosley, and that to the east (the current A6) proceeding to Penrith via the Heskets and Old Town. It would be surprising if the trade did not impinge on Thomas's activities. To judge from his inventory of May 1683, he practised mixed farming on a substantial scale but with an emphasis on stock-rearing. He grew bigg and barley and, besides two yokes of oxen, had cattle, sheep and pigs. What is striking for that time of year, the early summer, is the amount of fodder and straw he held, valued at over £5, suggesting that he too met at least some of the needs of passing drovers and their herds. He was, clearly, commercially active in other respects too: at his death he was owed nearly £19 by twelve separate individuals, while his own debts amounted to merely £3. 2s. 6d..[11].

---

10   W.T. McIntyre, 'The Fords of the Solway', *CW2*, xxxix, 154.
11   Pkr B, 28, Will of Thomas Parker, 5 July 1682, and associated inventory. One reason why the current A6 developed as a drove road was that, in addition originally to being the route of a Roman road, until the later 18th century its eastern flank was 'for the most part...wild moors and commons', which provided stances for drovers. – W.A.J. Prevost, 'A Journie to Carlyle and Penrith in 1731', *CW2*, lxi, 207.

As indicated earlier, his son and heir, Christopher, who died in his mid-to-late-30s less than three years later, was even more prosperous. He retained his relationship with Wreay, being a member of the body known as the 'Twelve Men' who have managed aspects of village life from that day to this[12]. We do not know when or how Christopher acquired the house at Carleton, on the outskirts of Carlisle and just north of Wreay – though on 15 April 1676 he obtained customary tenure of meadow land at Longholme, half way between Wreay and Carleton[13]. Nor are there records of when or how he got the property at Old Town where he built his second house although, located at the junction of two drove roads, it was certainly complementary to his existing business. What we do know is that cattle droving down the western routes from Scotland was of substantial proportions by the later decades of the seventeenth century; and that drovers might be asked to pay for temporary grazing at twice the rate charged to locals[14]. As indicators of the total volume of traffic, the statistics derived from the customs service are almost certainly underestimates because, by their nature, they took no account of smuggling and, in any case, no port books for the west Cumberland ports have survived as they have for some other coastal parts of England. Nevertheless, the customs figures provide a guide to the geographical flow of the trade, clearly indicating that the bulk of the traffic was through Cumberland. In 1675 Alex Campbell, a merchant in Ayr, maintained that 'this yeare our cattle have sold at [a] grait rate in England which hath occasioned many to be driven ther[e]'. By that date between 20,000 and 30,000 beasts a year from Galloway alone are reckoned to have crossed into Cumberland[15].

On the wider front prospects for the largely pastoral farmers of north-western England were steadily improving. Throughout western Europe the period from 1650 to 1750 saw prices for cereal products unsteady or on the wane as supply outstripped demand, whereas those for pastoral products, many of which supplied newly-emerging industries, rose or at least held up much better. The population of Cumberland and Westmorland grew and there was considerable house building and rebuilding in the region, of which that at Old Town was but one example[16]. The outlook for yeomen farming families such as the Parkers became more promising, particularly if their properties commanded economically strategic sites, as that at Old Town did. Following Christopher Parker's burial in St. Mary's churchyard at High Hesket in 1686, the key questions facing his family were whether hitherto

---

12   A.R. Hall, *Wreay* (Carlisle, 1929), 32.
13   A copy of the manorial record of this acquisition is held by Cathie Parker of Maughold, Isle of Man.
14   B. Tyson, 'The Cattle Trading Activities of Sir Daniel Fleming of Rydal Hall, 1656-1700', *CW3*, ii, 186, 188, 193.
15   Whyte, *Agriculture and Society*, 234-245; T.C. Smout, *Scottish Trade on the Eve of the Union* (Edinburgh & London, 1963), 217; Haldane, *Drove Roads of Scotland*, 169.
16   B.H. Slicher van Bath, *The Agrarian History of Western Europe A.D. 500-1850* (London, 1963), 206-220; R. Machin, 'The Great Rebuilding: A Reassessment', *Past and Present*, no. 77, 1 (1977), 33-56.

the successful enterprise at Old Town could be sustained during the ensuing long minority; and whether following his untimely death his legacy might be enhanced. During the next generation both questions were answered affirmatively.

EXPANSION AT OLD TOWN

If not in his longevity, Christopher was lucky at his death in having three healthy brothers to act as his executors and as the guardians of his young children during their minorities. All three lived till beyond the turn of the century. In their effect on families minorities were potentially double-edged: momentum could be lost and widows had to be sustained; and Christopher's widow, Jane, survived him by almost 30 years, dying in 1715. We do not know of the substance of any settlement on her or even if there was one, but she had to be supported appropriately. On the other hand, with no head of the family of age, conspicuous expenditure was low, allowing financial consolidation, especially under effective guardians[17].

The clearest evidence of the brothers' success as guardians was the marriage which they arranged – a decade after Christopher's death – for his only son and heir, Thomas. Initially, the match was not without its difficulties for, although Thomas did not attain his majority until 1699, he married in 1696. It was unusual for someone in his position to marry while still a minor. The fact that his first child, another Christopher, was born in 1696 suggests that his guardians and his prospective in-laws consented to the marriage because his bride-to-be was pregnant. Yet, while it may have got off to an impromptu start, the marriage significantly improved the family's standing in the local community. Only 16 years old when they married, Thomas's wife, Mary Nicolson, was of Park Broom, Linstock, which had come into her family earlier in the century on the marriage of Joseph Nicolson of Wetheral to Radigunda Scott, heiress of property at Linstock and Stanwix. Mary was the niece of Dr. William Nicolson, bishop of Carlisle from 1702, then of Derry in Ireland and, just before his death, archbishop of Cashel; her father, John, was chapter clerk and later registrar of the diocese of Carlisle; and the bishop's nephew and her brother was Joseph Nicolson who, with Richard Burn, was the early historian of Cumberland and Westmorland[18]. For a yeoman-farming family this was a very solid connection indeed and must in some measure have reflected their own prosperity and prospects.

Meanwhile, the cattle droving trade continued to grow. Although almost certainly an underestimate of total traffic, the customs figures for 1697-98

---

17   Roebuck, 'Impact of the Abolition of Wardship', 74.

18   2 Pkr B, 24, O. Parker, '[Ms] Outline of a Family', 17; C.M. Lowther-Bouch, *Prelates and People of the Lake Counties: A History of the Diocese of Carlisle 1133-1933* (Kendal, 1948), 289, 311-312; Nicolson & Burn; F.C. James, *North Country Bishop* (London, 1956), *passim*.

(long after the trade from Ireland had been prohibited and in what was by far the highest figure for legal traffic in these years) record the passage of 59,701 cattle from Scotland to England[19].   In 1707, a decade or so after Thomas's marriage, the trade was further boosted by the promulgation of full union between the two countries.   Previously disrupted by abrupt switches of policy by both the English and Scottish governments, it was now able to develop naturally in an open market.   The townsfolk of Penrith, nine miles south of Old Town, knew which side their bread was buttered on.   There were only four guilds in the town – merchants, skinners, tanners and shoemakers, all closely linked to the droving trade.   Celebrating the Union, the entire populace enjoyed a general holiday[20].   Lack of official statistics – customs duties having disappeared – has prevented calculations of the subsequent scale and rate of growth in cattle droving.   What we do know is that up to 30,000 beasts passed through three stances on a single estate – that of the Musgraves of Edenhall, just to the east of Penrith – in 1712; and that the overall scale of the traffic grew substantially in the years following the Union. Hitherto historians have generally accepted the estimate that around 80,000

Figure 6. Old Town House *c*.1950.

19   D. Woodward, 'A Comparative Study of the Irish and Scottish Livestock Trades in the 17th Century' in L.M. Cullen & T.C. Smout, (eds.), *Comparative Aspects of Scottish and Irish Economic and Social History 1600-1900* (Edinburgh, 1977), 153.

20   W. Furness, *History of Penrith* (Penrith, 1894), 126.

beasts a year were crossing the border, still mainly via the western routes, by 1750 but, in the light of the latest evidence from earlier years, this too appears to have been an underestimate[21]. Surviving to the ripe old age of 82, Thomas Parker witnessed this growth over many decades and there is ample physical evidence at Old Town of how he responded to it.

Thomas and Mary Parker raised a large family. Five children were born in the first decade of their marriage – four sons and a daughter; and five more – three daughters and two sons – during the second. Remarkably, in view of the normally monotonous regularity of infant mortality during that period, none died young and the eldest, Christopher, married while his youngest sibling, Beatrice, was still a child. Old Town House became their permanent home: but a family of that size was difficult to accommodate there and the house was extended on at least two occasions. As originally built *c*.1680 the house was small: a single bay with one large room upstairs and one downstairs, joined by a staircase or ladder which led from a straight passageway linking the front and back doors. By contemporary standards this was very small; most new houses in the region usually had two bays. Already having a house at Carleton (where his widow, Jane, may have lived after his death), it is likely that Christopher Parker had not wanted to overstretch himself financially, though he did want a base at the junction of the two drove roads. The subsequent extensions cannot be dated precisely but, in view of the steady growth of Thomas's family, the first at least (and possibly both) probably occurred around 1725, when an adjoining barn was built.

This first extension tripled the size of their home, which became a three-bay house with large rooms on both floors of each bay. Later, at some unknown date, it was further extended. The front elevation was raised by a couple of feet and an offshot running along the entire length of the house, was added at the rear, the whole being covered by an asymmetrical, or 'Westmorland', roof. The upper rooms now had higher ceilings and, easing congestion above and below, the offshot provided a kitchen, scullery, pantry and half-cellar, and a new passageway along the back of the house; together with a new staircase leading to additional sleeping quarters upstairs. The cubby-holes on the inside wall of the new passageway, which remain, had originally been on the external rear wall. The ceiling of the new kitchen was significantly higher than the others on the ground floor, allowing joints of meat to be smoked; and many of the beams downstairs were festooned with hooks to hold the meat once it had been cured.

As indicated in later manorial records, there were garden areas to the front and rear of the house (Figure 6)[22]. The back garden, which was used for

---

21   P. Roebuck, 'Cattle droving through Cumbria after the Union: the Stances on the Musgrave Estate, 1707-12', *CW3*, xii, 143-158; 'Cattle droving through Cumbria, 1707-12: New Evidence from the Musgrave Estate', *CW3*, xiii, 256-260; Haldane, *Drove Roads of Scotland*, 178.

22   CAS (C), D/MBS/4/32, Manorial Records: Forest of Inglewood, 1816-25, 6-7.

Figure 7. Old Town House today: the Westmorland roof and the barn.

growing vegetables, appears to have been laid out in the early years, for the wall surrounding it was made of the same local red sandstone as the house itself. The inside wall to the north was fashioned to provide four bee-boles where the straw 'skeps', or hives, were well-sheltered in winter from cold northerly winds[23]. With these embellishments and when finally extended, the property was roomy and comfortable, though not grand. It housed a family which, to start with, was prosperous rather than wealthy, but which later grew in both size and means. Nevertheless, few yeomen-farming families would have lived in so substantial a home; and for as long as they remained in Cumberland all heads of the family were described as 'yeoman farmer'.

All this illustrates the growth in the family's wherewithal and standing but reveals nothing of how this was achieved through servicing the droving trade. For evidence of this we must turn to the barn which Thomas built at Old Town (Figure 7). This was situated at right angles to the house, beyond a cobbled lane between the two. We have a firm date for its completion. Just after the millennium it was re-developed into three domestic units, when certain features, one in particular, disappeared. However, local people, who once lived in Old Town House and also used the barn, testify that before this re-modelling a date stamp of 1725 was inscribed at the apex of its northern gable[24]. The barn is, and particularly for its time was, huge: far larger than would have been required by a farmer engaged in stock rearing and associated

23   See B. Tyson, 'Architecture of Lakeland Beekeeping', *Country Life*, clxxi (18 Feb. 1982), 408-409.
24   I owe this information to Mr. (now deceased) and Mrs. Robert Ferguson of High Hesket.

arable farming. Towering above Old Town House and of three storeys, its proportions were more akin to those of a medium-sized country house than a substantial farm building. To have built it on this scale, Thomas Parker must have been heavily engaged in provisioning a large number of beasts on a regular, albeit largely seasonal, basis, as well as providing shelter and other facilities for those who accompanied them. His establishment constituted a very early version of a service station where people acquired whatever they needed for the rest of their journey, except that in his case many of the cattle probably spent some time on his surrounding grassland as they rested and were fattened for market.

How was the barn used? Until the 20th century its main door was at the rear and, therefore, away from the house. As old photographs indicate[25], carts were able, via a steep earthen bank or ramp, to enter directly into the first floor. This was where the oats, bigg, hay, and straw were stored, to be readily moved in or out. On the ground floor there was plenty of room for horses and dogs, for drovers usually travelled with both; in winter this would also have housed Thomas's own herd. A blacksmith's shop may have been located there too. In the later years of the trade cattle were increasingly shod for their long journeys, particularly when they crossed the border, where turnpiking with its firmer road surfaces gradually made droving more arduous for them[26]. The third storey of the building was probably where the drovers themselves were accommodated, no doubt in temperatures made more comfortable by the livestock below.

Little documentary evidence of Thomas Parker's business operations has survived. At one point he was summoned before the manorial court of the Forest of Inglewood 'for not making his hedge between Low Hesket field and Thomas Railton's barns', and was fined 6s. 8d[27]. This reveals what is not clear from other sources: that Thomas's holdings stretched northwards at least as far as the boundary with Low Hesket. Nor did he rely solely on servicing the droving trade. Between 1714 and 1718, at least, together with a partner, John Mallison, and for a joint rent of £50 a year, he leased the tithes of corn, wool and lamb at Hesket from the nearby estate of Hutton-in-the-Forest[28]. There are tantalisingly brief glimpses of the impact of the droving trade in the area. Another Thomas Parker, 'late of Wreay', and a cousin of Thomas of Old Town, had 'black [or Scots] cattle' worth £20 at his death in 1729[29]. Later 'Scotch droves of cattle rest on their passage at High and Low Hesket, which greatly enhances the value of hay and grass there'. And again, there is reference to 'good grass let at 30s. and 40s. an acre; it is applied partly

---

25   In the author's possession.
26   Haldane, *Drove Roads of Scotland*, 26, 33-35.
27   CAS (C), D/MBS/4/13, Manorial Records: Forest of Inglewood, 1715-23, 47-48.
28   CAS (C), D/Van, Box 71, Accounts 1714-18.
29   Pkr B, 28, Inventory, 28 Mar. 1729.

to dairying, and partly to the occasional grazing of droves of cattle, which in some seasons are daily pulling through [High Hesket][30]'.

Neither for the eighteenth century nor until the nineteenth century is there precise information about the extent and value of the Parkers' property at Old Town or, indeed, elsewhere. Because of the demand from drovers, land in and around the Heskets was much sought after and, once acquired, was difficult to augment. Their holdings at Old Town ran from the boundary with Low Hesket in the north to Petterill Green in the south, Old Town being between the two, and in total probably amounted to some 150 to 200 acres, some of which were scattered and detached from the main block around the house itself. From the late 1740s the context in which Thomas and his eldest son, Christopher, operated began to improve substantially, and did so steadily into the period of rapid industrialisation beyond the demise of both. The population of England and Wales, 6m in 1750, rose to 9m by 1800, propelled both by declining rates of mortality and a gradual fall in the age at marriage, which produced higher rates of fertility. Many types of industry developed more rapidly, creating a growing demand for agricultural raw materials, while population growth boosted the demand for foodstuffs[31]. Both factors further stimulated the droving trade.

Thomas Parker was pre-deceased by three of his younger sons, and by his wife, Mary, who died in 1747. He survived until the age of 82 in 1760. His business had continued to prosper, particularly perhaps towards the end of his life. Fortunately, his will of March 1758 and his inventory of May 1760, though brief in the first case and positively cryptic in the second, throw shafts of light on his achievement[32]. He left handsome legacies to two of his daughters: £100 to Barbara, who in 1724 had also married a Nicolson of Park Broom; and £200 to Mary, who had married William Nelson, a Penrith wig-maker, in 1738. Yet, although Thomas had become a man of means, there was still nothing grand about the family – Barbara could not sign a receipt for her legacy, and merely added her mark. Thomas's personal estate was valued at no less than £554, some £480 of which consisted of 'bonds and [promissory] notes'; and he had no significant debts. He was clearly a substantial net contributor to the rural pool of floating capital, taking money in and lending it out. Just as some of the cattle which came south were bought up by local farmers to be overwintered and then sold at a profit, or to swell their own herds, so some of the money which came with the drovers circulated locally. In effect Thomas was a precursor of the country banks which began to emerge during the last decades of his long life[33]. Promissory

30   W. Hutchinson, *The History of the County of Cumberland* (Carlisle, 1794), i, 497, 499n.
31   E.A. Wrigley, *Population and History* (London, 1969), 153; Wrigley & Schofield, *Population History of England*, 160-162, 174-179.
32   Pkr B, 28, Will of 18 Mar. 1758 and Inventory of 2 May 1760.
33   L.S. Pressnell, *Country Banking in the Industrial Revolution* (Oxford, 1956), 7.

notes were usually of relatively short duration, suggesting that the annual turnover of Thomas's business was very substantial indeed. Compared with what his paternal grandfather and father had left in the 1680s, his personal estate was of exceedingly handsome proportions for a yeoman farmer, its value far outstripping intervening inflation.

New Directions

Cattle droving through Cumberland continued to grow during the second half of the eighteenth century. The routes past Old Town House remained of major importance and property in and around the Heskets, still among the leading fattening areas for cattle coming south and where occasional fairs were held, provided a good living for those with holdings there. The trade from Scotland was augmented from 1759, when the long-standing ban on the import of Irish cattle was rescinded[34]. Together with the gathering pace of industrial activity, the onset of rapid population growth swelled the demand for both foodstuffs and agricultural raw materials. From 1793 war with the French was another factor, with successive governments having to victual large armed forces, both on land and at sea. By the end of the century the movement of cattle from Ulster to south-west Scotland and thence, along with Scottish cattle, through Cumberland was of large proportions. According to a touring French aristocrat, Jacques Louis de Bourgrenet, the Chevalier de Latocnaye, who sailed from Donaghadee to Portpatrick in the 1790s, 'on the day I crossed there were 400 horned cattle taken over to Scotland, and in the six weeks previous there had been transported nearly 30,000'[35]. Allowing for some hyperbole, it is clear that exports from Ulster were substantial as the droving trade neared its peak. By the turn of the century the number of cattle crossing from Scotland into England 'is believed to have reached 100,000'[36]. In the new century, however, drovers began to encounter serious problems. Expansion of the cultivated area led to increasing disputes with landowners and farmers; the spread of enclosure reduced the availability of overnight stances, which became more expensive; and the growth of turnpiking proliferated toll charges. A steady decline in the droving trade followed the emergence of new forms of transport for cattle

---

34   L.M. Cullen, *Anglo-Irish Trade 1660-1800* (Manchester, 1968), 69, 73.

35   Quoted in Allen, *Donaghadee*, 43-44. One contemporary feature of this very short crossing was its use by Irish couples who wished to marry 'irregularly', i.e. by declaration before witnesses rather than in church. Lord Hardwicke's Act of 1753 ended this in England (and soon also in Ireland), whereas under Scottish law the procedure was as legally effective as a church marriage. So Portpatrick did for the Irish what Gretna did for the English, and between 1759 and 1826 234 couples took advantage of this, most travelling by the mail packet which linked Donaghadee and Portpatrick from the mid-18th century. – A.A. Brock, (ed.), *Irregular Marriages, Portpatrick, Wigtownshire 1759-1826* (Dumfries, 1997), 3-4.

36   Haldane, *Drove Roads of Scotland*, 205; R.H. Campbell, *Scotland since 1707: The Rise of Industrial Society* (Oxford, 1965), 36.

from the second quarter of the 19th century – firstly coastal steam-shipping, and then the railways[37].

Unfortunately, there is no further evidence of the nature and scale of the Parker family's involvement in the trade, but for as long as they lived at Old Town they must have benefited significantly from it. However, we do know that family circumstances had begun to diversify some decades before the move to Lancashire. Who lived in the house at Wreay following the death of Christopher Parker's father in 1683 is uncertain. Yet, the property was retained.   John Parker (b. 1706), a younger son who pre-deceased Thomas, was ordained a deacon of the Church of England in 1733, and for the two years before his early death in 1735 served as curate of Wreay; thereafter, an older brother, Joseph, also in orders – first as deacon from 1738 and then as priest from 1763 – was curate there from 1738 to 1783, cementing the family's close relationship with the village. During the latter's curacy the old Parker home at the head of the village green in Wreay was sold to the incumbency and became the local parsonage, which it remained for many years, no doubt partially accounting for the fact that a property still exists on the site at 'Greane Head'[38].

Another development was of greater significance[39]. Christopher Parker (b. 1696), Thomas's eldest son and heir at Old Town, made a very good marriage indeed in 1731. His bride was Agnes, third daughter of Anthony Holme of Dillicar Park in Westmorland. Whether because she had no brothers and/or because of the early death of her two sisters, Agnes was, or became, an heiress: for Christopher was known not merely as 'of Old Town', but also 'of Orton and Gilse, Westmorland'. Later, as we shall see, 'Holme' was added to the Christian names of some of Christopher's descendants, a sure indication that this marriage brought a significant addition to the Parker family's landholdings. Moreover, although the marriage produced four sons, there were no daughters. If only in one sense this too was beneficial. There was no need for Christopher to provide dowries for daughters on their marriages – as his father had been obliged to do for his four daughters, all of whom married. Beyond these bald facts we know nothing about Christopher's career, but developments in the personal situation of other members of the family are revealing. His eldest son and heir, yet another Thomas (b. 1732), married twice, each time to a local woman. His first bride, in 1765, was Margaret, daughter of David Wray of Gowborough Hall, near Ullswater, who died without issue in 1782. Only a year later he married, Jane Faulden of Beaumont Hall, near Penrith, producing three sons with her – Thomas,

---

37   Haldane, *Drove Roads of Scotland*, 208-219; K.J. Bonser, *The Drovers* (London, 1970), 225-229.

38   Pkr B, 7, Licences & Ordination Papers, Will & Inventory of John Parker, 1735, and Conveyance of 1783; Hall, *Wreay*, 23-25, 69, 89-91, 93-94, 124-127.

39   Unless otherwise stated, the following two paragraphs are based on the annotated pedigrees at Pkr B, 5.

Robert and William – of each of whom we shall later hear a great deal more. At this stage, however, it is the careers of Thomas's brothers (Christopher's surviving younger sons) which provide further evidence of the family's burgeoning prosperity.

There were three of them: Anthony (b. 1735), John (b. 1737), and Robert (b. 1744). Anthony married Sarah Ireland in 1771 and later was known as 'of Carleton'. In 1775 Christopher felt secure enough to divide the ownership of Old Town and Carleton, together with the holdings that went with them; and he conveyed the latter to Anthony[40]. In addition, Christopher's third son, John, was curate of Orton (1762-1771), and then of Selside (1771-1779), both livings in the area of the inheritance (which appears to have passed to him) from the Holme marriage. And *his* heir, another Christopher (b. 1775) was also known, like his paternal grandfather, as 'of Orton and Gilse'; but also 'of Petteril Green', which lay just to the south of Old Town. Apparently, therefore, if we bear in mind the separation from the main line of 'Greane Head', Wreay, Parker property was divided four ways (Old Town, Carleton, Petteril Green and Wreay) at various points in the eighteenth century[41]. Among yeomen-farming families generally, there was a tendency during that period to consolidate landholdings, whether they were accumulated through marriage, purchase or by other means[42]. That a family of yeomen farmers (as all the Parkers continued to be described) were able, and chose, to do otherwise demonstrates growing confidence in their means and prospects.

However, it was Robert, Christopher's landless youngest son, who transformed the family's fortunes. We know nothing of his early life other than the hint (in the donations which he made many years later) that as a child he attended the new school established at High Hesket in the early 1750s[43]. Thereafter, because family property had been distributed among his older brothers, Robert was obliged to make his own way in the world. This he did to dramatic effect, no doubt helped by the fact that, apart from small legacies to the older brothers, all Christopher's personal estate was left to his widow and to Robert[44]. At some point in the later eighteenth century – probably during the decade from 1765 – Robert went south and became engaged in the cotton industry, whose meteoric rise as the leading sector in Britain's first industrial revolution was then underway. What prompted this move is uncertain. It is probably significant, however, that Robert's cousin, Thomas, younger son of the curate Joseph Parker of Wreay, became established as a woollen cloth merchant in London at about the same time. According to

---

40   Indenture of 4 April 1775 between Christopher Parker of Hesket, yeoman, and Anthony Parker of Carleton, yeoman, a copy of which is in the possession of Cathie Parker of Maughold, Isle of Man.
41   C.R. Hudleston & R.S. Boumphrey, *Cumberland Families and Heraldry* (Kendal, 1978), 250-251.
42   Beckett, 'Landownership in Cumbria', 150.
43   See below.
44   Pkr B, 28, Will of Christopher Parker, 22 Sept. 1770.

family testimony, having gained some experience as a merchant, Robert 'saw his way to make money. So he came back [to Cumberland] and his eldest brother, Thomas, agreed to mortgage Old Town to start Robert'[45]. In fact, Robert was not just financed by Thomas. The latter also left Cumberland and went south, where he entered into a working partnership with his younger brother in the cotton industry; and he and Robert were joined there not only by Thomas's three sons – Thomas (b. 1784), Robert (b. 1787) and William (b. 1789) – but also by their nephew, Christopher Parker (b. 1775), of the Petteril Green branch of the family. All six men worked together very successfully and, as we will see, rubbed shoulders with some of the leading manufacturers and merchants of their day.

All this lay some years ahead of the death in 1776 of Christopher Parker of Old Town, whose imminent birth 80 years earlier had precipitated his father's marriage in 1696; but following the inheritance in Westmorland of his own generation, these developments utterly transformed the family's fortunes and led to dramatic increases in their landholdings and social status in the early nineteenth century. While still retaining their property at Old Town, they ceased to be yeomen farmers and became major industrialists; and it was Old Town which provided the security for, and the capital to finance, this transition.

---

45   Pkr B, 24, '[Ms] Outline of a Family', 18. The late Oliver Parker of the Isle of Man, who was a regular correspondent of Robert Parker of Morecambe in the decade from 1981 (Pkr B, 11), produced the typescript 'Outline' in which this quotation appears. An exhaustive search for the original letter (written, according to Oliver Parker, by Anne Parker, 1843-1929) or a copy of it has been unsuccessful. A number of the documents cited in the 'Outline' have not survived but the work leaves no doubt that the citations are authentic.

Chapter 2:

Industrialists, 1791-1815

THE ACQUISITION OF HEATON MERSEY

The broader background to the family's involvement in the cotton industry lay well over a century earlier, in developments in English overseas trade from the mid-seventeenth century. Then, together with other new products such as sugar, dyestuffs and tobacco from the Caribbean and the Americas, and tea from the Far East, English merchants began to import cheap cotton cloths, or 'calicoes' as they were known, from India. These quickly became very popular; compared with the woollen cloth which had been the staple of fashionable clothing for centuries, cotton cloth was much lighter, more washable and, through printing on the fabric, more easily and variously embellished. However, such fabrics could not be manufactured in Britain because handicraftsmen could not spin yarn of the fineness produced in India. From the mid-eighteenth century calicoes and muslins dominated the quality end of the contemporary fashion market; and with raw cotton then being imported from the Levant and the West Indies, the search began for ways of improving spinning technology at home[1].

Along with James Hargreaves and Samuel Crompton, Richard Arkwright was chief among those who solved these technological problems, and Samuel Oldknow was among the first entrepreneurs to exploit their achievements by generating mass consumption.. Oldknow's father was a muslin manufacturer from Nottingham, while his mother hailed from Anderton in Cheshire, where the family lived. Samuel began his career as an apprentice to his uncle, who was a draper in Nottingham. In 1779 Arkwright, who subsequently became Oldknow's close friend and major creditor, invented the water-frame which, when combined with Crompton's spinning mule and Hargreaves' jenny, produced high-quality, wholly cotton yarn 'strong enough to serve as warp as well as weft...a new product – a British cotton cloth that was *not* a linen mixture'; it was soon in huge demand both at home and abroad[2]. Two years later Samuel returned to Cheshire as his uncle's partner in a muslin business in Anderton. Within three years he had become the largest muslin manufacturer in Britain and continued to prosper mightily. By 1784 he had acquired new premises in Stockport and at nearby Heaton Mersey, and in

---

1   R. Davis, 'English Foreign Trade, 1660-1700', *Economic History Review*, 2nd series, vii, 2 (1954), 150-166; 'English Foreign Trade, 1700-1774', *Economic History Review*,2nd series, xv, 2 (1962), 285-303.

2   P. Deane, *The First Industrial Nation* (Cambridge, 1979), 90.

1790 he opened the first steam-powered mill in Stockport. Samuel purchased yarn from Arkwright and others and, working through an energetic team of managers, had it made into cloth by employing large numbers of handloom weavers under one roof. By the late 1780s his sales were worth £80-90,000 a year; 90% of these were of fine muslins and many of them were exported, some to places as far away as Botany Bay in Australia[3].

The earliest evidence of Robert Parker's involvement with the cotton industry dates from October 1784, in the first of many letters he wrote during that and the following decade to Samuel Oldknow[4], who by then was clearly a close business associate. We do not know when or how they met, but by 1784 Robert was a partner – apparently the senior partner – in the firm of Parker, Topham & Sowden, cloth merchants of Watling Street, London. It seems likely that the mortgage on Old Town which gave Robert his 'start' was the means whereby he obtained the capital to secure this position, though in order to do so he must also have had several years of previous experience in the trade. As wholesalers the firm sold cotton cloth and probably other goods and took large quantities of Oldknow's output in the early stages of Samuel's career. The correspondence reveals that by 1784 Robert also imported raw cotton through Liverpool, that he had an impressive command of the complexities of the textile trade, and that he and Oldknow knew and respected each other well enough to be completely frank and mutually supportive in the midst of a fast-growing and turbulent industry.

The goods which Parker, Topham & Sowden ordered from Oldknow in Stockport, or from his warehouse in Manchester, were transported, mainly to London but also to other destinations, by long-distance wagons; but on many occasions urgent orders were dispatched by coach, and payments (at least) were sometimes sent by night coach. From 1784, under the radical reforms of John Palmer at the Post Office, mail-coach services in England and Wales were rapidly transformed, becoming safer, more reliable and very much faster – putting 'the mails ahead of even the fastest express riders'[5]. Manchester, Stockport and their environs were among the major beneficiaries of this change, as were Oldknow and Robert Parker. Though based in London, Robert periodically ventured much further afield, servicing existing and searching for new customers. His clients were widely dispersed – in Bristol, Sunderland, York, Scarborough, Hull, Sheffield, Wakefield, Kendal, Lancaster and Manchester – and no doubt elsewhere too. His travels encompassed Scotland and, on one occasion apparently, Ireland; and he also had clients (and competitors) in France. Meeting him in London, Stockport or Manchester from time to time, Robert was brusque in dealing

---

3   'Samuel Oldknow (1756-1828)', *Oxford Dictionary of National Biography*, xli, 700-701. For Samuel Crompton, see iv, 304-307, and for James Hargreaves xxv, 276-277.
4   The Oldknow Papers, SO/1/192-221, 234-241, The University of Manchester Library.
5   D. Campbell-Smith, *Masters of the Post: the Authorised History of the Royal Mail* (London, 2012), 95.

Figure 8. Map showing locations mentioned in the text: Lancashire and Cheshire.

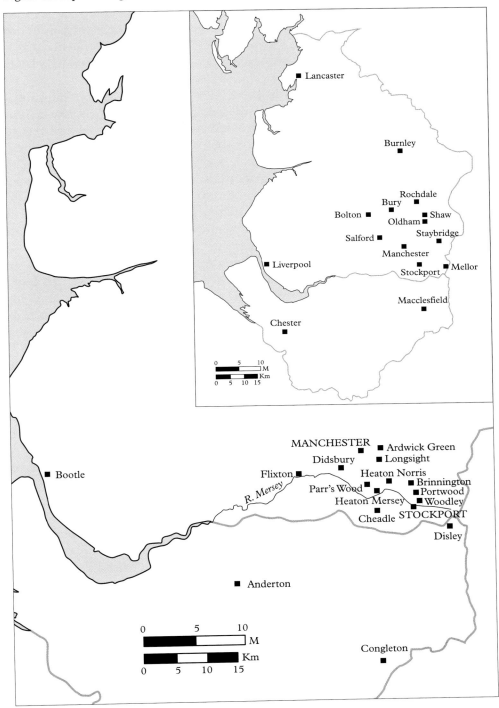

with inadequacies in Oldknow's services – partially delivered orders, some items of poor quality, and others which proved unsaleable; but he was also consistently supportive of the manufacturing pioneer whose goods underpinned much of his firm's business. He was vigorous, knowledgeable and self-confident enough to deal sensitively with Oldknow when the latter encountered difficulties.

At the height of his success in the 1780s Oldknow pursued additional interests and in 1787 he purchased the Mellor estate, near Stockport but in Derbyshire. There he engaged in extensive development for the rest of his life: building industrial and other premises and three reservoirs; farming; serving as a senior officer in the Volunteers; and, just before he died in 1828, becoming chairman of the local agricultural society. At his death Samuel Oldknow owed Richard Arkwright £205,000. He had always borrowed to finance the rapid expansion of his manufacturing business and the origins of this huge level of indebtedness lay much earlier. Although there were signs in 1790-91 that he might have overreached himself, worse was soon to follow. An economic downturn severely hampered trade from the autumn of 1792 and conditions deteriorated alarmingly when war with France was declared in 1793. Oldknow managed to weather the storm and to safeguard his Derbyshire property, but only by selling or letting all his industrial concerns in or near Stockport. The first to be jettisoned, in November 1793, was the complex at Heaton Mersey. The purchaser was Robert Parker[6].

It was from this period onwards that Manchester steadily overtook London as the commercial centre of the cotton industry and, having severed his connection with Topham and Sowden, Robert moved north himself and become engaged in manufacturing before his purchase of Heaton Mersey. By 1791 he was already operating on a significant scale in collaboration with a Samuel Stocks – with whose family the Parkers were subsequently to be involved for over half a century. From January 1792, having earlier sometimes paid him with goods, Robert undertook to pay Stocks a salary of £750 a year, which could have been afforded only from a substantial operation[7]. For a short period before purchasing Heaton Mersey he held the property on lease from Oldknow. While we do not know how much Robert paid for his acquisition, it is clear that it constituted a decisive breakthrough into large-scale manufacturing. The works there specialised in bleaching and calico-printing. In 1791 there had been 86 employees: 47 bleachers,

---

6   *Oxford D.N.B.*, xli, 700-701; G. Unwin, *Samuel Oldknow and the Arkwrights: the Industrial; Revolution at Stockport and Marple* (Manchester, 1924), 156. Heaton Mersey had been run by Thomas Oldknow, Samuel's brother, who was a bleacher. – Stockport Local Heritage Library, Typescript, S.M. Cobbing, 'Portrait of a Victorian Village: Heaton Mersey 1851-1881', 8. This last work was subsequently published as T.D.W. Reid (ed.) *Heaton Mersey, A Victorian Village 1851-1881* (Stockport, 1985).

7   S.D. Chapman, *The Cotton Industry in the Industrial Revolution* (London, 1987), 38-39; Pkr A, 1/17/23, Account & Agreement between Parker and Stocks, 1 Jan. 1795.

37 printers and two watchmen. Following the outbreak of war with France, Robert discontinued calico-printing at Heaton Mersey and remained engaged elsewhere with Stocks until 1795[8]. Nevertheless, particularly in the better times which lay ahead, his acquisition had great potential.

It was probably the purchase of 1793 which brought Robert's eldest brother, Thomas, south from Old Town to Heaton Mersey, though Thomas was mentioned fleetingly, and inconclusively, in a letter to Oldknow in 1787[9]. Whether they were joined there immediately by Thomas's second wife and their three children (then aged nine, six and four respectively) is doubtful; aged 18, their other accomplice, nephew and cousin, Christopher Parker of Petteril Green, may well have come south at that stage. All six of them were certainly working together during the first decade of the new century in what became a thoroughly family concern. With so much at stake in a cut-throat business, it was wise to share responsibilities among next of kin. It was also necessary because, with the exception of Robert senior, initially the rest knew little about the cotton trade. The transition from rural Cumberland to industrial south Lancashire, and from servicing cattle-drovers to manufacturing cotton, appears to have been smooth: but it may not have been so and was ultimately achieved through the experienced guidance of Robert Parker senior. He was undoubtedly their leader and, having got this far, he determined to build a solid basis for the family's future in the cotton business.

MANUFACTURING

As was sometimes the case at this stage of industrialisation, manufacturing at Heaton Mersey was carried on amidst a colony, a semi-rural industrial village. There was a substantial house on the site (where Robert Parker lived for several years) with associated stabling; a small farm and its outbuildings; a variety of manufacturing premises; and some 44 cottages, most of them occupied by employees and their families. The cottages are likely to have contributed significantly to the subsequent success of his operations; in the early stages of the industry operatives were notoriously mobile, and the provision of facilities additional to the workplace was often the key to retaining a workforce. The site at Heaton Mersey was large, on the Lancashire side of the Mersey and flanked to the south by the river. The plant was originally driven solely by water power; and, being upstream of Manchester and relatively clean, the river also supplied the water used in the dyeing and bleaching processes[10].

---

8   H. Heginbotham, *Stockport: Ancient and Modern* (London,. 1892), ii, 329; Pkr A, 1/17/23.
9   Oldknow Papers, SO/1/43, G. Bett to Oldknow, 19 Sept. 1787.
10   Pkr A, 2/7/9, Globe Insurance Policy, No. 27087, 6 Nov. 1807; Chapman, *Cotton Industry in the Industrial Revolution*, 46-47; S. Pollard, 'The Factory Village in the Industrial Revolution', *English Historical Review*, lxxix, no. cccxii (July 1964), 514, 517, 519, 529 and *passim*.

While the relationship with Oldknow was highly beneficial, not least in terms of the size and complexity of the premises purchased at Heaton Mersey, Robert Parker and his colleagues were doubly fortunate in the timing of their acquisition. Besides being extremely popular at home, the new cotton products also came to dominate overseas trade. Almost negligible in 1770, cotton goods accounted for nearly half of all exports by the early years of the new century. At first most sales were to North America, the West Indies and the African slave trade, but exports to Europe grew dramatically from the 1790s, for, despite French prohibitions and embargoes, it proved much easier to send fabrics to Europe than to bring raw cotton through the British blockade to supply European mills. There was startling growth in productive capacity in Lancashire where, for example, the number of cotton-spinning firms doubled from 51 in 1799 to 111 in 1802[11].

The complex at Heaton Mersey was valued at £10,980 for purposes of fire insurance in November 1807[12], when a wide range of manufacturing operations was carried on. Five storeys of a massive seven-storey factory building (by that stage equipped with a steam engine) 2,000 square yards in extent were devoted to cotton spinning. Together with additional premises elsewhere on the site, the two other floors were devoted to weaving. There was also a print house, a vitriol house, and a 'new building for machine-printing' (indicating a resumption of calico-printing); a steam room, a steam-powered still house, and a turning cellar; a dye house; a drying store and a dressing house; and several other premises, including a packing room and a joiners' shop. Commonly described by then as 'the Heaton Works', the establishment was a vertically integrated concern – rare indeed at that stage of the industry's development[13] – and able to deal with all stages of manufacturing from the receipt of raw cotton to the dispatch in bales of pieces of finished cloth.

The effective management of such a complex concern was no easy matter. Thomas Parker senior joined the enterprise only later in life and when he died, aged 75, in 1807 the younger Parkers were still learning their trade. Unsurprisingly, Robert senior enlisted additional help. His long-standing collaborator, Samuel Stocks, appears to have acted for many years as general manager at Heaton Mersey; and in 1802 he was joined there by a specialist bleacher, Thomas Pendlebury of Bolton, who took charge of that branch of the firm's operations[14]. Early in the following decade the Parkers established two partnerships, one with a Thomas Worthington, 'by all accounts a very good weaver', and the other with a Mr. Kinder[15]. Together with Worthington they

---

11   R. Davis, *The Industrial Revolution and British Overseas Trade* (Leicester, 1979), 9-10, 14-16; C. Hartwell, *Pevsner Architectural Guides: Manchester* (London, 2001), 14.
12   Pkr A, 2/7/9, Globe Insurance Policy, 6 Nov. 1807.
13   Chapman, *Cotton Industry in the Industrial Revolution*, 39.
14   Heginbotham, *Stockport: Ancient and Modern*, ii, 329.
15   For Worthington, see Pkr A, 3/12/4, Agreement of 1 Jan. 1813; for Kinder, Pkr A, 3/5/16, Solicitor's Bill, Sept. – Oct. 1812.

purchased 76 acres flanking the Mersey at Cheadle Wood[16]. With so many industrial concerns upstream of them, there was persistent anxiety about the strength of the Mersey's flow at Heaton and this further acquisition was an insurance against possible future difficulties. As this example demonstrates, they regarded undue caution as dangerous in itself and their enterprise was run with considerable pragmatism and flair. At some point before 1805 a colliery was acquired at Woodley, near Stockport, to ensure a steady supply of fuel[17]. Many conventional processes depended on this, but so too did the family's ability to remain competitive by applying steam power to other operations as soon as this became possible. Moreover, even when things were going well there, they were not always satisfied with the productive capacity at Heaton Mersey; and they eventually acquired additional spinning plant in a factory in Stockport[18].

More mundanely, there were also problems of security as well as workforce discipline. The Parkers did not hesitate to prosecute for theft, and one local man – caught stealing cloth laid out to bleach in the fields at Heaton Mersey – was convicted and transported to Australia[19]. Internally, their employees appear to have obtained promotion to certain positions only after signing formal agreements with the Parkers. On becoming a foreman in 1813 Christopher Kenyon agreed 'to do everything required of him'; and in July 1815 James Thain, signing merely as 'Jaimes', declared that 'I have nothing to do with any combination, nor will I endeavour to restrict my Employers in the fair exercise of their business. And I will be conformable to any rules and regulations that my Employers may lay down for the keeping of good order in their Works'[20].

By the second decade of the nineteenth century the Parker enterprise was producing a wide variety of cotton goods. A key question concerns the scale of the firm's output and, fortunately, one series of records throws light on this. Robert Parker's 'Cash Books'[21] run from mid-February 1813 to late September 1814, prompted perhaps by the disruption of overseas trade which occurred during the war of 1812-14 with the United States. For part of that period he listed the value of each bill of exchange received each week for each dispatched order, together with a sum total per week. Like most sources of this kind, which were working documents, the listings are not entirely systematic. The entries for a few weeks are not included: perhaps he was on holiday, indisposed, or simply too busy to complete his

16   Pkr A, 1/17/8, Lingard & Vaughan's Bill to RP, May 1813 – Dec. 1814; 1/17/18, Plan of the Cheadle Wood Estate, n.d.
17   Pkr A, 3/5/5, J. Bury to RP, forwarded to James Haughton, Manager of the colliery, 23 Dec. 1808.
18   Pkr B, 28, Inventory attached to RP's will of 17 July 1815, a typescript transcript of which is at Pkr B, 24, '[MS] Outline of a Family', Appendix D.
19   www.legarthm@levin.pl.net
20   Pkr A, 1/17/16, Statement of 14 July 1815.
21   Pkr A, 3/4/1.

books. Moreover, in July 1813 the recorded weekly value rose abruptly from £14,015 on 19 July to £27,159 on 26 July owing to the addition to the list of 'sundry bills', which were always included thereafter. Apparently, earlier lists related exclusively to overseas orders, while sundries consisted of bills forwarded for payment of sales in the home market. Bills of exchange became payable at different times according to the nature and, above all, the location of sales but, as each bill was cashed, it ceased to feature on the weekly list. These records, therefore, provide a nearly continuous bird's eye view of the value of the firm's turnover during a period of 19 months. It was clearly very substantial indeed. Until the aforementioned change of system in July 1813, the weekly lists fluctuated between a low of £9,314 and a high of £16,659. Subsequently, until mid-April 1814, weekly totals were only rarely below £20,000 and reached a peak of £38,015 in early May 1814. In the absence of any indication of production, transport and other costs, it is unwise to hazard guesses about profitability, although there is little doubt that labour was cheap. Production was large and varied; sales were extensive; and the enterprise must have brought substantial returns.

MARKETING

Stockport and its environs were among the earliest thoroughly industrialised areas in England. John Lombe's pioneering work in the silk industry at Derby had been widely copied in Stockport, Congleton and Macclesfield between the 1730s and the 1760s, and the silk mills there – later converted to cotton – anticipated structures in Manchester by a generation[22]. Nonetheless, once rapid growth in cotton manufacturing was underway, Stockport never rivalled Manchester as the nerve centre of the English industry. While their goods were produced at Heaton Mersey, and for a while also in nearby Stockport, the Parkers could never have doubted the need to establish a suitable presence in Manchester – which they did at the very central location of 47, High Street[23]. Their 'counting house', or main office, was on one floor, with the rest of the space, as was common in the trade, being devoted to warehousing. There they kept stocks of finished products for inspection by merchants, dealers and their agents. The business won a reputation for the quality of its printing on fabric and, during his later years, Robert Parker was known principally as a 'calico-printer'. Many of the pattern books which the firm produced have survived (Figure 9)[24]. At home these were widely distributed by 'travellers' and, in pursuit of orders from overseas, always accompanied consignments for export. Regularly updated with new designs, they illustrated, for both current and potential customers, what the firm was capable of producing in a

22   Chapman, *Cotton Industry in the Industrial Revolution*, 14-15.
23   Pkr A, 2/7/8, Sun Fire Policy 902928, 25 Jan. 1815.
24   There are several excellent examples at Pkr A, 1/19.

business which was a slave to fashion. In view of the port's key role in imports of raw cotton and exports of finished goods, Robert became a member of the Liverpool Cotton Exchange, established in formal headquarters for the first time from 1808; and he also joined the Cotton Exchange in Manchester, which was re-established in a new building in 1809[25]. Both bodies regularly circulated information about trends in trade, production, prices and other matters and membership brought with it access to a network of valuable contacts.

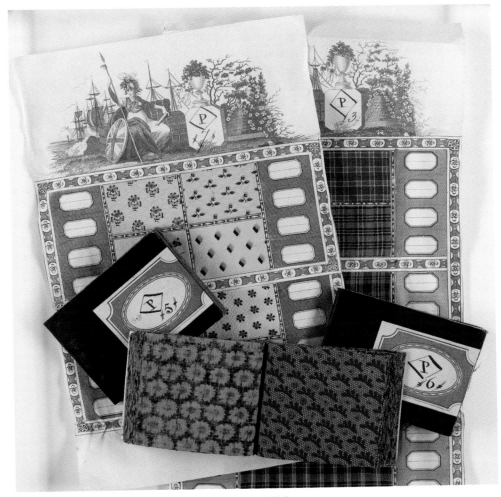

Figure 9. Pattern books from Heaton Mersey *c.* 1815.

---

25   Pkr B, 28, Inventory attached to Robert Parker's Will of 17 July 1815; Hartwell, *Manchester,* 18; J. Belchem, (ed.), *Liverpool 800: Culture, Character and History* (Liverpool, 2006), 144, 147-148.

Networking was vital to success. In a rapidly expanding industry the Parkers were constantly approached by would-be customers: but all too often, especially in the early years, they knew little or nothing about the ability of some individuals to pay for orders. This posed problems, particularly when orders were sought by merchants overseas or their agents in Britain; and when, therefore, the time lapse between meeting an order and receiving payment for it might be substantial – whether simply because of the physical distance involved or on account of international conflict, changes in import tariffs, exchange difficulties and a host of other factors. A business fraught with risk, it required sound judgement which, sometimes, in their ignorance of the substance and reliability of potential customers, was precisely what the Parkers could not deploy. So they turned for help to their contacts in the trade – in Liverpool, London and Glasgow, as well as in Manchester.

Sometimes matters were straightforward. For example, three separate references in regard to a Mr. T.J. Smith, two from London and one from Liverpool, were forwarded to the Parkers on 5 September 1814: all were glowing[26]. In 1813 they had been assured from Liverpool that the two firms they had recently enquired about were 'of the very first respectability and you may safely trust them to any extent'[27]. In December a London correspondent took 'pleasure' in reporting that 'Mr. George Greaves junior is considered a respectable young man. He is a cotton broker. His father is a reputable cotton merchant; and his son acts a good deal under his guidance and is in very fair credit in the cotton trade'[28]. Some positive recommendations were more nuanced. 'We think Robert and James Bathe of Bread Street [London] are steady and prudent men and *we* should credit them [with] £500 if they wished it...[but] we don't suppose they possess much property'[29]. Again, this time from Liverpool:

> From what we have heard of [the two brothers who ran Messrs. Rigg & Co.] we think you may, with their father's guarantee, trust them to the extent you mention without hesitation. We think it rather too delicate a subject to mention to the father personally, but we have understood that he guarantees the purchases of his sons and, as that has been mentioned to you, you need have no hesitation in applying for it direct[30].

In view of the distance involved in certain transactions, some responses provided a fuller background, for instance one reporting on James Spence & Co. of Montego Bay, Jamaica:

---

26   Pkr A, 1/1/11, J. Bibby & Co. to Parker Worthington & Co., 5 Sept. 1814; 1/1/12, Barclay, Tritton, Bevan & Co. to Parkers, 5 Sept. 1814; 1/1/13, W. Hardy to Parker, Worthington & Co. 5 Sept. 1814.
27   Pkr A, 1/1/4, W. Dixon & Co. to Parker, Worthington & Co. 13 Oct. 1813.
28   Pkr A, 1/1/6, Robinson & Bowman to Parker, Worthington & Co. 7 Dec. 1813.
29   Pkr A, 1/1/1, Same to Same, 16 Nov. 1813.
30   Pkr A, 1/1/3, W. Dixon & Co. to Thomas Parker of Parker, Worthington & Co. 4 Nov. 1813.

Our correspondence with this House commenced by their making us consignments of produce by one of our ships in the Spring of 1812, and we must do the parties the justice to say that they have conducted themselves in regard to us with great regularity. We know but little of the capital of the firm but, as they have never drawn upon us to the extent to which they were entitled, we should imagine that it is respectable... Their general reputation, both here and in the island, stands very fair[31].

Prompt responses to requests for information were necessary or potential orders might be lost. One correspondent, writing from London in 1815, knew 'nothing of William Henderson & Co. but I hope to get proper intelligence by Saturday's post'[32]. William Dixon & Co. in Liverpool, who corresponded regularly with the Parkers, neatly summarised the dilemma: 'it is really no easy matter to gain satisfactory information as to the respectability of people with whom you are totally unacquainted and equally at a loss to find out who does know them'[33]. When matters were so difficult, it was perseverance which paid off. Writing from London in November 1813, the firm of Robinson & Bowman confessed to knowing nothing of a Mr. Henry Oppenheim and they could not find a friend who did. Three weeks later, having pursued the matter, 'we cannot say much for Mr. Henry Oppenheim. The account we this day received at the Plate Glass Company (the credit of which by the bye we know nothing of) would not induce us to do *any* business with him; and if we *had* we should try to get out as fast as possible'[34].

Special vigilance was required in regard to conditions and developments in overseas markets. Reliable information was of critical importance, for example, when the Parkers sought to engage a company to act as their agent in some far-flung location. In 1814 they were delighted to receive the following assurance from Baring Bros. & Co. of London: 'we have much pleasure in bearing satisfactory testimony in favour of Messrs. Bogles & Co. of Jamaica with whom we have been many years in connexion. It is an establishment of solidity and we are of opinion you run no risk in confiding your concerns to their management'[35]. Though the Parkers' expectations of their overseas customers were by no means always fulfilled, they looked for prompt intelligence from merchant houses abroad: about the state of their markets, current exchange rates, the nature and impact of regional and local political developments, the types of imported cotton goods likely to sell well (on a seasonal basis), and so on. Anticipating that many replies would be unduly subjective, they also obtained independent advice from the cotton exchanges in Manchester and Liverpool, from financial institutions and, above all, from

---

31   Pkr A, 1/1/17, Boddington, Philips, Sharpe & Co. to Parker, Worthington & Co. 8 Oct. 1814.
32   Pkr A, 1/1/15, Anon. to Messrs. Parker and Nephews, 16 March 1815.
33   Pkr A, 1/1/10, W. Dixon & Co. to Parker, Worthington & Co. 21 July 1814.
34   Pkr A, 1/1/1, 6, Robinson & Bowman to Parker, Worthington & Co. 7 Dec. 1813.
35   Pkr A, 1/1/8, Baring Bros. & Co. to Parker, Worthington & Co. 23 July 1814.

their personal contacts in Liverpool, who were often the first to receive news from overseas. Inevitably, there were errors of judgement and, in the case of ships lost at sea, 'acts of God'. They insured their cargoes; where necessary took dishonoured bills of exchange through their solicitors and the courts, though sensibly they preferred informal means of restitution; and doggedly pursued meagre dividends from bankruptcies. While there is no indication of how the rewards of their efforts were divided between them, not all their individual endeavours were conducted under the umbrella of their firm. A proportion of Robert Parker's dealings were on his own personal account. Later the others did likewise and may also have done so in earlier years[36].

Through experience the Parkers gradually accumulated a deep knowledge of the wide variety of individuals, institutions and practices involved in the cotton trade but if a host of practical matters daily consumed their energies, the need to engage in extensive correspondence was certainly one of them; and monotonously regular meetings with their solicitors were another. The evidence suggests that their business was well organised and, indeed, punctilious in its attention to detail; and that with their peers they were accommodating but firm – at times unyieldingly firm, though not vindictive. Besides being successful, they were much respected in the trade. Robert Parker's cash books suggest that in 1813-14 around half of their sales were to the home market and half went overseas. Following the close of the war of 1812-14 there was a huge expansion of Liverpool's trade with the United States; and after the close of hostilities with France in 1815, well over half of British cotton manufactures were regularly exported[37]. It was from this period that the balance of the Parkers' marketing activities shifted steadily towards overseas trade. Primarily through Liverpool, they exported cotton goods to southern Europe and the Mediterranean, to the United States, the West Indies, Central America and South America. The pattern of their exports had been built up gradually over several, perhaps many, years and was to be further elaborated in the years ahead.

PRIVATE LIVES

During the early 1800s, if not earlier, the younger Parkers became actively involved in the business and by the 1810s were dealing with some matters individually. Robert junior and William never married, but the other two found partners after coming south from Cumberland. In 1806 Christopher married Mary, daughter of John Chadwick of Manchester. In 1809 Thomas married Mary Heald of Portwood near Stockport, whose father, James, was a calico-printer and merchant, operating at Brinnington and Disley in

---

36   See below, 49-50.
37   D. Lascelles, *The Story of Rathbones since 1742* (London, 2008), 59; Davis, *Industrial Revolution and British Overseas Trade*, 69-70.

Cheshire and from a warehouse in High Street, Manchester. Mary's brother, James, who very successfully took over the family business after his father's death, was a leading methodist; and later became a noted philanthropist, a magistrate for Lancashire and Cheshire, deputy lieutenant for Cheshire, and ultimately M.P. for Stockport 1847-52[38]. In the years to come he was regularly involved in assisting the Parkers, especially Thomas and William.

Two of the Parker brothers came to specialise in particular aspects of the business. At that stage William, being younger than the rest, remains a shadowy figure. His cousin, Christopher, encountered problems which led him to leave the business in 1810 with a payment of £20,000 from his uncle, Robert senior. His father-in-law, John Chadwick, who by then was living at Petteril Green, was ailing, and died in 1813; and he was followed to the grave in 1814 by Christopher's wife, Mary, and then by their eldest son, John - aged 28 and seven respectively. The first illness and bereavement persuaded him to return to Cumberland, while the later ones led to his return to Manchester, where he gradually got back into harness[39]. Meanwhile, Robert junior had always been more interested in operations at Heaton Mersey and was encouraged to oversee the manufacturing side of the firm. Thomas, on the other hand, was usually to be found at the counting house in High Street, Manchester. He developed expertise in marketing, particularly on the export side, and was to become among the more enterprising overseas traders of his day.

Outside work, again led by Robert senior, the family won a considerable reputation as philanthropists. While this reflected their growing wealth, it was also perhaps a means of quietening their uneasy consciences at the means whereby much of that wealth was accumulated. Many of those who worked in the cotton industry for the Parkers and others were very young – youths and, often, children. They worked 'long hours for abysmal wages'[40] from Monday through Saturday. Sunday was the only day available for their education. Robert senior's response to this situation was to build a Sunday school near the works at Heaton Mersey, which was opened in 1800. Wishing it also to be used as a church, Robert offered it to the warden and canons of the Collegiate Church in Manchester (later to become Manchester Cathedral) in the hope that they would secure a licence from the bishop. This, however, was refused on the grounds that divine service could not be held in an unconsecrated building. His next, more successful, move was to affiliate the school to another, much larger establishment, whose spiritual

---

38   Pkr A, 3/13/45, Memorandum, 29 Dec. 1824; I.R. Million, *A History of Didsbury* (Didsbury, 1969), 111, 123-124; M. Stenton, (ed.), *Who's Who of British Members of Parliament* (Hassocks, 1976), I, *(1832-1885)*, 185.

39   Pkr B, 5, Annotated Pedigree of the 3rd branch of the family. For the payment of the £20,000, see RP's Will of 17 July 1815. – Pkr B, 28.

40   Chapman, *Cotton Industry in the Industrial Revolution*, 47.

message was Wesleyan Methodist in emphasis, and in whose development Robert was also deeply involved – Stockport Sunday School (Figure 10) which, after operating for a time in temporary accommodation, moved into brand-new premises in December 1806. The new building was massive, 'the largest [Sunday School] in the Kingdom'. Available to pupils from 9 am to 6 pm on Sundays, it was four storeys high, and had 56 classrooms and a central hall with seating for 300. For many years its auditor, Robert was also a major benefactor of Stockport Sunday School, providing it, for example, with a new organ in 1810 at a cost of £500. He was also a regular subscriber to the Sunday School Trust Society, founded in 1810[41]. Nor did he neglect the parish of St. Mary's in High Hesket where he had worshipped in his younger days. Joining two local people – the current incumbent, Rev. John Harrison, and Henry Oliphant of Broadfield House in nearby Itonfield – he gave it £200 in 1811. On the strength of their combined gift of £600, the living received a grant from Queen Anne's Bounty of a further £900, making

Figure 10. Stockport Sunday School.

41   Heginbotham, *Stockport: Ancient and Modern*, ii, 248, 329, 388-389; M. Dick, 'Urban Growth and the Social Role of the Stockport Sunday School' in J. Ferguson, (ed.), *Christianity, Society and Education: Robert Raikes, Past, Present and Future* (London, 1981), 53-58; T.W. Laqueur, *Religion and Respectability: Sunday Schools and Working Class Culture* (London, 1976), 196-200 and *passim*. The younger James Heald was a 'pioneer' of the Sunday school movement in the north of England. – Million, *Didsbury*, 123.

£1,500 in all, which was used to purchase land to augment the income of the living[42]. In due course the younger Parkers made a wide variety of charitable donations; and Robert junior, who moved into the house at Heaton Mersey once occupied by his uncle, was from an early stage closely involved in supporting the Sunday school there.

For the family as well as for their friends and acquaintances, the most startling development of these years concerned Robert Parker senior. In 1808 at the age of 64, he married a Sarah Pollitt at the Collegiate Church in Manchester. At 33 years old, Sarah was nearly half Robert's age, young enough to produce children, and old enough fully to appreciate the financial prospects which her marriage gave her. Indeed, under a settlement executed before their marriage, she was granted £400 per annum for life. Family records are remarkably silent about her. To judge from Robert's will of 1815, the match caused unease, and possibly consternation; and for many years Robert's nephews, Thomas in particular, dealt with her cautiously and at a distance. A long search for Sarah's origins eventually revealed that a James and Sarah Pollitt ran the 'Black Boy' public house in Bridge Street, Stockport from 1795. This establishment was on or near the site on which Stockport Sunday School was later built; and, more significantly, before the school opened some classes were held in an upstairs room at the 'Black Boy'[43]. This strongly suggests that the Pollitts were Sarah's parents, or possibly her uncle and aunt. If either was the case – and it would be a remarkable co-incidence if it were not – it is easy to imagine an adverse reaction to the marriage among Robert's family and elsewhere. His nephews must also have been deeply concerned by the prospects for their own futures should his wife bear his child or children. For Robert senior was in rude good health and, as his 'Cash Books' demonstrate, remained thoroughly in charge of the family's affairs for some years to come.

A VIOLENT DEATH AND A WILL

Robert Parker's long and remarkably successful life ended suddenly, tragically and violently as a result of a carriage accident in 1815. According to a local newspaper:

> On Friday last, as Robert Parker Esq. of Heaton Norris was driving through Stockport in his gig, the horse took fright and ran against a

---

42 W. Parsons & W. White, *History, Directory and Gazeteer of the Counties of Cumberland and Westmorland* (Leeds, 1829), 482.
43 *The Monthly Magazine or British Register*, xxvi (Part II for 1808). Sarah's birth and death dates are recorded in F.C.F. Parker, 'Family Notes', 4 (in the possession of Cathie Parker of the Isle of Man). The pre-nuptial settlement is recited in RP's will of 17 July 1815 (Pkr B, 28). For the Pollitts and the 'Black Boy', see www. 'Old Family Names of Manchester and the North-West', *Papillon Graphics' Virtual Encyclopaedia of Greater Manchester*, n.p. but under 'Pollitt'.

post, which precipitated him with such violence on the pavement as to occasion almost instant death. His loss will be deeply felt and lamented by his afflicted widow and numerous friends. His purse was always open to assist in every work connected with religion and benevolence. The poor have lost in him a bountiful benefactor. He was in his 71st year[44].

In one respect, however, despite their shock, Robert's widow and the rest of his family were singularly fortunate, for his will had been finally signed and sealed on 17 July, only a week or so before his death. Had this not been the case, there would almost certainly have been a protracted legal dispute over the disposal of his extensive assets.

After the multiple wounds to his body had been repaired by a surgeon commissioned for the purpose, there was a grand funeral, followed by interment in the family's traditional burial ground, the cemetery attached to St. Mary's churchyard at High Hesket. We do not know where the funeral was held but several of the bills associated with it have survived. The corpse was laid in a series of four separate coffins: first, in a small oak one, furnished with a mattress and pillows, which was then placed inside a lead coffin; these were then set inside a large oak coffin which, in turn, was encased in a very large, strong oak coffin. This last was 'put together in a particular manner', with an engraved brass plate, 'and covered with cloth'. Mourning rings were distributed and funeral clothing was specially tailored for the leading mourners: 15 men's suits and stockings, and crepe dresses with elaborate buttons for the women; and there were sashes and 'servants' bonnets'[45]. All these arrangements were fitting for the funeral of a leading citizen and well-known and highly successful businessman. Predictably, Robert Parker's will was no less elaborate[46].

Revealing features of the lavish lifestyle to which Robert had grown accustomed, this began by making very substantial, additional provision for his widow, Sarah Parker. The £400 a year for life which she had been granted by the pre-nuptial settlement was now augmented by a further £600 a year during her widowhood. In addition she was left the bulk of her late husband's personal possessions: all the 'household furniture, plate, linen, china, horses and carriages, books and pictures' in the house where they had lived (almost certainly in Manchester), and use of the house for a year after her husband's death. She was also bequeathed, 'for life', 'my dwelling house and outbuildings at Tithe Barn Hill [in Heaton Norris] with the gardens and pleasure grounds surrounding' them, plus an adjacent field for her carriage horses. Sarah did not live in this latter property for long and, indeed, may

---

44   *Manchester Mercury*, 25 July 1815. There were derivatives of this notice in *The Exchange Herald: Aston's Manchester Commercial Advertiser*, 25 July 1815 and in *The Gentleman's Magazine*, lxxxv, 187.
45   Pkr A, 3/11/18-19, 21, Bills of n.d. & 25 July 1815.
46   Pkr B, 28, 17 July 1815.

never have done so – by the 1820s she had made a home for herself in the village of Longsight. The property at Tithe Barn Hill was not only close to the works at Heaton Mersey but also to the Healds, Thomas's in-laws, at Parr's Wood – too close for comfort, perhaps. Apparently, Sarah surrendered it, no doubt in return for a consideration. Whatever the precise configuration of the final arrangements, she received £1,000 a year for life from the Parker estate; and she outlived all Robert Parker's nephews, dying without marrying again, aged 81, in October 1856[47]. Significantly, the will began by establishing extremely strict safeguards against possible delays or non-payment of what was due to her; and only once these precise arrangements had been laid down did it proceed to establish a trust to govern the rest of Robert Parker's dispositions.

There were four trustees: three of Robert's nephews, Thomas, Robert junior and Christopher (though not William); and a close friend and neighbour, James Stubington Penny, 'gentleman', also of Tithe Barn Hill (who earlier had been lent over £6,000 by Robert senior). The will vested in them 'all my freehold and leasehold estates in Heaton [the works], Manchester [the High Street office and warehouse], Stockport [the 'spinning concern'], Woodley [the colliery], Cheadle [the 76 acres at Cheadle Wood] or elsewhere'. The trustees were also responsible for the personal estate not bequeathed to Sarah. Valued at over £153,000, this included stock and goods in the 'Heaton and Manchester concern' (£101,000), in 'Worthington, Parker & Co.' (£19,000), and in the 'Stockport spinning concern' (£15,000), as well as at Woodley, together with his shares in the Manchester and Liverpool Cotton Exchanges.. As with all rich men, there was no shortage of individuals keen to take advantage of his will, and the appraisers of his personal estate advised that, at £1,951, claims for debts owed by the deceased were exaggerated by 'above £500'[48]. So, perhaps influenced by his knowledge of the effects of Samuel Oldknow's heavy indebtedness, Robert was virtually debt free.

The trustees were charged with paying his debts and outstanding expenses. In addition, there was yet another bequest, of £500, to Sarah Parker; a similar one to James Stubington Penny; while a 'friend', Peter Appleton, together with his son, Robert, and a Joseph Plant, 'shall retain in their hands' £8,000 which Robert Parker had lent them in 1811. Most remarkable of all, a sum of £6,000 was bequeathed to *each* of Robert's five nieces – Mary and Nanny, daughters of his brother, Anthony; and Betty, Ellen and Isabella, daughters of his brother, John. Only one of these women, Betty Parker, was still single and, unsurprisingly, she got a husband within a year. No-one could accuse Robert Parker of failing to provide for the various offspring of

47   F.C.F. Parker, 'Family Notes', 4, in the possession of Cathie Parker of Maughold, Isle of Man.
48   There is a note to this effect at the foot of the Inventory attached to Robert Parker's Will of 17 July 1815. – Parker B, 28. For a typescript transcript of the Inventory, see Parker B, 24, '[Ms] Outline of a Family', Appendix D.

his extended family. There followed several substantial charitable bequests: £1,000 to the Manchester Infirmary & Lunatic Hospital, and £500 to each of the Manchester Lying-In Hospital, Stockport Sunday School, the British & Foreign Bible Society, and 'the School at Stockport under the Established Church on Dr. Bell's Plan'. Stockport Dispensary got £200 and the 'Free School at [High] Hesket' a further £100[49]. Robert Parker was buried only yards from this school, where he had probably received his early education and which then stood to the side and towards the rear of St. Mary's churchyard in the village. Finally, and as we shall see significantly, £500 was to be invested and the proceeds devoted by the churchwardens of Didsbury to the 'repair of the Sunday School at Heaton and for clothing for the children' who attended it. Nor was there to be any delay in discharging these bequests: all had to be, and were, paid within a year of Robert Parker's death[50].

Final clauses went on to dispose of Robert's real estate. His eldest brother and former partner in the business, Thomas of Old Town, who died in 1807, had not left a will. The two men appear to have agreed – at that early, delicate stage of family affairs – that Thomas's entire stake in the cotton business would devolve on Robert, on the understanding that ultimately he would provide for the members of the next generation – though the house and land at Old Town would devolve on Thomas's eldest son, Thomas junior, which it did in 1807[51]. Nevertheless, it is clear that at the time of Robert's death he still hoped to produce a child or children. Had he done so, all his landholdings would have gone to any sole heir and, if more than one, would have been equally divided between them. Moreover, being a self-made man with little formal education behind him, he was determined that any son or sons would 'have an [sic] University education at one of the Colleges in Oxford or Cambridge'. Yet, there was no issue of his marriage. In the event, therefore, and no doubt to their relief, everything devolved in equal parts on the four nephews who had joined him in the business – Thomas, Robert junior and William of the Old Town branch of the family, and Christopher Parker of Petteril Green.

But not immediately. Under the will partition could take place only 'at the expiration of seven years from 1 January last'. The nephews were obliged to wait till 1 January 1822 at the earliest to obtain their shares. If any of them left the business before then, £22,000 was to be their sole, individual entitlement. In the interim 'my will is that they shall carry on the trade

---

49   It seems likely that the Parkers donated the land on which this school was built. It was a few yards to the rear of the Salutation Inn in the village, which they certainly owned in the 1840s. See below, 125.

50   For confirmation of payment to this timetable, see Pkr A, 3/15/11, Lingard, Vaughan & Lingard, Solicitors, to TP, 3 Apr. 1826.

51   Contemporary Copy Admittances of Thomas Parker, the younger, Manorial Records, Forest of Inglewood, 11 June 1807 (in the author's possession, courtesy of Mr. & Mrs. Robert Ferguson of High Hesket).

and business at Heaton and Manchester'. Finally, the will confirmed that, by a formal transaction of 29 August 1810, as noted earlier, Christopher Parker had already received £20,000, which would have to be taken into consideration at the time of partition.

THE OUTCOME

Robert Parker's will reveals the extent of his meteoric rise to wealth and prosperity. While the contribution of other family members was considerable, and probably indispensable to him, the venture was his idea; and there can be no doubt that he was the major driving force behind its success. Having stayed in harness until his 71st year, he had become a leading industrialist, highly successful and respected in his business, and he died a very wealthy man. On the way and especially through his will, many members of his family, others and several institutions benefited enormously from his generosity. It was a massive achievement for the landless youngest son of a yeoman-farmer from Cumberland.

We can only speculate about why he included the seven-year clause in his will. Perhaps he had detected, or thought he had detected, signs among some or all of his nephews of a yearning for another way of life, away from the hurly-burly of manufacturing and marketing, and the overcrowding, grime and poverty of Manchester and Stockport; and against the background of his own lifelong efforts, he may have frowned on this. Alternatively, his feelings may have been more straightforward: in his view, having relied on his experience so very heavily during the early part of their careers, his nephews had yet fully to earn an inheritance. There is a third possibility. In the light of his very substantial bequests, he believed that the further development of the business was both desirable and necessary as a means of ultimately enhancing his nephews' shares. We shall never know, though what eventually transpired was more complex than anyone could have envisaged in 1815.

What of his nephews? Perturbed (as they appear to have been) by their uncle's late marriage to a very much younger woman, and shocked by his violent death, they nevertheless enjoyed one major consolation. Robert Parker's lack of offspring left them with much more to gain than if there had been children of his marriage. The discharge of his will would involve them and James Stubington Penny in a great deal of work; and they had until 1 January 1822 to maximise their inheritance if partition was then to take place. They had to get on before they could begin to consider getting out.

Chapter 3:

Interlude, Partition and Tragedy, 1815-1823

The Executorship

On 18 June 1815, a month before Robert Parker's death, two decades of war with France were brought to an end when Napoleon's army was defeated by the allied forces under Wellington at the Battle of Waterloo. The euphoria which followed this decisive victory was not mirrored in the ensuing economic conditions. Several years of post-war economic depression rendered the task of Robert's executors even more difficult than they might have envisaged and, although they discharged his substantial legacies promptly, during the next two-and-a-half years they made slow and very disappointing progress in recouping what was owed to him. They were never optimistic about the £13,134 of what they candidly described as 'bad debts', many of which had no doubt accrued years earlier, but the outcome was much worse than they expected. Of the £3,200 which they felt might be recovered, they had received only £1,238 by January 1818. By then only £2,848 of the £4,200 of 'good debts' had come in, though they had hoped for £3,700. Other calculations also proved unduly optimistic. Receipts from the sale of £2,063 of 'stock of goods', originally estimated to yield £1,500, brought in £1,286; and £96 of surplus office furniture only £65. 'Cash in hand' of £158 was the only item over which they had complete control. In sum, £20,489 of estimated assets yielded a mere £5,835 – a miserable return of just over 25%[1].

Bankruptcies played a part in this poor outcome, but not all of them resulted from the general economic downturn, and much of the correspondence of those years records unrelenting efforts to get debts repaid both at home and abroad, in cash where possible, but in kind if necessary. Mr. Cheesebrough, a cotton dealer in Liverpool, had got into difficulties before the close of the war. In July 1815 his solicitor reported that 'the bankrupt has been selling goods on commission for some of his creditors and has placed the amount of the commissions against the debts he owes them; [and] he is willing to do the same for you'. He went on to argue that Cheesebrough's need to support a wife and five children 'is certainly a claim on the humanity of his creditors'. Perhaps distracted in the aftermath of his uncle's death, William Parker did not reply on behalf of the executors till 4 September, to what effect we do

---

1   Pkr A, 3/5/4, 'Sketch of…Affairs', 17 Jan. 1818. For executors' activities prior to this statement, see 1/17/7, Mr. Shaw to executors, 2 Dec. 1815; 1/2/2, Mr. Vaughan to TP, 23 Nov. 1816; 1/4/7-9, 11-12, Misc. Papers, 1816; 4/2/6, Legal Papers, 1816.

not know[2]. In February 1817 the executors refused to sign the certificate of bankruptcy drawn up on behalf of Mr. John Formby of Bold Street, Liverpool, insisting on repayment of '20 shillings in the pound'; but two months later they had received no response from his solicitor[3]. In some cases strong personal ties were involved in their negotiations, and in none more so than in their dealings with Samuel Stocks, their uncle's close collaborator since at least the early 1790s. Stocks, then living at Peel Street, Manchester, got into serious financial difficulties in 1816, and owed Robert Parker's estate £740. A letter to him of 21 May from all four executors elicited no response and was followed by another, delicately but firmly couched, on 4 June:

> The present is to advise you that we have taken a legal opinion upon the question and are thereby fully confirmed of the justice of it. As it would be painful to us to urge the claim by *compulsory measures* we take this opportunity to suggest a friendly adjudication of the matter by referring it to arbitration. Your early answer is requested[4].

A reply, if it came, has not survived; and this hitherto immensely valuable connection came to an end – though one of Stocks's sons, Samuel junior, later established a key working relationship with the Parker family which redounded to the benefit of both for over two decades[5].

The executors, of course, were also responsible for discharging Robert Parker's own debts and unpaid expenses, of which, in comparison with his assets, there were very few. As the appraisers of Robert's personal estate had warned them, they needed to be wary of others' upward miscalculations. One claim – albeit, in the scheme of things, for a relatively small sum – came like a bolt from the blue. On 14 January 1817, some 18 months after Robert Parker's death and without having contacted them previously, Dr. Thomas Yarrold, a medical practitioner in Manchester, wrote to the executors, claiming a sum of 100 guineas for professional attendance on Robert 'and formerly and by his direction on some of his workmen'. This letter was the opening salvo in an acrimonious dispute which rumbled on for almost a year, and whose outcome satisfied neither party. The episode illustrates facets of the Parkers' circumstances not evident elsewhere; and, above all, reveals how, though normally extremely resilient, they were ultimately prepared to compromise in defence of their public reputation.

---

2   Pkr A, 3/5/21, J. Lea to Messrs. Taylor & Unwin, Solicitors, 17 July 1815, and Lea to Messrs. Parker, Kinder & Co. 24 July 1815, endorsed with 'Answered 4 Sept. WP'.
3   Pkr A, 1/20/11, RP's nephews to J. Formby, 13 Feb. & 17 Apr. 1817.
4   Pkr A, 1/17/14, Executors to SS, 4 June 1816.
5   In 1815, prior to the break with the Parkers, Stocks senior had partnered his son, Samuel junior, as cotton manufacturers and dealers in a warehouse at 6, Friday Street, Manchester, where they employed 20 people directly, together with a number of handloom weavers who worked in their own cellars. – R. Lloyd-Jones & M.J. Lewis, 'The Economic Structure of 'Cottonopolis' in 1815', *Textile History,* xvii (i) (1986), 80.

From the outset Dr. Yarrold maintained that his was a 'very moderate' claim. He insisted that his services had commenced in 1803, and that Robert Parker had summoned him regularly during the next four years. Then, when Yarrold moved from Stockport to Manchester, his attendance had been 'much less frequent', although he had been consulted 'during every succeeding year', the last occasion being 'a fortnight before [Robert's] lamented death, when he spoke of the excellent state of his health'[6]. In replying two days later, the executors indicated that they were 'extremely surprised at the claim...no part of the...family being aware that Dr. Yarrold [was] at any time considered [Robert's] regular medical adviser'. While acknowledging that he had treated Robert following an accident at Disley 'about five years ago', they reminded Yarrold that he had received a fee of five guineas on that occasion. Moreover, Sarah Parker had informed them that since then Yarrold had been 'in no instance sent for by her late husband'. They were, however, anxious to settle the matter justly and enclosed 20 guineas as a 'handsome consideration for any advice [Dr. Yarrold] may immediately and spontaneously have given to [their] late friend'[7].

Yarrold's vigorous reply accused the executors of charging him 'with dishonesty'. Simultaneously shifting his ground considerably and extending his field of fire, he went on to list a series of attendances, several of which had been of 'some duration'. A boy had been injured 'at the Mill'; Robert Parker had been treated for 'an ulcerated sore throat'; he had attended Thomas Parker for 'the duration of' some illness; a more prolonged attendance had been required in the case of a family living in one of the workers' cottages at Heaton Mersey; Thomas Parker had also suffered from a bad throat, 'when I stayed in the house three nights'; Yarrold had cared for one of the family's housekeepers; he had treated Robert Parker's legs; and 'at least once I have prescribed...for Mrs. Parker'. Christopher Parker in particular was challenged to confirm that Dr. Yarrold had attended his uncle since moving to Manchester. He had indeed been paid five guineas on one occasion but, that apart, he 'never did receive a farthing from Mr. Parker'. To substantiate his claim, Yarrold named witnesses and, in further corroboration, enclosed an earlier letter from Thomas Parker[8].

A lull followed until 23 January. Yarrold then suggested arbitration 'by any man of integrity that you can name'. There being no response from the executors, he called on Thomas Parker, who was out; and later wrote to both him and Christopher Parker. The latter had no wish to enter into correspondence about the matter; the executors saw no need for adjudication by a third party; and felt that the 25 guineas had entirely settled the issue.

6   Pkr A, 1/11/1, Yarrold to Executors, 14 Jan. 1817.
7   Pkr A, 1/11/2, Executors to Yarrold, 16 Jan. 1817.
8   Pkr A, 1/11/3, Yarrold to Executors, 17 Jan. 1817; Pollard, 'Factory Village', 520.

Shortly afterwards, things came to a head during a stormy meeting between the three men. At one point, according to Yarrold, Christopher Parker stated forcibly that 'as his uncle had paid me some money, he might have paid me more...After a time Mr. Christopher Parker repeated his remark and I put on my hat and left'[9]. Here, it seems, we get to the nub of the matter. While they queried some of Yarrold's assertions, the executors did not waste their energy in attempts to undermine the sequence of events outlined by him. They simply refused to believe that Robert Parker and those for whom he felt responsible had benefited from services over an extended period for which he had not paid. No doubt they also wondered why it had taken Dr. Yarrold so long to contact them in the first place.

Once the dust had settled somewhat, Dr. Yarrold returned to the fray in letters to Thomas Stubington Penny, James's father, and then to Daniel Grant, one of the Parkers' solicitors. In the second missive he threatened, should arbitration continue to be refused, 'to write the life of Mr. Robert Parker that I may have an opportunity of laying before the public this transaction'[10]. This was blackmail and, up to a point, it worked. All four executors wrote a joint letter to Yarrold on 14 August[11]. They deplored his threat in the strongest possible terms, but they did not dismiss it; they agreed to arbitration by two respectable men, with each party nominating one of them. His blackmail having proved effective, Yarrold replied two days later in calmly disingenuous terms:

> Had I written the life of the late Robert Parker Esq. it would have done his memory no discredit. I respected him and honour his memory. My object in the life would have been to show the progress of the manufactures of the place, and to have given the correspondence between the executors and myself as an appendix'[12].

He concluded by undertaking to devote any award to charitable purposes.

Taking time over their task, perhaps to let tempers cool, the two arbiters – Mr. Wood (for the Parkers) and Mr. Thomas Harbottle (for Dr. Yarrold) – delivered a brief judgement on 24 November, resolutely (yet somewhat vertiginously) perching on the fence between the two parties, though ultimately giving the Parkers the benefit of the doubt. While in their view the evidence did not sustain a conclusion that Dr. Yarrold 'was engaged as the late Mr. Parker's regular physician at a yearly stipend, yet we are of opinion that he...is justly entitled to a remuneration for various consultations'. They recommended that the executors 'make what compensation they may judge

9   Pkr A, 1/11/4, Yarrold to Executors, 23 Jan. 1817; 1/11/5, Yarrold to TP, 8 Feb. 1817; 1/11/6, Yarrold to CP, 19 Feb. 1817 & draft reply.
10   Pkr A, 1/11/7, Yarrold to TP, 27 June 1817; 1/11/8, Yarrold to D. Grant, 4 Aug. 1817.
11   Pkr A, 1/11/9, Executors to Yarrold, 14 Aug. 1817.
12   Pkr A, 1/11/10, Yarrold to Executors, 16 Aug. 1817.

proper'. The Parkers responded by sending Yarrold a further 20 guineas, together with '3 guineas for three tickets to Dr. Yarrold's lectures in Stockport which he now says were not paid for'[13].

To judge from this and other evidence, the executorship was no mere formality. In economically difficult times garnering a rich man's assets was a hard, slogging business, requiring close attention to detail and sound judgement, both in a legal and a wider human context. In the face of attempts to divide them, the Parkers stuck together. They were nobody's fools in regard to money and extremely wary of exploitation. Moreover, they turned few, if any, blind eyes towards their debtors, although there are many examples of their supporting other people in need. While unwilling to pay over the odds in wages, they made free accommodation available to many of their workers and otherwise looked after their health and welfare: not just by providing educational facilities, but in more personal and practical ways. Irrespective of other considerations, this made sound commercial sense. They were also convinced that their own prosperity depended, to a considerable degree, on their public reputation. When they asked others in the cotton trade for judgements about people's credit worthiness, great emphasis was placed – by both parties – on the perceived 'respectability' of potential customers. In business circles this was a key touchstone of their era and the Parkers knew that they could not afford to risk their own standing in this regard. They had learned the cost and the value of their reputation and feared that a publication by Dr. Yarrold would jeopardise it.

Albeit with a keen sense as to what was feasible and sensible, the executors relentlessly maximised income and minimised expenditure. They never relinquished this task. When they took over responsibility in 1822 for insuring the 'Stock & Utensils & Goods' in a warehouse in Burnley, it appears that they had obtained them in lieu of unpaid debts. One debt, dating from 1810, was discharged only in June 1825; in November 1826 they collected '3d. in the pound [from] the bad debts belonging to the estate of J.T. Koster & Gilfillans' in Liverpool; and the residue of bad debts which had originated in 1811 – from Hunters, Rainey & Co. in London, and from Hunters, Rainey & Morton in Glasgow – was still being pursued as late as October 1837[14].

Rationalisation and New Trends

Meanwhile, there were other matters to be attended to. Under Robert Parker's will three of his nephews were not only executors but also trustees. Thus,

---

13   Pkr A, 1/11/11, Executors to Yarrold, 23 Aug. 1817; 1/11/12, Award of Harbottle & Wood, 24 Nov. 1817; 1/11/13, Executors' Decision, 4 Dec. 1817. There is a contemporary summary of events at 1/11/14.

14   Pkr A, 3/13/2, Endorsement to Sun Fire Office Policy 984893, 20 Mar. 1822; 2/11/3, JM to TP, 23 June 1825; 3/10/63, Anon. to Parkers, 8 Nov. 1826; 3/18/66, JM to WP, 21 Oct. 1837.

with the ready consent of the fourth, William Parker, there was much more they could do to augment their inheritance, which had, perhaps, been Robert Parker's intention in formulating the various arrangements in the first place. As a result, the years after his death saw significant adjustments to the family business, no doubt partly in response to deteriorating economic conditions in the domestic market.

Success in a volatile industry such as cotton manufacturing required, among other things, not just a keen eye for opportunity but also a sure sense of when to reduce capacity. In January 1815, some months before Robert Parker's death, the partnership with Thomas Worthington, having run its allotted two-year span, was dissolved by mutual consent, though Worthington continued to share the cost of insuring the finished goods stored in the High Street warehouse. In April of the following year the partnership with Kinder was also dissolved[15]. Meanwhile, in September 1815 an estate agent had been assured that 'the executors...have no intention whatsoever of continuing the spinning concern' in Stockport. 'We will insert it in next week's paper [and] if you can sell the factory, the purchaser can have the machinery low'[16]. Before long, therefore, manufacturing capacity was located solely in the works at Heaton Mersey.

Major problems arose there due to marked fluctuations in water levels in the Mersey and occasional floods, both of which disrupted production. These difficulties originated in the operations of a Mr. Fielden and his associates at a mill and weir nearby. Problems first arose in the months prior to Robert senior's death and persisted for several years, resulting in what Lingard & Vaughan, the Parkers' solicitors in Stockport, described as 'a voluminous correspondence'; this reveals successive legal manoeuvres, and threats and counter-threats by both parties. The matter came before the Cheshire magistrates in the spring of 1819 and, with the Parkers retaining a London barrister, was scheduled to proceed from there to the Court of King's Bench. However, Fielden ultimately proposed an out-of-court settlement: in addition to various undertakings, he would pay the Parkers £40 per annum for two years in compensation. Although the Parkers had incurred legal costs of over £1,000, they accepted this offer and the matter was closed with relief if not satisfaction[17]. It is also from the period following this settlement that we get the first evidence of substantial purchases of cloth which had not been manufactured at Heaton Mersey. In a series of transactions in 1821-22 Thomas Parker bought goods worth over £2,000, largely from Leonard Cooper's cambric, muslin and calico warehouse at Bridgewater Buildings

15   Pkr A, 3/12/2, Dissolution, 17 Jan. 1815; 2/7/8, Sun Fire Office Policy 902928, 25 Jan. 1815; 1/20/9, *London Gazette*, 9 Apr. 1816.

16   Pkr A, 1/17/3, Copy, Parkers to J. Beard, 2 Sept. 1815.

17   Pkr A, 1/6/1-4, 6-9, 13-16, 18, Misc. Papers, Parkers in account with Lingard & Vaughan, Solicitors, 1815-20; 1/17/1, 20, Papers to TP from J. Vaughan, 19 Feb. & 19 July 1820.

in Manchester[18]. Why he did so is unclear, though there may have been a connection with the earlier dispute. By then production at Heaton may have been less diverse than previously. Falling prices, one of the continuing consequences of technological advance, may have made the deals particularly attractive. Also, as Robert Parker had done in the past (though he had bought his cotton goods from Parker, Worthington & Parkers), Thomas bought on his personal, rather than the firm's, account. It was a sign of things to come, for he later became a substantial purchaser on the open market.

There was another shift of emphasis. Many years before 1821 the family had acquired office and warehousing facilities at 47, High Street in Manchester. Following Robert Parker's death, his nephews began to scrutinise sale catalogues for other property in the town centre. At least one property which interested them was put up for auction, perhaps a sign at a time of falling prices that another type of sale had proved difficult[19]. In the autumn of 1821 the executors almost reached agreement with a Mr. Clegg for the purchase of premises in Birchin Lane, Manchester. There were legal difficulties, however, and they eventually pulled out of the deal, Clegg 'being unwilling to be at any expense in making the title marketable'[20]. Moreover, at some points before March 1825 (and in certain instances, it seems, before the partition of 1822) they acquired additional properties – a house and a warehouse in Mosley Street, and other premises in Market Street and Tib Street as well as on a large site at Albion Buildings next to Piccadilly[21]. These acquisitions were not designed to augment the warehousing facilities which they themselves used but, instead, to generate rental income from inner-city properties, which eventually became substantial.

The clearest evidence relates to their sales of goods abroad which, in common with British overseas trade in general, expanded and diversified considerably in the years after Waterloo[22]. In the two years from 1817 details of 36 bills of exchange relating to overseas business, for sums ranging between £100 and £700, have survived. Most of their shipments went direct from Liverpool but some were via London. In southern Europe and the Mediterranean there were consignments to Lisbon and Cadiz, to Malaga, Alicante and Gibraltar, and to Livorno and Izmir[23]. Livorno was an entirely new market for them and the first cargo, scheduled to arrive there in March 1818, was of 'summer articles'. The Parkers carefully gathered intelligence of recommended lengths and widths of material, and of prices, as well as the most up-to-date advice available about how to cope with local customs

18   Pkr A, 2/1/23, J. Higgin to Parkers, 1 Dec. 1821; 3/13/ 25, 27-28, 30, 34, Bills for Purchases, 1821-22.
19   Pkr A, 3/5/22, Printed Catalogue, 29 July 1818.
20   Pkr A, 1/17/10, Bill from Taylor & Sheriff to Executors, Oct – Dec. 1820.
21   See below, 83-84.
22   Davis, *Industrial Revolution and British Overseas Trade*, 16, 69-70.
23   Pkr A, 3/4/6, 8-9, 12, 19-20, 22-23, Bills of Exchange, 1817-19.

procedures:

> The larger the packages are, the better, as the duty is charged per case or bale; but for facilitating the sale, 3 or 4 small bales might be enclosed in one large one...A bale should only contain one quality of goods and all the pieces should be of the same length, width and fineness. A strict attention to the assortments etc. recommended is absolutely necessary[24].

In the following year the Parkers were joined in this venture by their friends and in-laws, the Healds; and the two firms engaged William Jago & Co. of Livorno as their local agent on a guarantee of sales worth at least £2,000 from the commission house of Orr & Robinson in Liverpool[25]. Transatlantic cargoes went to Quebec, and to Baltimore, Philadelphia, New York and New Orleans. Other consignments proceeded to Jamaica (where they had successfully secured Messrs. Bogles and Co. as their agents) and to Vera Cruz in Mexico. In addition there were longer-distance ventures to Argentina through Buenos Aires and (round Cape Horn) to Santiago in Chile[26]. These latter were entirely new markets. The break-up of the Spanish and Portuguese colonial empires led to the emergence of a series of independent republics which were keen to trade with Britain, and exports to them grew rapidly during the 1820s[27]. There are no records of sales in northern Europe, though in April 1818 Thomas Parker solicited detailed advice on how to negotiate the complex exchange mechanisms in Hamburg[28]. This wide range of overseas trading involved the Parkers in a welter of intricate business. It also underpinned a continuing growth in their wealth, despite occasional disasters. Following one of these they received what was probably their most cryptic and least sympathetic communication. In October 1821 G.J. Sealy, a regular correspondent, wrote from Liverpool: 'I am sorry to inform you that the *Emperor Alexander* [en route from Liverpool to Bahia] is totally lost on the coast of Ireland. I hope you are fully insured'[29].

PARTITION

The nephews lost no time during 1821 in preparing for partition in the following year. This confirms their determination – for there was no compulsion – to strike out on their own as soon as possible. Copies of the formal agreement between them, of 13 April 1821, have not survived, but

---

24   Pkr A, 1/9/1, 'Scheme of Summer Articles', n.d. but 1817-18.

25   Pkr A, 3/13/35, J. Orr to Parkers & the Healds, 27 Mar. 1819; 3/13/37, Orr's Memorandum of Guarantee, 30 Mar. 1819.

26   Pkr A, 3/4/7, 10-11, 13-18, 21, Bills of Exchange, 1817-19.

27   Davis, *Industrial Revolution and British Overseas Trade*, 18-19.

28   Pkr A, 3/5/6, Anon. to TP, 27 Apr. 1818.

29   Pkr A, 2/1/64, Sealy to Parkers, 24 Oct. 1821. See also 2/1/64, G.B. Highfield & Co. Liverpool to Parkers, 25 Oct. 1821.

very detailed solicitors' bills, common at that time, reveal the broad outline of what transpired[30].

The outcome for Christopher and William Parker is least certain. The £20,000 which the former had received in 1810 must have been augmented, probably substantially, because he surrendered his share in the premises at 47, High Street, no doubt for a material consideration. He was certainly engaged in extending his property holdings in Petteril Green around the time of the partition. Later, Thomas Parker left him £10,000 in his will, suggesting a residual feeling at least on his part that Christopher had received somewhat less than he deserved[31]. Yet the settlement had to be deemed to be equal: and there is no doubt that it was mutually agreed, and that Christopher's relations with his cousins were not only untroubled but close. Both he and William were indemnified by the other two against any responsibility for making annual payments to Sarah Parker which, as things turned out, was an exceedingly valuable element in their settlements.

The outcome for William, while still uncertain, was also more complex. He too surrendered his share in the High Street premises and, 'in part satisfaction' of this, received £6,000. However, he also retained a significant interest in some of the inner-city properties acquired since 1815 and was sole owner of a house in Mosley Street, Manchester. Moreover, whether or not this was part of his settlement – it could have developed informally – he shared in some of Thomas Parker's overseas trading ventures, though to a much lesser degree than did his older brother. In view of William's purchase after partition of the Skirwith Abbey estate in Cumberland[32], the amount transferred to him was probably much more than the £22,000 he would have received had he left the business earlier. Physically, he was never strong and, of all Robert Parker's nephews, appears to have had the least aptitude and stomach for business. Since his estate was initially small – only 150 acres – and on poor land, he could not afford to eschew business activity entirely. He joined Thomas in exporting abroad from time to time; but customers dealt with him through Thomas; he seems never to have been involved independently on his own account; and he settled quickly and comfortably into a quiet, private life at Skirwith.

All Robert Parker's real estate passed to Thomas and Robert junior. The latter got the works at Heaton Mersey. He had long been closely engaged in manufacturing there; and, once his uncle had acquired a home more suited to his standing in the trade, Robert had lived in the house at Heaton Mersey. Now he himself acquired a much finer home – the house at Tithe Barn Hill, with its gardens and pleasure grounds, surrendered by

---

30   Pkr A, 3/12/16, Bill from Lingard, Vaughan & Lingard, 6 Dec. 1822; 1/17/11, Bill from Taylor & Sheriff, Dec. 1821 – Jan. 1822.
31   See below, 103.
32   See below, 52-53.

Sarah Parker. He also obtained the colliery at Woodley. Always primarily interested in marketing cotton goods, Thomas got the wharf at Heaton and the premises in Manchester, together with the Cheadle Wood estate; and a 'House in the Park' in Stockport where the 'Spinning Concern' had been located. The two men quickly established a joint company, T. & R. Parker & Co., to manage and co-ordinate their business affairs; and, also jointly, they assumed responsibility for the annual payment of £1,000 to Sarah Parker (70% by Thomas and 30% by Robert).

Thus, the legacy in cotton manufacturing and marketing left by Robert Parker senior was not dismembered. While in terms of ownership it was divided in two, the division was coherent and the formation of the new company ensured that, essentially, operations were akin to those of a single concern, though with the freedom for both men also to operate on their own account. The evidence suggests that, in agreeing to this, William and Christopher actively wished to disengage, and that they received what they regarded as adequate compensation for doing so. The bridge between the founder of the business and his successors had been crossed safely and amicably. Henceforward, Thomas and Robert Parker junior were firmly in charge of the family's endeavours in the cotton trade. A new era was underway.

A FLYING START

In Cumberland tongues must have wagged incessantly about the Parkers in 1822. While Robert began to enjoy his new home at Tithe Barn Hill in Heaton Norris, Christopher spent most, if not all, of his time at Petteril Green; and, having moved there very quickly, William chose to live permanently at Skirwith Abbey. And then, before the year was out, Thomas too acquired a seat in Cumberland, purchasing the Warwick Hall estate, five miles east of Carlisle and near the village of Warwick Bridge, for the substantial sum of £45,000[33]. Clearly, three of the cousins wished to re-engage with their family's native heath and their efforts to do so got off to a flying start.

After many years in India where he made a fortune, a John Orfeur Yates had returned to Cumbria in 1767. In the following year he married the 18-year-old Mary Aglionby, bought the Skirwith estate and, employing Thomas Addison, proceeded to build a house there which was completed in 1774. In view of the property's supposed origins as the site of a religious house of the Knights Templar, Yates called his new home Skirwith Abbey. It was a fine, four-square, two-storey Palladian mansion, with a front of seven bays and a full basement sunk in a broad railed area, the whole set within 'pleasure grounds [of] good taste'. At the turn of the century it was described as 'fit for the reception of a genteel family, with a good garden, walled, and

---

33   J.M. Robinson, *A Guide to the Country Houses of the North-West* (London, 1991), 140.

well stocked with fruit trees [and] in a sporting country'. The marriage was an unhappy one and, once the couple's five children were reared, Mary became thoroughly miserable and lonely in an isolated house which she also found cold and uncomfortable. Subsequently, Yates lost control of his assets in India and, facing mounting debts, the family was obliged to let Skirwith Abbey and to move to a much smaller townhouse, Hutton Hall in Penrith. There, using her own inheritance, Mary steadily discharged her husband's debts, while their eldest son, Francis, similarly constrained, pursued a career in the army. Following his mother's death in 1816, Francis moved back to Skirwith. Then, in 1822, he inherited from an aunt a sizeable estate at Nunnery, but only on condition that he lived there and changed his name to Aglionby. Although he quickly sold Skirwith Abbey to William Parker, Francis was loathe to leave it – 'I will never love any place so well'[34]. All the evidence indicates that William Parker came to hold the same view. We do not know how much he paid for Skirwith Abbey, but the sum must have been considerably less than the £45,000 Thomas paid for Warwick Hall. Some 20 miles to the south-east of Warwick Hall, William's fine house but much smaller property – around 150 acres at the time of the purchase – was on much poorer land underneath the high Pennines.

Thomas Parker's situation, of course, was rather different from that of the rest in another way. As Thomas senior's eldest son and heir, he had inherited Old Town from his father in 1807. What the latter had done with the house and its adjacent land after moving south to join his younger brother, Robert senior, is unknown; the property was probably let to relatives or others. In June 1807, at the manorial court held 'under the Thorn[tree] in Hesket Lane'[35], Thomas had exercised his right to be admitted to the property as a customary tenant (akin in all respects, except for manorial fines, to a freeholder) inheriting from his father. The lands he came into there were of very small compass, which leaves one wondering whether, in addition to the mortgage which started Robert Parker in the cotton industry, some of the property at Old Town had also been sold for that purpose. Thomas subsequently kept in touch with developments in the locality and, of course, attended Robert senior's burial at High Hesket in 1815. In the post-war years which followed, poor agricultural prices made life very difficult for insubstantial yeomen farmers and between 1815 and 1819 Thomas snapped up six parcels of land adjacent to Old Town for a total of £2,066, plus a £40 life annuity to one vendor[36]. There was never any question of Thomas living

---

34 *Carlisle Journal*, 9 July 1803; H. Summerson, *'An Ancient Squire's Family': the History of the Aglionbys* (Carlisle, 2007), 120-127.

35 For the origins of this outdoor location, see W.T. McIntire, 'The Court Thorn', *The Cumberland News*, 22 Jan. 1944, 4.

36 The manuscripts dealing with these transactions are in the author's possession, courtesy of Mr. & Mrs. Robert Ferguson of High Hesket, but see also Pkr A, 3/11/1-2, Solicitor's Bill from Grace & Blaymire to TP, May - Sept. 1815.

permanently at Old Town House – though a forwarded letter of May 1825 suggests that he did so temporarily during developments at Warwick Hall[37]. Nor, however, had he any wish to sell: the property was, after all, at the heart of the family saga. His new property at Warwick Hall was of a quite different order and quality from that at Skirwith Abbey. It was a compact estate in a beautiful location by the banks of the River Eden – to the east of Carlisle, a few miles to the north-east of Old Town, and on the main route across the Pennines to Newcastle.

It only remained to set a formal seal on these various developments. As soon as his purchase had been completed and he had become a rural landowner as well as a commercial proprietor, Thomas applied to the College of Arms for a grant of armorial bearings. Supported by a family pedigree drawn up by William, his application was successful and a coat of arms was granted on 10 February 1823. Under the terms of the grant the arms were to be borne by all male-line descendants of the grantee's late father, who had died in 1807: but, significantly, this limitation was specifically extended to include Christopher Parker of Petteril Green and his male-line descendants[38]. Thus, the three brothers and their cousin continued to stick together. Having moved in less than two generations from the ranks of yeomen farmers, they had finally arrived, collectively, as landed gentry.

A FAMILY TRAGEDY

Just before the grant of arms came through, the Parkers suffered a bewildering and appalling calamity. At his new home at Tithe Barn Hill, Robert Parker's mental health failed completely and permanently. According to a later family record, 'he was quite normal until the age of thirty-six [in 1823] when he became a mental case and never recovered'[39]. Apparently, there was no prior warning of this catastrophe. He had played a vigorous role in the family's industrial activities, had continued to do so after his uncle Robert's death, and was scheduled for the future to mastermind manufacturing at Heaton Mersey. From 1815 he had espoused his late uncle's commitment to philanthropy with more enthusiasm than the others. He had become a member of the committee which managed Stockport Sunday School, contributed to its building fund, and was a signatory of a letter circulated in the district appealing for further contributions. In 1822, following the partition and in what appears to have been a statement of intent, he had been chiefly responsible for financing a major extension to the Sunday school at Heaton Mersey: Thomas and William each subscribed £50 to the venture,

---

37   Pkr A, 2/11/7, JSP to TP, 28 May 1825.
38   Timothy H.S. Duke, Chester Herald, College of Arms to Fiona M. Roebuck, 16 Dec. 2010, in the author's possession.
39   Pkr B, 24, '[MS] Outline of a Family', 15.

but Robert paid the several hundred pounds which it took to complete and furnish the extension (Figure 11). On 27 July 1822 he had laid its foundation stone, which was inscribed 'for the education and religious instruction of the children of the labouring classes'[40].

Figure 11. Heaton Mersey Sunday School following extension.

Strenuous efforts were made to have Robert treated successfully. At least three practitioners were consulted. Beginning on 27 January 1823, a Dr. Holme of Brown Street, Manchester (possibly a relative) saw Robert at Heaton Norris 28 times between then and the end of February, on five of those occasions twice in a single day. In March and early April there were six further visits 'at Flixton'; and, after Robert had been taken to live with Thomas in the Manchester suburb of Ardwick Green, two final visits before the end of that month[41]. A Dr. Hull and a Mr. J.A. Ransom were also engaged, apparently as frequently for, compared with Dr. Holmes's bill of £108, they charged £138 and £73 respectively[42]. It was all to no avail

40   Heginbotham, *Stockport: Ancient and Modern*, ii, 389; Parker B, 20, Judith Higgins to Robert Parker of Morecambe, 7 Aug. 1991.

41   Pkr A, 1/17/27, Dr. Holme's Bill to TP, 26 Feb. 1824.

42   Pkr A, 1/17/26, Dr. Hull to TP, 12 Mar. 1824; 1/17/28, Ransome's Bill, 1823-24. The only one of these practitioners to be positively identified is J.A. Ransome (1779-1837), who lived at 1, St. Peter's Square, Princess Street, Manchester , had 'a high and well-deserved reputation as a surgeon', and later treated the politician William Huskisson following the railway accident which killed him in 1830. For a short biography, see Sir D'Arcy Power (reviser), *Plarr's Lives of the Fellows of the Royal College of Surgeons of England*, ii (1930), 213-214. I am grateful to Adrian Allen for this reference.

and for the rest of his life Robert was 'incapable of managing his affairs[43]', living firstly with Thomas at Ardwick Green and Warwick Hall, and later with William at Skirwith Abbey.   Latterly, Robert was known as 'of Old Town, Stockport, Warwick Hall and Skirwith Abbey', but these were only courtesy addresses and did not signify control over property.

While there are no precise details of his condition, he was not confined to bed and did not have to be constrained in any way.   He lived very quietly and was capable of little other than regularly reading the newspapers[44].   He probably suffered a severe and permanent nervous breakdown, of which there was little understanding at that time, and for which there was no effective therapy.   The breakdown, if that is what it was, may have been due to the stress of overseeing the works at Heaton at a particularly difficult time and, latterly, of having become formally vested with responsibility for doing so for the foreseeable future.   So, just over a year after the partition had come into effect, Thomas Parker found himself facing a daunting prospect: he would have to manage affairs, both at Heaton Mersey and in Manchester, as well as at Warwick Hall, entirely on his own; and also, with his wife, to care for a mentally incapacitated brother.   It was a challenging situation.

---

43   This was the phrase used in Thomas Parker's will of 28 Mar. 1828. – Pkr B, 28.
44   Pkr A, 1/14/5, WP to Rev. Kidd, 1 Feb. 1841. See below.

Chapter 4:

A Landed Entrepreneur, 1823-28:
Manufacturing and Overseas Trade

ADJUSTMENTS

The sudden onset of Robert Parker's incapacity produced a crisis in the family's affairs. Despite the progress made over three decades, the plans laid in recent years were, if not stopped in their tracks, severely threatened. It was necessary to review strategy and tactics, and to assess how the objectives of the partition might be carried forward most effectively in a radically altered situation. Great and abiding sadness remained but, after due consideration, there was no going back. The agreements ratified in advance of partition were left undisturbed, as were William and Christopher at Skirwith Abbey and at Petteril Green. The joint company of T. & R. Parker & Co. was retained and Thomas took on both his own and his brother's responsibilities for running it. In view of Robert's condition, this sometimes gave rise to legal and procedural difficulties but, with the ingenuity of the Parkers' solicitors and apart from an occasional, consequent delay, these were safely overcome[1]. To all intents and purposes, and certainly as far as the outside world was concerned, Thomas Parker took the tragedy in his stride. He was a strong, resourceful and talented man and needed to be.

In one key respect, however, there was fundamental change. Even had he possessed the time, energy and inclination to do so, Thomas could not have managed operations at Heaton Mersey effectively. He had never developed the necessary expertise and, in any case, was now in charge of complex marketing ventures overseas and premises in Manchester, as well as his newly-acquired estate in Cumberland. Perhaps in the light of the family's past experience with Samuel Stocks senior, the employment of a salaried manager at Heaton was also judged to be inappropriate[2]. What Heaton needed was the personal commitment and flair of an experienced cotton manufacturer, which were available only at a price, and a considerable one at that. The right person would want unfettered managerial control and a large stake in the profits of the enterprise; and in the prevailing circumstances these could only be made available under a leasing arrangement. In return for shouldering responsibilities as landlord, Thomas had to settle for a rental income from Heaton, plus certain marketing advantages arising from his working relationship with the lessee. Particularly in the fluctuating years for

---

1   See below, 60-61.
2   See above, 44.

the cotton industry which lay ahead, this proved to be a wise judgement; but it must also have been a painful one. He granted a lease of the Heaton works to Samuel Stocks junior, son of the late Robert Parker's long-time collaborator, who had broken with his father. In return Stocks became responsible, as part of his annual rent of c. £2,000, for paying the £1,000 a year due to Robert's widow, Sarah Parker, a neat rationalisation which, from Thomas's viewpoint, kept her at arm's length. The two men also entered into a formal business partnership over and above their relations as landlord and tenant[3]. Dealings between them were not uniformly smooth for, though often at a distance, Thomas kept in close touch with developments; and Stocks could always be relied on for blunt comments, not just on conditions in the cotton trade but on any other matter which came or was brought to his attention. Despite and partly perhaps because of this, the arrangement stood the test of time; and Samuel Stocks junior became a valued and trusted (if still blazingly candid) collaborator, not just at Heaton Mersey but in numerous instances in Manchester too.

In view of the elaborate plans which Thomas began to formulate for developments at Warwick Hall, other key personnel also became involved in the management of his business affairs further south. Chief among these was James Stubington Penny, a fellow executor of Robert Parker's will. His early home was at Heaton Norris and by the 1820s, and probably long before then, his family owned a cotton factory in Manchester[4]. Penny, however, spent most of his later working life in Liverpool, where he ran a shipping business with his son, Edward. In 1826 another son, James, became a partner in a merchant house in Mexico City where he was joined by his two other brothers; and, together, Thomas Parker and Penny senior subsequently sent many consignments to Mexico. Throughout that decade Penny also collaborated with Thomas Parker in a wide variety of other overseas trading ventures. He regularly sought his advice, and was happy to accede to what he clearly perceived to be Thomas's superior business acumen and trading experience but it was Penny who fixed things at the cotton trade's chief port – receiving goods from Manchester, providing advanced notice of shipping schedules, choosing vessels, organising insurance, dealing with officialdom, accounting for outgoings and remittances, and regularly providing his partner with the latest news of market conditions overseas. Their personal accounts were kept separately but, albeit informally, they worked largely but not exclusively in partnership. During this period Penny was but one of numerous individuals who moved from Manchester to Liverpool, subsequently blending their earlier experience of manufacturing with growing expertise in the import of raw cotton and the export of cotton cloth[5].

---

3   Pkr A, 2/5/72, Anon. to Parker, Stocks & Co. n.d. but 1823-24

4   See Pkr A, 3/10/68, JSP to TP, 1 Dec. 1826. In Robert senior's will of 1815 Penny's address was given as 'Heaton Norris', which was adjacent to Heaton Mersey.

5   See below, 71-82; Chapman, *Cotton Industry in the Industrial Revolution*, 38-39.

By the early nineteenth century the port of Liverpool had come to play an indispensable role in the rapid development of the cotton industry. A century earlier it had begun to prosper through exporting coal and salt, the chief raw materials of its hinterland, and for long continued to do so. On the import side, besides a growing commerce with Ireland, it also moved into the Baltic timber trade. Subsequently, however, and for many decades, Manchester textile merchants dominated the promotion of schemes for the improvement of water carriage to and from the port, so that by the last quarter of the eighteenth century an effective transport infrastructure linked Liverpool to the economic region of south Lancashire, Cheshire and north Staffordshire. By the time Robert senior's career began to blossom Liverpool was connected with most parts of the world, serving the cotton industry in particular, as well as many overseas producers of primary products, including raw cotton. Thereafter, new contacts emerged in India and China following the end of the East India Company's monopolies, and in South America during and after the wars of independence from Spain and Portugal. There was a ninefold increase in Liverpool's dock area in the eight decades down to 1836, with the massive Prince's Dock being completed in 1821, and the tonnage of shipping using the port doubled between 1815 and 1830[6]. Irrespective of the apparently close relations between their two families, it made eminently good sense for Thomas Parker to collaborate with James Stubington Penny, someone who, from personal experience, knew the cotton industry well, but was also now based in the industry's chief avenue to and from international markets.

Although a textile industry (of mixed linen and cotton) had emerged in Manchester from the early seventeenth century, development quickened with the steady improvement of the town's transport links with Liverpool. Spectacular growth in cotton manufacturing began during the 1770s with the inventions of Arkwright, Crompton and Hargreaves and the beginnings of the factory system under Oldknow and his contemporaries. Down to the early 1790s large parcels of land from great estates near the centre of the town were sold for development in response to increasing demand and soaring property values. Through a combination of natural increase and immigration, Manchester's population grew from 22,481 in 1773 to 126,066 in 1821, the year before partition of Robert senior's assets – an expansion which was accompanied by 'seemingly unprecedented levels of poverty'[7]. In some years during this period the growth in manufacturing capacity was faster

---

6   F.E. Hyde, *Liverpool and the Mersey: An Economic History of a Port, 1700-1970* (Newton Abbot, 1971), 3-79, 247; Belchem, (ed.), *Liverpool 800*, 126-138, 247-248, 259.

7   Hartwell, *Manchester* , 17-18. As Hartwell points out, the deplorable situation in Manchester was highlighted in J. Kay, *Moral and Physical Conditions of the Working Classes* (London, 1832) and in E. Chadwick, *Report on the Sanitary Condition of the Labouring Population* (London, 1842), both being 'more influential' than F. Engel's latterly better-known *The Condition of the Working Class in England* of 1844, which was not published in Britain until 1892.

than anything previously experienced. Even before the turn of the century emigration to the suburbs had already begun, one such being Ardwick Green where later Thomas Parker went to live. There was a massive expansion of exports to the United States following the end of the war of 1812; and a much more widespread proliferation of overseas trade after Waterloo[8].

Particularly when he became distracted by affairs in Cumbria, Thomas needed a competent and trustworthy agent in this hectic environment and he found one in the person of James Marchanton, who was a third member of his core team. For some years employed jointly by Thomas and Samuel Stocks, and walking over every weekday to 47, High Street from his home in neighbouring Salford, Marchanton managed a welter of business. Like Penny, he kept meticulous accounts and was a very frequent correspondent with his employer. Above all, he acted as Thomas Parker's eyes and ears in the town. He sought precise instructions from him, partly because he was occasionally unsure of exactly how to handle matters, but primarily because he recognised that his boss was a stickler. The Healds, Thomas's in-laws, were also major confidants. Not, of course, in Thomas's employ, they nevertheless stood ready to facilitate his business, particularly when sensitive issues were involved. Invariably helpful were their regular visits to see Mary Parker (*nee* Heald) and Thomas at Warwick Hall.[9] Beyond this inner circle lay an outer one of business associates, dealers at the Cotton Exchange, solicitors, bankers and insurance agents.

Thomas's correspondence with these individuals was incessant. Leaving aside other qualities, he was an immensely hard-working man, juggling a variety of concerns in many different locations at home and abroad. It might be thought that his heavy reliance on correspondence created problems of communication. In general, this was not the case. While difficulties with overseas customers certainly arose (often through their tardiness in communicating when things were not going well), by the 1820s the British postal system was remarkably efficient (though, before the advent of the national penny post in 1840, expensive). Many letters – whether they were to or from Manchester, Liverpool, London, Glasgow, Carlisle, Newcastle, Warwick Hall or Skirwith Abbey – were received within 24 hours; and it was, therefore, entirely feasible to have a three- or even four-way exchange within a single week. From 1821 post was delivered by letter carriers throughout Manchester and Salford, immediately after the arrival of the London mail coach. Moreover, a local penny post became more readily available, letters

---

8   Hartwell, *Manchester*, 10-18; Davis, *Industrial Revolution and British Overseas Trade*, 16-19.
9   In 1825 Mary's brother, James Heald (1796-1873), sold manufacturing concerns in Cheshire and bought a fine Georgian property at Parr's Wood, near Heaton Mersey, where he lived for the rest of his life. He became a shareholder in many Manchester companies and, following its difficulties during the financial crisis of the mid-1820s, was heavily involved in the reconstruction of the Manchester and Liverpool District Bank. – Million, *Didsbury*, 123; *Dictionary of National Biography*.

posted in Manchester before 5.30 pm being delivered the same night, along with the letters from London.[10]. Transport of other goods was also effective. While quite large parcels also went by mail coach, heavier goods were carried by wagons. Marchanton regularly used those of Hargreaves & Co. which were based close to the High Street office and warehouse; and which, taking three days, made daily trips in both directions from Manchester to Penrith and Carlisle[11]. Liverpool was accessible by road as well as by navigable river and canal, and there were frequent sailings to and from Carlisle, not just in conventional vessels but, from 1826, via one of the earliest steam packet services to be established around Britain's coasts, with two vessels, the *Solway* and the *Cumberland.* The first recorded use of the packet by Marchanton was in September 1827, when he sent timber (for the new Warwick Hall) from Liverpool to Carlisle [12].

Sometime after the onset of Robert Parker's illness his home at Tithe Barn Hill in Heaton was let to a local businessman, Thomas Salter. Before partition Thomas and Mary Parker had made a home for themselves at Ardwick Green; and both then and for some time afterwards, they actively refurbished it. In December 1823 Thomas also arranged to let for a year from the following April 'Rose Cottage', near Bootle, the village where James Penny lived. Apparently, this was designed to enable him to familiarise himself more thoroughly with shipping and other matters in Liverpool and to review arrangements for their collaboration in the export trade[13]. Because he planned to build a new house at Warwick, it proved impossible for Thomas to move north immediately. He took up permanent residence there (punctuated by trips to Manchester) only from 1825. Before then, in any case, he was pre-occupied with matters further south, not least at Heaton Mersey.

DEVELOPMENTS AT HEATON MERSEY

From December 1823, when a significant improvement in Robert Parker's health must have begun to seem unlikely, a major re-equipment programme was instituted at Heaton Mersey. While this was probably planned, or at least contemplated, by Robert before he fell ill, it was now led by Thomas Parker. For some years before then the two men had conducted business with the

10   Campbell-Smith, *Masters of the Post*, 89-105; A Redford, *Manchester Merchants and Foreign Trade,* I, *1794-1858* (Manchester, 1934), 189-190. Pkr A, 1/17/9 provides comprehensive details of the arrival and departure times of mail at Manchester during the period Dec. 1823 – Dec. 1824.

11   Parsons & White, *History, Directory and Gazetteer*, 509.

12   S. Towill, *Georgian and Victorian Carlisle* (Preston, 1996), 7; Pkr A, 3/17/43, JM to TP, 8 Sept. 1827. Whether Christopher Parker of Petteril Green was among the original members of the management committee which ran the *Cumberland* is uncertain, but he was a member in 1830. – D/Hod/13/50, Legal Papers, 1830.

13   Salter: Pkr A, 2/11/17, Salter to TP, 12 July 1825; Ardwick: 1/17/20, J. Vaughan to TP, 19 Feb. 1820; 3/12/9, Bill, 29 July 1823; Rose Cottage: 3/13/7, Memorandum, W. Cross to TP, 1 December 1823.

younger members of the Stocks family, Samuel junior and his brother, Bernard, who had manufacturing in their blood[14]. Precisely when the Heaton works were formally let to Samuel junior (who was then in his mid-30s) is uncertain, but for marketing purposes he and Thomas entered into formal partnership, and Stocks was closely involved in the refurbishment programme and partly responsible for financing it. Stocks himself acknowledged some years later that the works were 'old in many parts [which] occasions much more expense than if [they] were newer'[15]. We do not know how much change had occurred before Robert senior's death in 1815, but there was little, if any, in the following seven years as his successors worked out who was going to get what. In a fast-moving industry that was a long time. There was little problem on the bleaching side of operations; in addition to Stocks's own work, sub-contracts from other firms were regular and substantial. Elsewhere, however, much of the machinery was outdated and, in particular, there was an imbalance between capacity in spinning and that in weaving, to the detriment of the latter. Indeed, the 1820s were the decade when the weaving of cotton cloth began to be done on power looms instead of handlooms, in a development almost as momentous as the transformation of spinning in the 1770s and 1780s[16].

At a cost of £1,200 refurbishment began with the repair of the existing boiler, and the installation of a new steam engine linked to it, which together generated 36 horse power[17]. The next endeavour was to boost weaving capacity by installing a huge new waterwheel (18 feet in diameter and 18 feet wide, with two spur wheels) at a cost of £863. A few months later, through gearing, belts and straps, this transmitted power to the factory's warping and dressing machinery, and to most of its looms[18]. In January 1824, under a separate contract, J. & F. Sharratt of the Salford Ironworks – a large family firm which, since the 1790s, had played a leading role in meeting the local demand for advanced textile machinery – undertook 'to make two firing machines [for the bleaching process] with the apparatus for regulating the same by steam'[19]. Another dramatic development – to equip the factory with gas-lighting – followed in May. Henry Worthington (perhaps related to Robert senior's former partner, Thomas) had devised a method of 'preparing and improving coal gas'. He installed two large gasometers, 'put up on a plan to be a self-acting regulator on the burners without any attendance'; together with the necessary piping, these enabled some manufacturing to proceed

14   Pkr A, 3/5/12, Parker Accounts with S. & B. Stocks, 7 July 1818.
15   Pkr A, 3/17/6, SS to TP, 2 Apr. 1828.
16   Chapman, *Cotton Industry in the Industrial Revolution*, 24, 51.
17   Pkr A, 3/13/46, Agreement with TP, 6 Sept. 1823.
18   Pkr A, 3/11/17, Statement to TP, 20 Nov. 1823; 3/13/4, 13, Estimates, 28 Nov. & 13 Dec. 1823; 3/13/14, Tender for Gearing Factory, 11 May 1824.
19   W.H. Chaloner, 'Manchester in the Latter Half of the Eighteenth Century', *Bulletin of the John Rylands Library*, 42 (1959-60), 49; Pkr A, 3/13/36, Memorandum to TP, 26 Jan. 1824.

around the clock[20]. A further £744 was invested in new millwork and gearing for the 'Blowing Room', an adjunct to the bleaching and finishing processes[21]. There were other changes. Calico-printing (which could be sub-contracted at keen prices) was again discontinued and the redundant materials, which included a large stock of chemicals, were sold[22]. It was also decided to put the property at Woodley on the market. Relations with the operators of the colliery there had been punctuated by friction, particularly over accounts, since Robert senior's time; one coal seam was almost exhausted; and a steady supply of fuel at competitive prices was available via the canal system. Thomas refurbished the farmhouse on the property, built a new barn, stable and shippen, and eventually sold the holding for £5,600[23].

Taken together, these changes constituted the most substantial re-modelling of operations at Heaton Mersey since the acquisition of the complex in 1793; and in installing power looms Thomas was in the vanguard of technological change on the weaving side of the industry. By the spring of 1825 the new systems were beginning to have an impact on production. While a little weaving was still done on handlooms, power looms generated the bulk of cloth output: in April and May some 750 'pieces' were being produced each fortnight for a wage bill of around £110. Bleaching was also going well, with output well in advance of wage costs[24]. However, operational changes also led to some reductions in pay, which met with resistance from the workforce. When weavers' wages were reduced in June 1825, 'all the weavers turned out'. Most returned before long and, as for those who did not, Stocks felt that 'we can do better without them than they can without us'. By August he felt able to report that all was 'going on in the way of renewal with all speed'. Sharratts had returned to make adjustments to the machinery installed earlier and improvements were being made to some of the cottages adjacent to the works[25]. In October Stocks ordered 18 more 'fancy looms' and a dressing frame, both of which he expected to be in use within a month. He dismissed two staff at his Manchester warehouse (one of whom was James Marchanton, who henceforth worked exclusively for Thomas Parker); and replaced them with a clerk, a salesman and a collector of goods and money. Soon afterwards, Thomas bought 4,000 pieces of shirting from him – a huge order, though James Penny grumbled that Stocks's prices were higher than

---

20   Pkr A, 1/17/13 & 3/13/1, Worthington to TP, 6 Apr. & May 1824, and 'Notes of Progress', 27 Nov. 1824. Some factories began to be lit by gas in the early 1800s. – Chapman, *Cotton Industry in the Industrial Revolution*, 58.
21   Pkr A, 3/13/3, Fairbairn & Co. to TP, 8 Oct. 1824.
22   Pkr A, 1/16/6, 'Sundry Drugs sent from Heaton', 5 & 7 May 1824.
23   Pkr A, 3/6/6. Improvement Accounts, 1824; 3/15/23, Sale, Lingard, Vaughan & Lingard, to TP, 15 Apr. 1826. For earlier difficulties, see e.g. 3/5/5, J. Bury to Robert senior, 23 Dec. 1808 and 1/2/3,5, Accounts, 1816-17.
24   Pkr A, 2/11/ 1-2, Reports, Apr. & 25 May 1825.
25   Pkr A, 2/11/16, 32, SS to TP, 2 July & 6 Aug. 1825.

could be obtained elsewhere, and that the finish on the goods was 'inferior'[26]. While much had been achieved in less than two years, there was no room for complacency.

Thomas was taken aback by another development at Heaton Mersey. At some point during the early 1820s, a William Wilson had joined the partnership between Thomas and Stocks. Operations became tripartite between a landlord and fairly regular purchaser on the one hand, and two manufacturers (each of whom brought capital to the venture) on the other. Stocks, however, became thoroughly disenchanted with Wilson and in July 1825 announced his intention of dissolving the partnership: 'he has no abilities for a Master and he is spoiled for a servant'. Thomas's reaction was to wait and see, but within days Stocks insisted that 'you must part with either him or me'. Significantly, James Heald agreed with Stocks, and so too did James Penny. Thomas put up little resistance; nor indeed did Wilson, and a formal agreement to dissolve the partnership with Wilson was signed and published in early October 1825[27]. This was the back drop at Heaton Mersey to a major crisis affecting the entire industry, and indeed the national economy, which developed during that year.

The first intimations of trouble ahead – though few realised it at the time – were reports in late 1824 that future imports of raw cotton from the United States were likely to prove inadequate. This led to feverish speculation and a doubling of the commodity price, which were soon followed – when supplies proved adequate – by equally sharp falls at Liverpool in the sale price of imported raw cotton. Earlier most imports had come from the Levant and the West Indies, but by now the bulk came from the southern United States. Thomas Parker was among those caught up in this in June, having imported 31 bags from New Orleans. Despite Penny's frantic efforts, a 50% loss was recorded when the last 19 bags were eventually sold in early August[28]. Able to acquire their key raw material at very low prices, Stocks and other manufacturers initially reaped the benefits: 'cotton gets lower and I think goods [are] better to sell'[29]. Thereafter, cloth was overproduced and prices for finished goods fell precipitously. In the lead-up to Christmas 1825 many firms went bankrupt and there were numerous failures in the banking system, both in London and the provinces. According to Stocks, 'it is not possible to describe....the consternation the whole Town and Trade is put into'. Two months later he urged Thomas Parker to 'take goods' in lieu of rent. Following further failures in all types of business, 'the state of affairs

26   Pkr A, 2/11/49, 58-59, 62, 64, 66, 68, SS to TP, 18 Oct. 17 & 22 Nov. 1, 6, 10, 13 Dec. 1825.

27   Pkr A, 2/11/18, 24, 29, 32, 46, SS to TP, 16, 23 & 30 July, 6 Aug. & 6 Oct. 1825; 2/11/45, W. Wilson to TP, 5 Oct. 1825.

28   Pkr A, 2/11/10, 12, 15, 19, 26, 30-31, JSP to TP, 9, 13 & 23 June, 18 & 26 July, 1-2 Aug. 1825; Redford, *Manchester Merchants*, 76-77; Davis, *Industrial Revolution and British Overseas Trade*, 39-40.

29   Pkr A, 2/11/64, SS to TP, 6 Dec. 1825.

gets blacker and blacker. Never did I witness dismay written so plainly on almost everyone's face'[30].

Within a week Stocks himself was in acute difficulties and sent Thomas Parker an abject begging letter:

> If I were to lay my life down I cannot make sales. Good people won't buy and to bad I cannot sell. Money I cannot get it for bleaching and blocked up I am in all points. The stock of white [cotton] goods in [the] Manchester Warehouse exceeds 4,000 pieces, [in] value about £3,400, and it forms the means of carrying on which are not available. And the conclusion is I *must* stop the spinning and weaving concern except I can raise money. You are my first resource...[In] two months...the whole trade will become bankrupt if there will be no alteration....I should like to keep my people on but, if the means are wanting, I cannot do it[31].

There was no response to this initial plea and a week or so later Stocks was in desperate straits. Although by then 'we are giving satisfaction to our employers in Bleaching', the situation on every other front was dire:

> As my Cotton works out the Mill stops...my money is done and my credit at [the] Bank is running great risk, to collect what is owing is impossible, and get on I cannot. More money is invested in machinery etc. than I have of yours and my own, and the floating capital is wanting...I ask you in perfect calmness, but with all the feelings of deep distress, what must I do? My money and yours was [sic] not invested in Heaton in expectation of such times as these. The times as such are not [of] my individual making and I don't think I should be left and deserted as is now the case...The works are coming into better play than ever...The fatigues of body and soul I have had to undergo to bring about this state of things [are] known to many, and my prospects are on [the] one hand as bright as any man's in the county, and on the other as dark as any. For this day Mr. Lloyd [his banker of Jones, Lloyd & Co., Manchester] informed me that I must pay up *all my account*. And all my *disposable property* if sold tomorrow will not do it...I rely on a letter from you on Tuesday morning and will wait the issue. I cannot say or do more than I have done. All my concerns good or bad are known to you...for I have no other friend[32].

This time Thomas Parker acted decisively, travelling from Warwick Hall to Manchester for negotiations; the outcome was the dissolution of their formal

---

30   Pressnell, *Country Banking in the Industrial Revolution*, 482-492. Pkr A, 2/11/ 66, 68, 77, SS to TP, 10, 13 & 21 Dec. 1825; 2/4/7, 16, 7 & 18 Feb. 1826. As at least one sporting event demonstrated, the crisis impinged heavily on the national consciousness. The hot favourite for the Derby in 1826 was a horse named 'Panic' which, on the day of the race, failed to start! – Pressnell, *Country Banking*, 507.

31   Pkr A, 2/4/4, SS to TP, 22 Feb. 1826.

32   Pkr A, 3/15/54, SS to TP, 4 Mar. 1826.

partnership; and a hefty rescue package for Stocks and Heaton Mersey whose chief component was financial – the floating capital hitherto sorely lacking. Although their agreement took immediate effect, in early May 1826 its key clauses were laid down in a legal instrument – a bond – which instituted draconian penalties for non-fulfilment by Stocks.   Subsequently, with characteristic bravura, Stocks continued to express the deepest gratitude to his landlord whilst simultaneously bewailing the 'dreadful instrument' to which he was now subjected[33]. Financially, their agreement encompassed not just immediate needs but also what Thomas Parker judged he was owed from the outset of the refurbishment programme, through the break with Wilson, and down to the current crisis. One memorandum, in Stocks's hand, identifies a total debt of £24,554. The successful impact of the arrangements is evident from the fact that the amount owed to Thomas Parker had been reduced to £13,539 by 31 December 1826, and a further £4,700 was discharged during 1827[34]. Meanwhile, Stocks had signified his gratitude in a very personal way: when his second son was born in 1826 the baby was christened Thomas Parker Stocks[35].

Whether or not they formed part of the agreement, two other features of future arrangements are clear. Henceforward, Thomas Parker and James Penny bought finished goods more regularly from Heaton Mersey, despite the availability via the Manchester Cotton Exchange of other supplies. Both men continued to urge Stocks to improve the quality of his product. In October 1826 when ordering 1,000 pieces, Thomas advised him not to put 'quite so much starch in them, although it will not do to have them soft and flabby'. Moreover, the owner of Thomas's main outlet in Portugal, in Lisbon, had recently described some goods from Stocks as 'coarse, which they certainly are [in] comparison with those sent him by Mr. Penny. Your yarn seems more uneven and the cloth not so mat as that made about Stalybridge. I hope you will soon improve'. Thomas also indicated that he detected in Stocks's latest missive an implication that he needed more capital. He was adamant: he had gone as far as he was prepared to go[36]. However, the persistent emphasis on the need for quality control, together with the increased incidence of orders from Heaton Mersey and the speed with which the debt was reduced, strongly suggest that their agreement permitted Stocks to discharge his obligations through the value of goods as well as in cash.

Secondly, following the rescue package, Stocks and some members of his workforce at Heaton Mersey were very active in support of Thomas's business interests in Manchester. Stocks discharged a variety of commissions, often

---

33   Pkr A, JSP to TP, 14 Mar. 1826; 3/15/45, SS to TP, 18 Mar. 1826; 3/15/41, 23 Mar. 1826; 1/16/7, 13 May 1826.

34   Pkr A, 1/16/7 & 3/17/23, SS to TP, 12 May 1826 & 16 Feb. 1828.

35   Wikipedia, 'Samuel Stocks (c.1786-1863).

36   Pkr A, 3/10/58, TP to SS, 25 Oct. 1826.

in collaboration with James Heald, and from his warehouse at 1, Mosley Street (let from Thomas) was on hand to substitute for, and often to lead, James Marchanton; and was, along with Marchanton, recognised by many customers and other contacts as Thomas's *alter ego* in the town. Moreover, some of the key workers, particularly William Buckley, in the warehouse development programme in which Thomas invested heavily in the later 1820s, were on the payroll at Heaton Mersey[37]. So the resolution of the crisis of 1825-26 ushered in change in more ways than one.

None of this is to imply that following the rescue package the solution to the crisis was either assured or straightforward – far from it. Many months passed before deep recession gave way to faltering recovery. Thereafter conditions fluctuated for almost a decade and full recovery did not take place until the mid-1830s[38] Numerous businesses failed and thousands of workers faced cuts in wages, were laid off, or both; and there was serious industrial unrest in Manchester and the surrounding area during April and the early days of May 1826. Weavers rioted and, according to Stocks, broke into six factories; five had all their looms destroyed and a sixth lost 73 out of 400. At Bury, 'after repeated provocation', soldiers opened fire:

> and six are dead and many wounded. The weavers declare they will visit all the county. A large meeting of operatives was held at Stockport last night [26 April] and it is said something is about to be done in that neighbourhood. James Kennedy's people are out about wages and he has obtained others in place of the old ones, and these beset the new hands last night and killed two of them and injured many[39].

On the 28th Stocks reported that 'at one o'clock' there had been 'thousands of people' in and around Oldham Street in central Manchester. Three factories were attacked, one being set on fire, but 'the soldiers came in time to save the looms. Magistrates on horseback, military in motion, and all on the alert. [However] all safe at Heaton'. John Burton, one of Thomas Parker's regular suppliers of finished goods, confessed on 4 May to having been 'very much afraid of the rioters last Sunday, but providentially they were turned to Shaw and Oldham. We have now soldiers to defend [Manchester] but all seems very peaceable – many of them are taken up. We expect to see no more of them in our neighbourhood'[40].

Although the works at Heaton Mersey were not attacked, there were serious industrial disputes there. Earlier, in March 1826, when his spinners

---

37   See below, 90.
38   C.N. Ward-Perkins, 'The Commercial Crisis of 1847' in E.M. Carus-Wilson, (ed.), *Essays in Economic History*, iii (London, 1962), 275 which, while dealing authoritatively with the short-lived crisis of 1847, contrasts it with the much more protracted one from 1825.
39   Pkr A, 3/15/14, SS to TP, 27 Apr. 1826.
40   Pkr A, 3/15/13, SS to TP, 28 Apr. 1826 & 3/15/12, JB to TP, 4 May 1826.

had been without work for two to three weeks, Stocks went to Liverpool to buy cotton to set them going again. On his return, the spinners refused to work for a reduction of 'half a penny per 100 hanks of twist and one penny on weft, i.e. I offered 5d. per 100 when…others give less than 4d'. So he sold on his cotton at a profit. According to Stocks:

> Mules working upon Mules make themselves into Asses and are quite as stupid. So these fellows won't give place to the times, no not for a halfpence, and the poor card room hands, who don't earn half their amount, must starve before they will move. I have taken measures to get some people who will work. Three-quarters of the people in Stockport are out on the same ground[41].

Some months later, in August, Stocks was utterly ruthless, and got away with it. Following a pay-cut, the 'dressers' at Heaton Mersey went on strike. He brought them before the local magistrates, 'who sent them to work or to prison – they might take either'. When they returned to work, he sacked them all. Then his spinners also planned a strike. Stocks immediately informed them that 'the man that gave me notice [of a strike] at this time should never work again at Heaton under any circumstances, and I had not one notice'[42]. Times were exceedingly tough for everyone, but Heaton Mersey survived relatively unscathed.

During the early autumn of 1826 there were clear signs that Stocks had weathered the storm. Not only had the works escaped physical damage during some of the worst industrial unrest the north-west had experienced, but in September he felt 'persuaded of the place answering'. Two weeks later 'wages in many parts are improving which I take to be a sure sign of bettering'. By then, using the capital provided by Thomas Parker, he had added no fewer than 120 looms to his complement, substantially rectifying the previous imbalance between spinning and weaving; sales were much brisker, albeit still at disappointingly low prices; and, somewhat less pre-occupied with his own affairs, he was increasingly out and about in Manchester on Thomas Parker's business. Nonetheless, investment in new plant at Heaton Mersey continued. He acquired 'a set of preparations very cheap [and] very good in quality, which with two new cards just launched leaves me only two new cards short of filling the mill… When you next visit Heaton you will see all agoing and find us progressively improved'[43].

The fall in the sales prices of finished goods gave Thomas Parker and James Penny additional incentive to purchase cloth for export, to which they were quick to respond. While they had many customers overseas, they were keen to exploit opportunities which opened up for them, not only in South

---

41   Pkr A, 3/15/34, SS to TP, 31 Mar. 1826.
42   Pkr A, 2/4/39, SS to TP, 17 August 1826.
43   Pkr A, 3/10/48, SS to TP, 30 Sept. 1826; 3/10/53, 14 Oct. 1826; 3/10/61, 1 Nov. 1826.

America but also in Cuba and Mexico. Sales in Cuba were substantial, profitable and generally trouble-free. Above all, Penny's sons in Mexico traded very heavily with them. In the months surrounding the new year of 1827 Stocks supplied Parker and Penny with large orders, not just for those markets but for many others too[44]. He himself had 'won new customers, primarily because he continued to improve the quality as well as to expand the scale of his output. In this regard one episode in September 1827 is revealing. Penny had placed an order for six bales of goods for shipment to Gibraltar. When the bales failed to arrive on schedule at the dockside in Liverpool, both Parker and Penny asked what had delayed them. Stocks explained that he 'had an opportunity to *keep out* the stiff finish [previously complained of] and was glad of it; and kept the lot a few days to supply them with the finish that I knew would do well'[45].

In December 1827 Stocks, feeling more relaxed and self-confident, wrote to Thomas Parker with an account of the distribution, which took place each year at Christmas, of the 'bounty' for the children who attended Heaton Mersey Sunday School, which Robert Parker senior had left by his will. The 'most needy' recipients, some 300 of them, were chosen by their teachers. Each got stockings, clogs and cloth, and there were arrangements for the cloth to be made up by the second Sunday in the new year, 'when all should appear at School in their new clothing'[46]. It may have been the record of benevolence at Heaton Mersey which saved it from damage in the violent disturbances of 1826.

Meanwhile, ever since becoming the lessee of Heaton Mersey, Stocks had been responsible for handing over the £1,000 a year due to Robert senior's widow, Sarah Parker. Paid in cash, there were two equal instalments of £500, one paid in January and the other during the summer. In view of the strictures in the will of 1815, the need for prompt payment was emphasised. Stocks invited Sarah to dinner in October 1826 and found her 'quite fat and good looking'. He evidently got on well with her, which may have bred some complacency on his part. In the following January, when everyone found cash hard to come by, he looked for some leeway in the date of payment to Sarah; asked if Thomas might lend him the money for a short while; and paid it on 8 February. The next instalment was paid promptly on 4 August 1827. As late as 26 January 1828, Stocks again announced that he needed a loan of the £500 then due, as he wished to use his cash for some purpose connected with Heaton Mersey. At that stage William Parker was resident at Warwick Hall because Thomas was seriously ill – not too ill, however, to prevent a stinging rebuke to Stocks, who confessed that he remembered 'what was said'. On the

44   Pkr A, 3/10/58, 61, 65 & 3/14/23, SS to TP, 25 Oct. 1 Nov. 18 Nov. 1826 & 8 Feb. 1827. See below, 80.
45   Pkr A, 3/17/38, SS to TP, 20 Sept. 1827.
46   Pkr A, 3/10/33, SS to TP, 27 Dec. 1827.

evening of 31 January, just in time, Stocks rode over to Longsight with the money for Sarah, apologising to Thomas and William for being the 'ground of alarm'[47].

Shortly afterwards Stocks visited Thomas's bedside at Warwick Hall, just as his lease of Heaton Mersey came up for renewal. Thomas announced his decision to raise the rent, asking £2,300 a year for the works alone, quite apart from any payment for the surrounding land. On 2 April 1828, in what proved to be the last communication between the two before Thomas's death, Stocks delivered his customary combination of solicitude and candour:

> It will be a great pleasure to us to hear of your better health. We continue to remember you before the Lord and some of us have still strong hope. [Yet] I take this opportunity to say that [the proposed rent for Heaton Mersey] is too high, in consideration that I am to keep the place in good and substantial repair, 'within and without'...The amount should not exceed £2,000 for the works, leaving the rent of the land as it is...The whole case is before you...it would be difficult...to find a person who would take more care of the property and be more liberal in keeping it in repair. With every good wish and kind regards[48].

And so to the very end Thomas Parker was left in no doubt as to what Samuel Stocks thought. It was not Stocks's style, even in such circumstances, to be anything other than candid with the person who had rescued him; and while Thomas was more socially skilled, frankness was clearly a trait which they shared. In the midst of the most severe difficulties, they enjoyed a productive working relationship.

Despite the fact that both the Parkers and Stocks junior had severed business relations with Samuel Stocks senior, this co-operation was also based on the long-standing interaction between their two families, which went back to the early 1790s, and possibly even further. They also had broader interests in common: following the onset of Robert Parker junior's illness, there was no stronger supporter of the Heaton Mersey Sunday School than Stocks. Furthermore, for Thomas Parker to have taken over the works there in 1826 was, practically, out of the question; and in the circumstances of that year in particular it would have been exceedingly difficult to attract an alternative lessee, and dangerous to have set about trying to do so. In fact, instead of parting ways, they worked even more closely together. Stocks owed his survival as a manufacturer to Thomas Parker, who came to depend heavily on Stocks's interventions in Manchester on his behalf. Because he presided over a diverse portfolio and yet was often absent from Manchester, Thomas needed ready access to local knowledge and street wisdom, which Stocks

---

47   Pkr A, 3/10/58, 3/14/12, 3/17/ 23, 27-28, SS to TP, 25 Oct. 1726, 20 Jan. 1827, 26 & 31 Jan. 1828; 1/20/3, Receipt from SP, 4 Aug. 1827.

48   Pkr A, 3/17/6, SS to TP, 2 Apr. 1828.

provided in abundance. Thomas drew rents from property in Manchester, at Heaton Mersey, and at Woodley and elsewhere in Cheshire, as well as at Warwick Hall. He also had returns from investments in government funds, though these appear to have been modest. And through his extensive network of clients and contacts, he both lent to and borrowed from others[49]. On the other hand net income from rents was relatively low. Half of that from Heaton Mersey was devoted to Sarah Parker's life annuity. Developments at Warwick Hall were costly, the house and demesne there took up much of the land, and there was little to let beyond them. And the rest of his property yielded little income until towards the end of his life, following investment in warehousing facilities in central Manchester. The key question, therefore, is: how did Thomas Parker manage to finance his wide range of activities?

The answer lies in the success of his endeavours prior to the partition of 1822. Otherwise, even with the proceeds of that exercise, he could not have afforded the £45,000 paid for Warwick Hall, the substantial sum involved in bailing out Stocks, and other investments in a host of ventures. His uncle, Robert senior, had traded on his own account as well as on that of the family firm, and it seems that members of the younger generation, particularly Thomas, did so too. By the early 1820s Thomas Parker had already won a firm reputation as an importer of raw cotton and, primarily, as an exporter of cotton goods. His correspondence in 1821 reveals substantial imports from New Orleans and extensive exports to the southern Mediterranean, North America, and Buenos Aires, Bahia and Pernambuco in South America[50]. It is equally clear that prior to his untimely death in 1828 the bulk of his income continued to come from the latter source.

OVERSEAS EXPORTS

Although in the face of difficulties from prohibitions and embargoes trade in cotton goods had expanded throughout the hostilities, the prize for Britain's success in the Revolutionary and Napoleonic Wars (1793-1815) was secure command of the high seas. Thereafter, despite occasional problems, British traders were able to carry on their business much more confidently right around the globe, and Thomas Parker did so. In the period 1822-24 there were frequent consignments to Gibraltar and there are scattered references

---

49   For investment in government funds, see e.g. Pkr A, 3/13/19, 44, W. Marriott, Stock Exchange, to TP , 8 Jan. & 8 July 1824. He lent Thomas Worthington £2,000 in 1827 (3/14/36 & 3/17/19, TW & JM to TP, 7 Mar & 19 Sept. 1827). For the mortgage which Thomas took out to part-finance his warehouse developments, and for what was his largest loan – of over £6,000 to John Burton, one of his cloth suppliers – see below,

50   Pkr A, 2/1/1-140, Various to TP, 1821. Mainly with shippers, insurance brokers and the like, these letters are not as revealing of cargoes, markets and profits as later correspondence, though they deal in detail with destinations.

to exports to Philadelphia, Jamaica, Buenos Aires and Calcutta[51]. In mid-decade, the wholesale cost of finished goods fell, which enhanced the terms of trade for exporters. Other services were improving too, while their costs were falling. Decades of improvement in road and canal transport, and competition between the two, made for cheap and fast transit of goods from Manchester to Liverpool, the main embarkation point for exports of cotton cloth. The decade had its dark clouds but there were significant silver linings.

No general accounts of Thomas Parker's export business have survived. However, there is a wealth of correspondence and associated papers which, together, provide a tolerably clear picture of what transpired. Utilising two separate accounts (one for T. & R. Parker & Co. and the other a personal one), Thomas operated largely, though not exclusively, in informal partnership with James Stubington Penny through the latter's office in Liverpool. While continuing to trade with long-established markets in southern Europe (Lisbon and Gibraltar), the Mediterranean (Sicily, Naples, Livorno and Izmir), and the U.S.A. (particularly New York), as well as with India (Calcutta) and the Far East (Singapore), they increasingly targeted markets in the Caribbean (particularly Cuba), in Central America (Mexico), and in South America (Brazil, Argentina, Chile and Peru). A chief associate was James Burt, a dealer on the Manchester Cotton Exchange who, in addition to what they got from Stocks at Heaton Mersey, managed much of their supply of finished goods. There were also other, individual suppliers such as John Burton[52], for, seeking to meet demands from many far-flung markets, they invested in a wide variety of cotton goods.

An initial impression of the scale, costs and rewards of their endeavours may be gauged from details of their trade with Lima in Peru during the period 1823-25. Between October 1823 and March 1824 Parker and Penny exported 7,078 pieces of assorted cloth (quiltings, one- and two-colour stripes and imitations) to Lima at a cost of £6,831. Lima was an emerging market, though the voyage round Cape Horn was a very long and dangerous one. Four vessels were involved. Having embarked on 13 November 1823, the *Wavertree* was expected to arrive at the end of March 1824. The *Andes* set sail on the 21 January 1824 and was scheduled to dock at Lima in late May. Both *Jane* and *Erin* set off in March 1824 and were due to complete their outward voyages in July and August 1824 respectively. There are fuller details of one of these shipments in March 1824, to John Beggs & Co. via *Jane*. At source the exported cloth cost £1,307; carriage and shipping charges from Manchester to Lima came to a mere £47; Parker and Penny paid insurance of £67; and there were commission and other charges of £84. The entire venture involved an outlay of £1,505 and earned £2,204, leaving

51   Pkr A, 1/3/23, Memorandum, 29 Oct. 1825.
52   See above, 67, and below, 82, 117-118.

a profit of £699 (over 35%) to be divided equally between Parker and Penny. There were five remittances from Beggs & Co., the first in May 1825 and the last in February 1826[53]. Though there was some lapse of time between initial investment and final return, the profit was far in excess, for instance, of the 3.5 to 5% available on deposits in Jones & Lloyd, Thomas Parker's and Stocks's bank in Manchester[54], or from other conventional investments. When things went well in the export trade the returns were handsome. On the other hand, things did not always go well and, at times and for a variety of reasons, overseas trade was fraught with difficulty.

Parker and Penny established contacts with merchant houses around the world, almost all of which were in the hands of British expatriates who had agents in Liverpool or London. While this infrastructure was indispensable, the trade in cotton cloth was peculiarly susceptible to the vagaries of fashion, which fluctuated unpredictably from one market to another. Each market had a prime season for sales; and even if they delivered an appropriate range of goods in time for that season, local or regional developments might make sales difficult or impossible. Remittances of the proceeds of sales were far from straightforward. Local exchange rates fluctuated and, especially in new markets, bills of exchange – the normal means of remittance – might be difficult to arrange or be dishonoured back in Britain. There was, therefore, a substantial speculative element in their endeavours. That both men persisted is testimony to their confidence in ultimate success, though Thomas Parker demonstrated a much steadier nerve than did James Penny.

Their first tasks were heavily dependent on advice from their contacts: to choose appropriate goods for export to a particular market; and have them delivered punctually for sailings, from Liverpool or occasionally from London, in order to arrive at markets at the optimal time. To achieve this they had to be well organised in Manchester, which they were: but, with Thomas frequently at Warwick Hall and Penny normally in Liverpool, only up to a point. At times Stocks was less than prompt in his deliveries, and so too was Burt. Both often had to cope with short notice of designated sailings and sometimes prompt delivery proved impossible. According to Penny, who was frequently very critical of him, Burt employed poor-quality staff; and, to judge from Burt's scarcely decipherable correspondence, he was habitually rushed off his feet. In August 1826 Penny was:

> exceedingly vexed that the 400 prints for Jago and Carey [at Izmir] are *not yet* done! And Mr. Burt can give no promise of them. It is

---

53   Pkr A, 1/3/12, Consignments to Lima, 1823-24; 1/3/10, Shipment to J. Beggs & Co. 1824-25.
54   Established in Manchester in 1772 on the basis of wealth from tea dealing, with a London office by 1784, and with 42 'correspondents' in various provincial centres by 1820, this 'carefully run bank... ranked amongst the greatest of the country banks'. – Pressnell, *Country Banking in the Industrial Revolution*, 20, 51, 80, 106, 177, 255-56, 379. In 1827 James Stubington Penny obtained 4% on bank deposits, though Burt charged 5% on unpaid bills. – Pkr A, JSP to TP, 14 May 1827.

most provoking because I have actually shipt a large quantity for other friends to Jago and Carey in a vessel which is to sail tomorrow - she closed today. Another vessel with a large cargo is to sail on Tuesday and thus you will see my goods will arrive after the fair is over[55]. I am quite tired of Mr. Burt's management of prints.

The prints had still not arrived in Liverpool almost two weeks later[56]. To be fair to Burt, there were often problems at the printers – to whom unprinted goods were sub-contracted – over which he had little or no control. In December 'Mr. Burt has not expedited these goods as I expected'. And in January 1827, 'I am very much disappointed again by Mr. Burt. My prints are not ready [to] go…180 pieces being still behind, and the assortment therefore cannot be completed'. In May 1827 Penny was once more 'very much disappointed by Mr. Burt (the cause is doubtless with the printers) that 200 pieces [of] single-colour furnitures are kept back a most unreasonable time. They are for Havana and have missed two vessels, to my great mortification'[57]. There was no change in arrangements, however. Thomas Parker judged that they got as good a service from Burt as they might from anyone, and the harassed dealer continued to source many of the goods which they exported. Between January and June 1827, for instance, Burt was paid £1,604 for goods which he forwarded to Parker and Penny in eight separate transactions[58]. He too was occasionally lucky: earlier that year bad weather delayed the departure of *Anne* for Mexico, unexpectedly enabling Burt to get 19 bales on board[59]. Clearly, however, Thomas's move to Warwick Hall and Penny's to Liverpool were not without cost to their joint endeavours.

Once the goods were ready, they were carried to Liverpool on canal barges or by road on wagons or 'carrs'. Rates were competitive and, while goods were usually sent by canal, Burt was instructed to send them by road if that seemed more likely to meet shipping schedules[60]. On their arrival in Liverpool the location of Penny's office in the dock area proved immensely valuable. He got good notice of sailing schedules, could watch ships being loaded and, if necessary, could oversee that process. He was also among the first to receive 'advices' from incoming vessels.

After embarkation quite different hazards arose. As with the *Emperor Alexander* in 1821, some vessels failed to complete their voyage. Particularly where far-distant destinations were involved, efforts were made to ensure, where possible, that cargoes were carried in the best available vessels. In

55   Most sales in Italy were also conducted at periodic fairs, and the biggest in Italy – from 15 September – was at Livorno, where Casey was agent for Parker and Penny. – Redford, *Manchester Merchants*, 25-26.
56   Pkr A, 2/4/36, 40, JSP to TP, 12 & 23 Aug. 1826.
57   Pkr A, 3/10/68, 3/14/18, 55, JSP to TP, 1 Dec. 1826, 30 Jan. & 10 May 1827.
58   Pkr A, 3/14/64, JB to TP, 23 June 1827.
59   Pkr A, 3/14/35, EB Penny to TP, 3 March 1827; 3/14/37, JSP to TP, 7 Mar. 1827.
60   Pkr A, 2/4/18, JSP to TP, 26 Jan. 1826.

March 1826, for example, several ships were scheduled to sail from Liverpool to the west coast of South America. Parker and Penny were advised by their London insurance agent to use the *Superior* for a shipment to Valparaiso in Chile: besides being likely to be the first to embark, it was 'a larger vessel than the others'. On seeing her at the dockside, Penny's assistant, William Brown, confirmed that she was 'first-class'[61]. Inevitably, although cargoes were routinely insured, negotiation of final settlements was often protracted. One total loss, by the *Eliza Mary*, was settled in July 1825; another claim, following the sinking of the *Hindostan* in 1823, was still outstanding in February 1826; and another, from the loss of the *Acorn*, 'long pending' in January, was only settled in September 1826[62]. Later that year the two men arranged to ship goods, unsold in the United States, to Mexico. *Emma* left New York but failed to reach Vera Cruz and was never seen again. Penny was still deeply embroiled in December 1827 in revising the paperwork required by New York insurers who, he believed, were wilfully raising 'absurd objections'. A clause in the policy forbade final settlement within less than a year of a loss, but that period had long passed by then[63]. Such clauses catered for the possibility of unexpected returns from shipwreck and Penny gleefully reported one stroke of good fortune. Remittances from both the United States and Mexico were regularly sent by one of the recently established packet, or mail, ships from New York. In January 1827 the packet *Panther* was wrecked off Holyhead. Some mail, however, was retrieved, including a bill of exchange for £2,344, payable to Messrs. T. & R. Parker. In this instance the Pennys were lucky too. Penny's son, Edward, 'received one letter, quite saturated and almost defaced by sea water, which contained bills [of exchange of] about £6,000, one of which [for] £550 was for me [Penny senior]'. Penny's only regret was the loss of 'advices' from customers on the other side of the Atlantic[64]. Apart from foul weather, there were other dangers, despite the British navy's post-war command of international waters. Already dealing with merchants in Livorno and Izmir, Parker and Penny used those ports for onward shipments to Malta, and thence to Alexandria. In 1826 a ship carrying a consignment from Malta to Alexandria was boarded by Greek pirates, who stole 151 pieces of cloth; but Penny assured Thomas that 'my policy covers me'[65].

Notwithstanding these hazards, most shipments arrived safely, though it was sometimes many months before this was confirmed. However, the network of packet-ships steadily extended to cover most of the ports

---

61   Pkr A, 3/15/44, Thompson & Poole to TP, 20 Mar. 1826; 3/15/22, JSP to TP, 23 Mar. 1826; 3/15/29, W. Brown to TP, 25 Mar. 1826.

62   Pkr A, 2/11/19, JSP to TP, 18 July 1825; 2/4/9, JM to TP, 15 Feb. 1826; 2/4/23 & 3/10/41, Thompson & Poole to TP, 21 Jan. & 9 Sept. 1826.

63   Pkr A, 3/14?28, 44, JSP to TP, 23 Feb. & 2 Apr. 1827; 3/10/ 26-27, E.B. Penny to TP, 10 & 14 Dec. 1827.

64   Pkr A, 3/14/11, E.B. Penny to TP, 17 Jan. 1827; 3/14/16, JSP to TP, 27 Jan. 1827.

65   Pkr A, 2/4/32, 40, JSP to TP, 12 & 30 Aug. 1826.

to which they traded; and by the mid-1820s 'advices' were received more quickly and regularly than had been the case only a decade earlier. The pattern of their exports thereafter is clearly discernible. While shipments were made to Calcutta and Singapore, they were infrequent and exceptional. The bulk of their exports were to southern Europe and the Mediterranean; and, increasingly, to South America, Cuba, and Mexico. Their dealings with the first of these broad areas were well established and conducted chiefly through a Mr. Studart in Lisbon, Mr. Casey in Livorno, and Messrs. Jago and Carey in Izmir. The markets there were 'dull' or sluggish in the mid-1820s and recovered only slowly as the decade progressed. Penny complained bitterly about the slow rate of remittances and the incidence of bad debts, and frequently feared serious losses. Thomas Parker was uniformly calmer, insisting that they maintain shipments; and Penny, despite his habitual pessimism, almost always bowed to his colleague's judgement. Westwards, across the Atlantic and beyond, they met with much greater, albeit not unblemished, success; and their ventures in Cuba and particularly to Mexico were very successful.

While warmer climates made cottons attractive throughout southern Europe, much of the area remained economically depressed in the post-war years and also politically unstable following the collapse of the Napoleonic regime[66]. However, being relatively close to Britain, the region was readily supplied with goods and the steep price falls of 1825-26 led to markets being flooded as British merchants sought salvation in exports. J. Duffield & Co. reported very poor sales in Gibraltar in May 1825 and in June their remitted but unaccepted bill of exchange for £500 was formally protested by James Penny. Duffield returned briefly to Manchester in August and brazenly recommended that his suppliers invest a further £2,000-3,000 in goods for Gibraltar. For once, Penny was adamant, having 'no disposition to do any more business in Gibraltar, chiefly because of the great competition' there from another merchant house, Barrow's[67]. There was a similar problem at Lisbon, where the market was dominated by a single large operator, a Daniel Hardie. At one point the situation was exacerbated by the sort of unpredictable event which severely disrupted local trading patterns: the death of King Jao of Portugal in March 1826 created a surge in demand for black and white mourning cloth and greatly reduced sales of everything else. Prospects improved when Hardie went bankrupt in May 1826 but for months afterwards prices were depressed by the sale at auctions of Hardie's huge stocks[68]. In the southern Italian states the key problem was the low level of regional purchasing power. In February 1826 a power of attorney

---

66   Redford, *Manchester Merchants*, 87.
67   Pkr A, 2/11/8, 38, JSP to TP, 4 June & 27 Aug. 1825; 2/11/37, J. Duffield to TP, 27 Aug. 1825.
68   Pkr A, 3/15/4, 33, JSP to TP, 1 Apr. & 20 May 1826.

was employed so that a Mr. Dawson could take over goods sent by Parker and Penny to Close & Co. at Messina in Sicily, but which remained unsold. However, in contemplating further supplies to Dawson, Penny had to search for new patterns, those he had being 'too fine and expensive to trust to a profit coming from them'[69]. Moreover, earlier misjudgements proved costly. At Naples in August 1826 a Mr. Pater of Cumming, Woods & Co. reported as still unsold 149 pieces of prints sent over two years previously. The patterns were 'totally out of the taste of the Naples market'. Pater recommended that fresh goods be sent and the two mixed up, to be sold as job lots[70].

A possible solution to these difficulties was to search out new markets in the Mediterranean. Alexandria in Egypt seemed promising. Through their established bases at Livorno and Izmir Parker and Penny were already dealing in Malta (a key staging post for Alexandria). However, their agents there, Messrs Robinson & Co., were in substantial debt to them. In March 1826 they were actively searching for a more 'respectable' merchant house in Malta and when they found one, Messrs John Bell & Co., they used a power of attorney to enable Bell to salvage their interests. By 1827 they were shipping successfully to Alexandria[71].

Meanwhile, with periodic outbursts of pessimism from Penny countered by steadfast resolve from Thomas Parker, they persisted with other endeavours in the region. In 1825-26 this was difficult amidst the alarms and excursions of the cotton trade at home, but falling prices for finished goods sustained their efforts. It was disturbing that their main collaborators in southern Europe, in difficulties themselves, became increasingly infrequent correspondents - it was always more congenial to report successes rather than failures. By late December 1825 Studart had allowed three mail packets from Lisbon to come and go without sending a letter; and that which reached Thomas at Warwick Hall in the following March spoke briefly of the market being 'very flat, and goods selling remarkably low, in consequence of the many failures that have taken place here and at home'. By June 1826 he held £3,000 worth of goods from Parker and Penny and a month later Penny feared 'great losses' at both Lisbon and Livorno[72]. However, as with Stocks at Heaton Mersey, matters improved from the autumn of 1826, when all three main

---

69 Pkr A, 2/4/1, 10, JSP to TP, 11 & 24 Feb. 1826.
70 Pkr A, 2/4/37, JSP to TP, 19 Aug. 1826. The Italians had a taste for fancy patterns. Specially prepared for their markets and fairs, they were generally found unsuitable elsewhere. – Redford, *Manchester Merchants*, 36.
71 Pkr A, 3/15/33, JSP to TP, 1 Apr. 1826; 3/15/15, TP to Robinson & TP to J. Bell, 24 Apr. 1826. Trade through Alexandria had expanded following the construction between 1817 and 1820 by the ruler Muhammad 'Ali of a canal linking the port more effectively with the River Nile. Subsequently, Alexandria's population grew rapidly; Muhammad 'Ali's favourite summer residence was there, as was a growing European community, both factors generating a 'large market for goods'. – E.R.J. Owen, *Cotton and the Egyptian Economy: A Study in Trade and Development* (Oxford, 1969), 22.
72 Pkr A, 2/4/52. 60 & 2/11/70, JSP to TP, 27 Dec. 1825, 12 June & 3 July 1826; 2/4/2, Studart to TP, 28 Feb. 1826.

collaborators in southern Europe began to report more frequently and more favourably. Casey was busy in Alexandria in February 1827. Although he annoyed Penny later that month by turning up unannounced in Manchester – so that Penny, accidentally hearing of his arrival, had to seek him out for urgent talks – he was able to report sales when he returned to Manchester in August and to order more supplies. Studart still encountered disappointing prices but began remitting more regularly; and in December shipments to Gibraltar were resumed[73].

Fortunately, the evidence enables us to place these developments in sharper perspective. Although they always hoped for more, it is clear that Parker and Penny were content to trade for a profit of 10% on overall costs: for, despite the risks involved, this was a better return than could have been obtained through many other avenues. In the light of this, shipments to southern Europe before the onset of the crisis of 1825-26 produced satisfactory returns – 10% from Casey in October 1825; and, on separate consignments, 10%, 15%. 7% and 15% from Studart at Lisbon in January 1826. Losses ranging from 8% to 12% were recorded later in 1826, but these were comparatively modest; and, though some debts were initially recorded as 'bad', they were pursued into better times. By early 1827 Studart was reaping a 'fair profit' on some consignments and a 5% loss on others, and matters improved thereafter[74]. 1826 was a poor year at home and abroad, but it was atypical. While many goods remained unsold, awaiting better times, there were no catastrophes. Against the background of his previous experience, which James Penny – hitherto a manufacturer in Manchester – did not share to the same extent, Thomas Parker knew that steadiness was all. And before his death trading prospects in southern Europe began to improve markedly.

Transatlantic ventures were in one case thwarted by uncontrollable factors; in others they fluctuated but were generally promising; and in two instances they were extremely successful. Dealings with Buenos Aires were a huge disappointment and a classic example of the disruption of overseas trade following a deterioration in external relations in the region. Consignments were shipped to at least one merchant house, Hardisty, McGregor, Wilson & Co., who had an agent from the Hardisty family in Liverpool, a promising arrangement. Initially, prospects were apparently good: in July 1825 shirtings were 'scarce and in demand'. Later, 'advices' were conflicting and one in November spoke of a 'bad market', possibly anticipating future developments. The situation changed dramatically in the new year when Brazil declared war on Buenos Aires. The Brazilian navy blockaded the

---

73   Pkr A, 3/14/22, 28 & 3/17/61, JSP to TP, 7 & 23 Feb. & 27 July 1827; 3/17/52, F. Casey to TP, 18 Aug. 1827; 3/10/20, EB Penny to TP, 29 Nov. 1827.

74   Pkr A, 2/4/10, 24-25, 2/11/53, 3/10/42, 57, 69 & 3/15/ 28, 77, JSP to TP, 25 Oct. 1825, 18 & 19 Jan. 11 Feb. 1 Mar. 8 Apr. 9 Sept. 2 Dec. 1826 & 24 Oct. 1827.

coastline, no further consignments could get through and, with the blockade being strengthened in August, there were no sales in 1826. In December the British government despatched Lord Ponsonby to mediate between the two sides and subsequently he engaged in shuttle diplomacy between Rio de Janeiro and Buenos Aires. Preliminaries of peace were agreed in August 1827 but nothing was finally agreed by the time of Thomas Parker's death early in the following year. Meanwhile, the proceeds of meagre sales had been invested in local government funds, producing a meagre and long-delayed return of $99 on $1,455[75].

Elsewhere in South America Parker and Penny experienced mixed fortunes. Some of their goods – shirtings and prints – were selling for a 10% profit at Rio de Janeiro in October 1825. However, their agents there went bankrupt and they tried unsuccessfully to replace them; subsequently they did little, if any, business at Rio[76]. As we have seen, they began regularly trading round Cape Horn to the west coast of Latin America before the partition of Robert senior's business and they were successfully exporting to Lima during the autumn of 1825. By then they were also doing business in Chile and a large consignment of 27 bales was shipped to Valparaiso in March 1826. As elsewhere, however, as that year progressed their operations in the Pacific got into difficulties. There were problems with remittances from both Peru and Chile. On one earlier occasion, in 1819, H.M.S. *Warspite* had carried 2,940 'hard [metal] dollars' from Valparaiso Bay to London via Rio de Janeiro; and during the 1820s two boxes containing 5,652 Peruvian dollars were brought back to England by a British frigate. Both agents in Peru began to struggle, with one of them managing to sell only 160 out of a consignment of 2,000 pieces. By August 1826 there was 'no expectation of improvement at Lima for twelve or eighteen months'. Yet, by the following March 'advices' from both Peru and Chile were much more optimistic. Several cargoes were despatched to Valparaiso from April 1827 and by October there was much better news of sales at Lima[77].

In the Caribbean the Parkers had been active in Jamaica for some years and Thomas and Penny continued to be, though apparently on a modest scale. By far their most successful operations there were at Havana in Cuba, where they shipped to Tennant & Co. and Keith & Co. In August 1825 the

75   Pkr A, 2/11/3, JM to TP, 25 May 1825; 2/11/46, SS to TP, 6 Oct. 1825; 2/11/ 13A, 19, 55, 3/15/3, JSP to TP, 18 & 27 July, 5 Nov. 1825, 26 May & 3 July 1826; 2/4/27 & 2/11/3, Hardisty, McGregor, Wilson & Co. to TP, 23 July 1825 & 14 Jan. 1826; 2/4/34, 38, 51 & 61, 3/10/21, 36, 59, & 71, 3/17/17, 59, Wilson, Hardisty & Co. to TP, 7 June, 4 July, 19 Aug. 27 Oct. & 12 Dec. 1826, 1 Aug. 30 Nov. & 31 Dec. 1827, 26 Feb. 1828.
76   Pkr A, 2/11/44, JSP to TP, 5 Oct. 1825; 1/3/23, Memorandum, 29 Oct. 1825
77   Pkr A, 2/4/ 32, 40, 52, 63; 3/10/4, 72; 3/14/44, 54-55; 3/15/ 22: JSP to TP, 23 Mar. 3 June, 3 July, 30 Aug. 6 Sept. & 13 Dec. 1826; 2 & 27 Apr. 10 May & 8 Oct. 1827; 3/10/ 66, 3/14/40 & 3/17/49: A. Comber to TP, 29 Nopv. 1826 & 20 Mar. & 30 Aug. 1827; Proclamation of Transit by H.M.S. Warspite, Carlton House, 12 July 1819 (in the possession of Cathie Parker of Maughold, Isle of Man).

former sent the 'usual strong assurance of selling at a good profit', which was borne out. In April 1826 a profit of 'at least 40%' was obtained from very rapid sales, and Keith & Co. sold at a profit of 75% in September and 40% in October. In January 1827, having received a remittance from Tennant & Co. together with an order for a further 900 pieces, Penny paid what for him was an uncharacteristically fulsome tribute: their 'doings at Havana', he enthused, had 'uniformly succeeded'[78].

Even this success was dwarfed by their profitable business in Mexico. In sharp contrast to those elsewhere, operations were managed exclusively by younger members of the Penny family. At home Penny senior and Thomas Parker benefited enormously from this, there being no need, for instance, to read between the lines of letters from Mexico. J.S. Penny's eldest son, J.P., together with his brother, Edward, arrived in Mexico City in June 1824 and established a merchant house in partnership with a Mr. Hodgson. A year later the two were joined by their other brothers, Henry and Charles. Even at that stage their habitually anxious father was writing to Thomas Parker of 'the golden harvest of Mexico'[79].

From the start shipments to Mexico, usually to Vera Cruz on the Gulf coast, were very large – 6,500 pieces of striped prints and, from Stocks at Heaton Mersey, 1,000 pieces of shirtings. Although this first consignment was spoiled by mildew, shirtings were generally 'well adapted to this market [and] 1,000 pieces sent out per every vessel would sell immediately on arrival [for a profit] of 10% or 15%'. Gratifyingly, this estimate proved too conservative. Profits of 140% were reported in July 1825, 20% in August, and 19% at the end of the year. In February 1826 even the damaged shirtings fetched a profit of 10% which, the brothers maintained, 'would have been five times as much had not the goods arrived in a mildewed state'. In October a 60% profit was reported, with a further 25% being expected on goods in hand; a year later profits were still running at 60%. Shipments were regular and some consignments were huge – 75 bales in January 1826, 117 bales in May, 26,500 yards in October, 30 bales a month later, and 1,000 pieces in February 1827. Although there is no continuous record of remittances, when they arrived they were large: £5,000 in August 1826, for example, and £1,000 in August 1827. In January of that year, having organised the shipment of a further 1,000 pieces of prints, Penny senior was told by his sons that they 'had not a tenth part of what they could sell', so he sent a further 1,000 a month later[80].

78   Pkr A, 2/11/35; 3/10/ 42 & 55; 3/14/18; 3/15/28: JSP to TP, 18 Aug. 1825, 8 Apr. 9 Sept. & 23 Oct. 1826, & 30 Jan. 1827.
79   Pkr. A, 1/3/15, J.P. Penny to TP, 24 Aug. 1824, giving his first impressions of the commercial situation in Mexico; 2/11/7, JSP to TP, 28 May 1825.
80   Pkr A, 1/13/15 & 2/11/74: J.P. Penny to TP, 24 Aug. 1824 & n.d. but Nov.–Dec. 1825; 2/4/15 & 32; 2/11/19 & 35; 3/10/4, 54 & 64; 3/14/18 & 37; 3/15/8; 3/17/51: JSP to TP, 18 July & 18 Aug. 1825; 3 Feb. 13 May. 30 Aug. 17 Oct. & 13 Nov. 1826; 30 Jan. 7 Mar. 17 Aug. & 8 Oct. 1827; 3/10/56 & 3/14/20: E.B. Penny to TP, 24 Oct. 1826 & 2 Feb. 1827; 1/3/9, Bill of Lading, 2 Jan. 1826.

Edward Penny suffered ill-health during his early months in Mexico and returned to Liverpool in June 1826. Whether these two developments were connected is uncertain – Penny senior needed assistance with his shipping business in Liverpool – but the consequences were beneficial[81]. Henceforward, Edward managed the Mexican trade at the Liverpool end, so that on both sides of the Atlantic it was presided over by men who from personal experience knew that market intimately. This knowledge prompted the export of brandy, wine and paper as well as cotton goods in December 1825; a further consignment of wine in October 1826 would have been profitable but for leakage from some of the barrels[82]. News of the buoyancy of the Mexican market spread quickly and the possibility of shipping round Cape Horn to the west coast – through Acapulco, Guadalajara, Tepia or San Blas – was contemplated, but there is no evidence that it occurred[83]. There were problems in Mexico but, in one way or another, they were overcome. Despite attempts to evade raised duties on certain goods – by the manner in which they presented and packaged them – Parker and Penny had to pay some; but a subsequent change in the ministry in Mexico City saw them reduced again. For many months they encountered no difficulties with remittances; mining companies in Mexico had excellent contacts in the London money market and bills of exchange were regularly transmitted through them. When this conduit became temporarily unavailable in December 1827 arrangements were made to return specie. This was risky because bandits lurked on the month-long journey from Mexico City to Vera Cruz and military escorts were untrustworthy on account of substantial arrears of army pay. Ever the courteous but extremely hard-nosed businessman, Thomas Parker persuaded the Penny brothers to guarantee the sum involved in exchange for a 1% commission, and the specie arrived safely shortly after his death[84].

During his last months one large remittance arrived from an unexpected source. While Parker and Penny had done business in Calcutta in 1824-25, little was subsequently exported there because the merchant house involved (Willis, Latham, Gair & Co.) ceased to make remittances, though in substantial debt to them. In September 1827 Thomas's patience finally snapped and he had a power of attorney prepared in an attempt to break the impasse. This did the trick. The earlier partnership was dissolved and a new one (D. & T. Willis & Co.) was established. The latter delivered a remittance of some £5,995 in December 1827[85]. There is no doubt, therefore, that

81 Pkr A, 2/4/63, JSP to TP, 3 June 1826.
82 Pkr A, 2/11/61 & 3/10/50, JSP to TP, 1 Dec. 1825 & 7 Oct. 1826.
83 Pkr A, 3/10/51, T. Kinder to TP, 9 Oct. 1826.
84 Pkr A, 2/4/32; 3/10/50, 54 & 69; 3/14/55: JSP to TP, 30 Aug. 7 & 17 Oct. & 2 Dec. 1826; 10 May 1827. 3/10/5, 25, 27, 56, 62 & 69; 3/14/3, 37: E.B. Penny to TP, 24 Oct. 3 Nov & 2 Dec. 1826; 1 Jan. 7 Mar. 11 Oct. 7 & 14 Dec. 1827
85 Pkr A, 1/16/4, TP to M. Gisborne, 21 Sept. 1827; 3/10/8 & 24, D. & T. Willis to TP, 17 Oct. & 6 Dec. 1827.

although losses were made and some remittances were long delayed, the returns from Thomas Parker's exports of cloth, particularly those from his ventures with the Pennys in Mexico, constituted his major income stream during these years.

Inevitably, in view of the problems associated with moving large sums of money from one side of the world to another, despite the availability of bills of exchange, there were occasional returns in kind. Coffee was sent in lieu of bills from Singapore in October 1826, although Francis Casey was forbidden to send raw cotton (probably from Alexandria) during the calamitous fall in the sale price of that commodity in August 1825[86]. Personal needs were also catered for. Several pipes of port and madeira, no doubt despatched from Lisbon by Studart, were shared from time to time between Parker, Penny and the Healds, and in January 1826 Samuel Stocks took delivery of a barrel of olive oil[87]. There was also the occasional present, most bizarrely in August 1827 from John Burton in Manchester. Having obtained a New Providence turtle through a contact in Liverpool, Burton had it taken by coach to Carlisle. The advice was: 'have the goodness to let a tenant take it from the coach as soon as it arrives. If it die[s], its throat should be cut and allowed to bleed'[88].

Thus, the locations, cargoes, profits and other outcomes of overseas trade were many and varied. Perhaps most remarkable of all was the fact that Thomas Parker conducted the overwhelming bulk of this business by correspondence from his desks at Ardwick Green and Warwick Hall.

86   Pkr A, 2/11/35 & 3/10/50, JSP to TP, 18 Aug. 1825 & 7 Oct. 1826.
87   Pkr A, 2/4/22, 25 & 2/11/8, JSP to TP, 4 June 1825, 18 & 21 Jan. 1826.
88   Pkr A, 3/17/55, J. Wright to TP, 9 Aug. 1827.

Chapter 5:

A Landed Entrepreneur, 1823-28:
Property and Estate Development

PROPERTY DEVELOPMENT IN MANCHESTER

Property development in central Manchester was the third element in Thomas's diverse portfolio. The arrangements which the Parkers had established for themselves were characteristic of the cotton industry as a whole in that they sold their cloth from a base in Manchester, but manufactured it elsewhere. Of course, there were mills and factories in Manchester, John Burton's being among them[1]; but the majority were located elsewhere in the region – at Stockport, Stalybridge, Oldham, Rochdale, Bolton, Bury, Burnley and elsewhere. Manchester was 'dominated less by production than by wholesale distribution and marketing…factories [were] swamped by warehouses'[2]. Most of the warehouses which have survived – grand buildings by any standard – date from the later nineteenth century. Modest establishments emerged much earlier, particularly from the 1790s when the town overtook London as the industry's commercial hub. However, the rapid expansion of trade after 1815 created a strong demand for display and storage facilities, especially for 'shipping warehouses', which were built on a grander scale than hitherto. In 1820 126 buildings were officially described as 'warehouses' in the rate books; by 1829 this number had risen to almost 1,000. Thomas participated energetically in this surge of urban development, much of which took place in and around High Street and behind Piccadilly, as existing tenements were cleared and converted, and new buildings were erected.[3]

Besides the main office and warehouse at 47, High Street, he owned other, similar property: no. 1, and also probably 1A, High Street, let to Samuel Stocks; and various other buildings, some owned in conjunction with William Parker and acquired since 1815; and there is fragmentary evidence of 'new building' there in the autumn of 1823[4]. Thomas decided to secure additional

---

1   His firm, J. Burton & Co., had a workforce of 205 spinners and 135 weavers. – R. Smith, 'Manchester as a Centre for Manufacturing and Merchanting Cotton Goods 1820-30', *University of Birmingham Historical Journal*, iv (1953-54), 50, Table III.

2   Lloyd-Jones & Lewis, 'Economic Structure of 'Cottonopolis' in 1815', 78.

3   H.R. Hitchcock, 'Victorian Monuments of Commerce', *Architectural Review*, 105 (1949), 61-75; Hartwell, *Manchester*, 24; Smith, 'Manchester as a Centre for Manufacture and Merchanting', 63. Despite its scale and commercial significance, research on warehouse development has remained relatively neglected, but see also M.M. Edwards, *The Growth of the British Cotton Trade 1780-1815* (Manchester, 1969), 172-174.

4   Pkr A, 2/12/96, Bill from T. Mycock, 'Messrs. Parkers for New Building 9 Oct – 26 Dec. 1823'.

holdings and, in a series of transactions in early 1825, he purchased several for a total of £19,200: firstly, on 2 February premises in Pall Mall, Manchester, from a Mr. Christie for £4,200 – a dwelling house, two warehouses and adjacent premises; and next, on 9 February, premises in Stable Street from 'Messrs. Grants' for £4,500. Then on 21 February came a deal with 'the Trustees of the late Mr.Lomas' for £4,000: three houses, a warehouse and other buildings in Oldham Street, Dale Street and Spear Street. Finally, on 16 March 1825, for £6,500, Thomas bought a further warehouse in High Street from a Mr. Joseph Marshall[5]. All these acquisitions backed onto, or lay just behind, Piccadilly in the very centre of Manchester. His carefully co-ordinated foray into the market may have been prompted by the first signs of the ensuing crisis in the cotton trade and its associated effect on prices. For instance, in June 1826 Thomas was offered, but declined, a further warehouse in Oldham Street for £1,800: the owner had replaced the roof since purchasing the property for £1,950 in 1819[6]. To judge from the differentials in the cost of the various properties, borne out by further evidence, some of them were run down and in poor condition. Thomas went on to invest heavily in their major refurbishment, and in most cases in their demolition and complete rebuilding to high specifications. By the end of his life he had begun to reap returns from increased rents, though most of the rewards of his efforts went to his successor.

Though then involved in much other complex business, Thomas quickly decided where property renewal should start (Figure 12) and by July 1825 he had secured an estimate of £8,900 'for the creation of your buildings in Stable Street', more generally described as 'back Piccadilly'[7]. The tenant of the substantial existing premises on a large site, Samuel Newton, had sub-let to numerous undertenants, creating a teeming slum. In due course all the occupants had to move on (or bid for one of the proposed new units) before demolition and rebuilding could begin. After some hesitation, Newton determined to make life as difficult as possible for his new landlord. Thereafter, together with James Marchanton, Thomas was frequently engaged with John Taylor, one of his solicitors in Manchester, in proceedings which dragged on till December 1826 when vacant possession was finally secured.

At first Newton was compliant and, at his request, some undertenants vacated the premises: but when they heard that he had changed tack and was digging in his heels, some began to return. Counsel firmly recommended formal ejectment proceedings. Both Newton and his undertenants (many of whom had sub-let even further) would each have to be served with formal notices: but, to be safe, Taylor advised, this should happen only when he fell

5   Pkr A, 3/12/7, Account, Taylor & Son, Solicitors, to T & WP, Feb. – Mar. 1825.
6   Pkr A, 2/4/53, J. Taylor to TP, 30 June 1826.
7   Pkr A, 3/13/29, J. Whirter to TP, 11 July 1825. Successive development led to the disappearance of Stable Street.

Figure 12. Central Manchester: locations (in bold) of urban development by the Parkers.

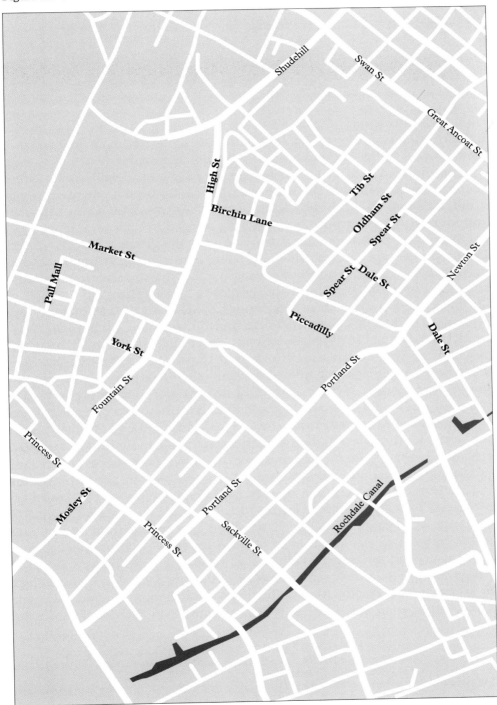

into arrears with his rent. Stocks's reaction was typical. Thomas was:

> in bad hands between bad people and a *poor* lawyer...[and I] am inclined
> to think the latter is the most to be dreaded. If it were mine I should take
> it out of the lawyer's hands and...get the people out in a very short way...
> I would begin to pull down and they would soon run. It is easier to defend
> than to prosecute...It would not be endured by any British jury that
> a parcel of strumpets should keep you out of your property by mere
> menace[8].

By early August 1825 it had become clear, as Stocks had implied, that
Newton was 'filling the place with bad women at great rent'. However,
Thomas decided to stick to due process, causing considerable delay as the
cautious Taylor waited in the hope that rent would become overdue, which
it did in March 1826. A deputation visited Newton, demanding both rent
and immediate possession. Newton flatly refused to 'quit until he had got
another place to suit him', and his wife paid the arrear a few days later.
Formal notices of ejectment were served on Newton and his 19 undertenants
in April, whereupon his attorney proposed either that the matter be referred
to arbitration or that his client be rewarded for delivering up possession.
Taylor pointed out that there was nothing to refer; and, 'as to money, from
Newton's conduct' his client 'had determined now not to give him 6d.'[9].

Newton decided to oppose ejectment; he was 'making as much money...
as will repay him the expenses he may have to pay for'[10]. As Taylor prepared
a barrister's brief, evidence mounted against their adversary. Inadvertently,
but before witnesses, Newton had confirmed the date of his first entry to the
premises, and would be unable to dissemble about that. Moreover, according
to Joseph Wilcock, an unfortunate former undertenant then in Lancaster gaol
for debt, Newton's wife had proceeded against him, and anyone else whose
rent was overdue even by a day, in order to convert the property 'into one
of ill-fame'[11]. The case came before successive assizes in Lancaster during
the late summer and autumn of 1826. While Newton's lawyers called no
witnesses, Taylor was accompanied to Lancaster for a week by a retinue of
assistants and witnesses; a few of the latter had moved from Manchester
in the interim; all of them had to be paid for travel, accommodation and
subsistence; and some also for the cost of their time 'from home'. A writ of
possession was eventually secured and, joined by the local sheriff and a posse
of workmen from Heaton Mersey, Taylor and Marchanton entered the Stable
Street premises in mid-December 'by breaking open the doors'. Newton

---

8   Pkr A, 2/11/29, SS to TP, 30 July 1825; 2/11/13 & 18, JM to TP, 23 June & 16 July 1825.
9   Pkr A, 2/11/32, SS to TP, 6 Aug. 1825; 3/15/27 & 36, JM to TP, 28 Mar. & 8 Apr. 1826; 3/15/20 & 37, J. Taylor to TP, 25 Mar. & 21 Apr. 1826.
10   Pkr A, 2/4/55, J. Taylor to TP, 26 June 1826.
11   Pkr A, 2/4/53, J. Taylor to TP, 30 June 1826; 3/10/46, J. Wilcock to TP, 27 Sept. 1826.

had fled[12]. By February 1827 he was in the Fleet prison in London for debt. Having discovered that - apart from what he had occupied himself, which with stabling for up to 20 horses was worth 'upwards of £100' a year – Newton had got a further £362 annually from sub-letting the property, Thomas went to court to oppose his discharge from prison. He was furious at his failure to be awarded either costs or compensation for unpaid rent; but, as an insolvent, Newton was released from prison[13]. After a delay of one-and-a-half years, the premises in Stable Street were available for re-development from December 1826.

Thomas meanwhile had pursued other projects. The first of these involved the property – a warehouse and other premises in Mosley Street – bought from Joseph Marshall in March 1825. At £6,500 this was the most expensive purchase of the series and much, if not all, of this money was obtained via a mortgage from Marshall. Another businessman, Thomas Cardwell of Cardwell, Longworth & Co., was anxious to lease the property. Thomas must have known and trusted him because, subject to regular reports from Marchanton, he was content for Cardwell to oversee the re-development; and the latter offered, should they be unable to meet in Manchester, to travel to Warwick Hall for discussions. Demolition of the old premises was completed in the summer and in September two builders, J. Wallace and D. Bellhouse – the latter and other members of his family being 'the most successful building contractors in Manchester of the day'[14] – submitted estimates of £1,840 and £1,880 respectively. As both firms were highly regarded and it was 'late in the season', it was decided to proceed with the lower of the two. Delay arose because of problems with the foundations, which had to be cut more deeply than in the original specification in order to accommodate a well. Nevertheless, the new building was up and roofed by early December and work on the interior was completed in March 1826. The contract catered for interim payments to Wallace who, owing to the extra work required, ultimately received £2,020. As part of his agreement Cardwell insured the new warehouse for £5,000[15].

While this was underway Thomas had refurbished one of the two warehouses in Pall Mall which (together with a house and other premises) he had bought from Mr. Christie for £4,200 in February 1825. Following refurbishment, he had let it to the sitting tenants, Martin & Hartwright, at an increased rent – originally set at £120 a year but, following an intervention by Christie, agreed at 100 guineas for one year. So began another chain of

12   Pkr A, 3/10/ 52 & 70, J. Taylor to TP, 10 Oct. & 4 Dec. 1826; 3/10/73, JM to TP, 16 Dec. 1826.
13   Pkr A, 3/14/21 & 27, J. Taylor to TP, 7 & 23 Feb. 1827.
14   Hartwell, *Manchester*, 130.
15   Pkr A, 2/11/8, JM to TP, 16 July 1825; 2/11/22 & 25, J. Burton to TP, 21 & 25 July 1825; 2/11/ 33, 41 & 65, T. Cardwell to TP, 7 Aug. 2 Sept. & 7 Dec. 1825; 1/3/19, 'Estimates etc. for Warehouse in Mosley St.', Sept. 1825; 3/13/8, J. Wallace to TP, 24 Sept. 1825; 1/16/10, TP's Account with J. Wallace, March 1826.

events which stretched well into the following year. In April 1826, just as the crisis in the cotton trade was at its worst, the lessees gave notice to quit at the end of that year – they could not 'afford to pay so much rent these times'. A week later, however, they changed their minds, even though they had an offer of alternative premises. Instead, they began to haggle over the rent. They claimed to have beaten down the rent of their alternative from £100 to £80 per annum, and were willing to take Thomas's premises at that price, although it was 10% more than they had previously paid Mr. Christie. After many more weeks of stand-off the tenants finally agreed to pay an annual rent of £86 for a seven-year lease commencing in the new year[16]; but this was not the end of the matter. In August, having engaged a jobbing builder to make repairs in their packing room, they reported that he had declared the building dangerously unsafe, 'the principal of the roof' having 'given way eleven inches towards the street'. Not only was the matter extremely urgent but the cost of repair had been estimated at between £50 and £70, which would have to be allowed out of their rent. When in late August Thomas despatched Stocks and William Buckley, the builder at Heaton Mersey, to assess the situation, they advised that 'the roof must be taken off or it will fall in'. For once, and for some unknown reason, they heard nothing from Warwick Hall for several weeks, by which time Martin & Hartwright were on the verge of moving out. Stocks seized the initiative and got Mr. Wallace and his men to start the repairs 'by day work'[17]. By the end of September Stocks felt able to report 'favourably', but the workers 'want some drink. I have no authority over your barrel [kept apparently at 47, High Street]. Will you allow me to give any? I am told it will get the job on faster'. And so it did. By mid-October the work was 'near a close [and the] job would soon be done'[18]. The tenants were very happy with the outcome, their landlord having paid for the extensive repair work.

A few weeks later on 4 December the writ of possession against Newton was secured and work began on the demolition of the existing premises in Stable Street, with Stocks selling off old materials to defray costs. By early January 1827 precise boundaries were under negotiation with surveyors from the local authority and building materials were being assembled. Many balks of timber were brought in from Liverpool and two sawyers from Heaton Mersey set about planking them. By early February Marchanton was armed with a precise ground plan. Using some 'cleaned' bricks from the old premises, building commenced in earnest in mid-February and was up to the first floor and 'going on well' by early April, when Buckley was fashioning doors for

---

16   Pkr A, 2/11, 50 & 51, R. Christie to TP, 21 & 24 Oct. 1825; 3/15/27 & 36, JM to TP, 28 Mar. & 8 Apr. 1826; 3/15/22 & 2/4/48, Martin & Hartwright to TP, 17 Apr. & 10 July 1826.

17   Pkr A, 2/4/35 & 3/10/37, Martin & Hartwright to TP, 24 Aug. 1826 & n.d. but Sept. 1826; 2/4/33 & 3/10, 38 & 43-45, SS to TP, 30 Aug. & 2, 12, 16 & 23 Sept. 1826.

18   Pkr A, 3/10/48 & 53, SS to TP, 30 Sept. & 14 Oct. 1826.

the 'teagles' – lifting apparatus for bringing goods up from and down to the street. A month later work was going on apace, by sawyers, 'soughers' [drain and sewer diggers], joiners, glaziers, plasterers, painters, carters and a gang of labourers. External work on an entirely new complex was completed during June including an eight-foot-high cellar, and a building of five storeys built to detailed and high specifications[19].

None of Thomas's other plans for property development in central Manchester proved as problematical as that in Stable Street, but a host of issues arose, all of which had to be dealt with; and it was as well by this stage that Marchanton worked solely or primarily for him. On receiving notice to quit, most sitting tenants either moved on without fuss or declared an interest in negotiating fresh terms following refurbishment or re-building. Indeed, in anticipation of future developments some put down very early markers. One tenant of that part of Pall Mall not developed in 1825-26 indicated willingness to renew once his current lease expired in three or four years time[20]. Some current leases were for terms which Thomas felt likely to prove uneconomic, preventing any interim increase in rent; and when another tenant in Pall Mall requested a 14-year term, he was told that a seven-year one was the most he could hope for[21]. Most leases were of shorter duration. Against the background of the Stable Street episode, sub-letting was strongly discouraged, except with Thomas Parker's express, written permission. Unsurprisingly, as happened with a Mr. Wilkinson 'who occupies part of the warehouse in Dale Street', some tenants got into difficulties with their businesses in 1826 and failed to pay their rent. Marchanton considered seizing goods to the value of the rent 'but doubted....finding sufficient on the premises to pay it'. One of Wilkinson's suppliers stepped in to pay the arrear, expecting (and probably hoping) to 'have to take the concern into his own hands' eventually[22].

Some properties scheduled for re-development became vacant – one in Dale Street for example – but it was often possible to set these on short terms for correspondingly modest rents. Mr. Hall, a cloth dresser, offered to take it for one year at £20, which was accepted. Hall had a shop in Oldham Street but needed additional storage space; he intended building his own place in Salford and would have plenty of room there by the end of the year[23]. At times vacant properties encouraged petty crime. In November 1826 Stocks reported the theft of windows from some premises, 'and the lead was

19   Pkr A, 3/9/27 & 3/14/ 5, 51, 59-60, JM to TP, 4 Jan. 6 Feb. 12 Apr. 17 & 25 May 1827; 3/14/7 & 23, SS to TP, 9 Jan. & 8 Feb. 1827; 3/9/30 & 3/14/13, Gregson & Co. to TP, 17 & 20 Jan. 1827; 3/14/57, Satterfields & Cresswell to TP, 12 May 1827; 1/3/26, 'Specification...in Stable St.', n.d. but 1825-26.
20   Pkr A, 1/3/24, JM to TP, 29 Oct. 1825.
21   Pkr A, 2/11/8, JM to TP, 16 July 1825.
22   Pkr A, 3/10/47, JM to TP, 28 Sept. 1826.
23   Pkr A, 3/15/36 & 40, JM to TP, 24 & 28 Mar. 1826.

rolled up ready to be taken away'. He recommended 'pulling them down' immediately[24]. Much of the traffic through Marchanton's office concerned relatively minor repairs: for instance, in March 1826 a cellar wall, made only of half-bricks, collapsed 'owing to the pressure of cotton or other matter in the adjoining cellars'. At a cost of £6 the tenant was willing to organise the repair work but, as in all such cases, he expected an equivalent reduction in his rent[25]. Many of Thomas Parker's warehouses, old and new, contained numerous separate rooms which were let to a variety of different businesses, and squabbles between them were not uncommon. The entire area was a hive of activity, news and gossip travelled quickly, and the issue of 'respectability' was, as always, not far from the surface. When one tenant, a Mr. Barker, was about to vacate his property, two other individuals, Messrs Faulkner and Paul, vied with each other to succeed him. Faulkner, who already leased adjacent premises from Thomas, heard that Barker had promised to recommend Paul as his successor. Faulkner immediately complained that Paul 'was in the habit of taking respectable premises and letting...off...the cellars as fruit shops etc.'. He had no need of additional premises but was keen to get this one in order to prevent Paul from facilitating outlets for mere consumables[26]. Unfortunately, the outcome is unknown.

None of this was allowed to undermine the main agenda and, as economic conditions gradually improved towards the close of 1826, significant changes occurred in the way in which Thomas Parker conducted his development programme. Firstly, no doubt partly as a result of his own periodic visits to Manchester, he came to trust William Buckley's capacity to co-ordinate major building work. Because Buckley had previously worked at Heaton Mersey, Thomas probably knew little or nothing about him until Stocks seconded him to resolve problems in Manchester. Thereafter, outside firms were called in to assist with particular aspects of development but none was contracted to undertake an entire project, as had been the case earlier. From the time of the Stable Street development, the work was done either by direct labour or under sub-contract. With Marchanton permanently on hand and Stocks regularly overseeing him, Buckley organised demolition, assembled new materials (sometimes travelling beyond the town to do so), engaged craftsmen and labourers, and supervised the building process[27]. And by then, of course, he had examples nearby of the quality of work required, and Thomas Parker often referred to them. Secondly, the growing success of Thomas's overseas trading ventures eliminated cash-flow problems and made him more ambitious; never one to let money lie, he preferred to put

---

24   Pkr A, 3/10/65, SS to TP, 18 Nov. 1826.
25   Pkr A, 3/15/36, JM to TP, 28 Mar. 1826.
26   Pkr A, 3/14/29, JM to TP, 24 Feb. 1827.
27   See e.g. Pkr A, 3/12/62 & 3/17/19, 30 & 54, JM to TP, 13 June & 14 Aug. 1827, 22 Jan. & 20 Feb. 1828.

it to work. Whereas during 1825-26 individual projects had proceeded in sequence, in 1827 activity became much more extensive. Several projects proceeded simultaneously and building activity rose to a crescendo in the months immediately prior to Thomas's death in April 1828.

Hence, scarcely a letter passed between Thomas Parker, Stocks and Marchanton without reference to aspects of the re-development programme. Before the Stable Street complex was completed, there were substantial repairs to premises in Pall Mall. At an unidentified site 'two or three warehouses' were up to the fourth floor and at the roofing stage in July 1827 and all external work on them was completed in August. By then too the dates of first entry of the tenants of properties in both Dale Street and Spear Street were being checked, with a view to their being vacated to allow re-development from New Year 1828[28]. Apart from Stable Street, the two major projects in 1827 were in Tib Street and at Albion Buildings 'next Piccadilly', properties which had been acquired sometime between 1815 and 1825.

The work in Tib Street got underway in May. The very narrow street had originated as a footpath alongside the River Tib. The river had been culverted in 1783, but not very successfully[29]. Progress with establishing foundations was delayed because parts of the site became waterlogged, and anxious deliberations ensued about what sort of drainage system to deploy. Yet bricks were delivered in early June and by the middle of that month activity was hectic. The walls were up by mid-August, whereupon plasterers and painters began touting for business. Progress was steady throughout the autumn and in January 1828 Marchanton was able to report that there was 'little [external] work remaining undone at the Tib Street building'[30]. Meanwhile, having also commenced in the preceding early summer, external work at Albion Buildings was nearly finished too; indeed, some tenants were already in residence in advance of the completion of internal work. This was almost certainly Thomas Parker's largest single re-development project. The site was a very extensive one on which he erected no fewer than ten warehouses (with nos. 9 & 10 'communicating'). Great care was taken with what appears to have been his flagship project and on the completion of building work the complex was insured for £5,000. The stonework was of the finest quality; ten black marble chimneypieces were installed; the door cases were specially fashioned; the glazing alone ran to some 4,300 square feet; the 'areas' in front of each lot were fenced with iron railings; and, finally, perhaps in view of the disorder in the town centre during 1826, the site was

---

28   Pkr A, 2/17/63, 3/14/60, 3/17/37, 41 & 60, JM to TP, 25 May, 20 & 31 July, 15 & 22 Sept. 1827.
29   Hartwell, *Manchester*, 226.
30   Pkr A, 3/14/56, R. Winder to TP, 12 May 1827; 1/20/2, T. Evans to TP, 27 Aug. 1827; 3/12/62, 3/14/61, 3/17/30 & 54; JM to TP, 2 & 13 June, 14 August 1827, & 22 Jan. 1828.

surrounded by an elaborate 'palisade'[31]. Full details of the rents charged have not survived though, inevitably, there were the customary haggles. In December 1827, however, the rents of nos. 2-6 were set at between £130 and £180, producing an annual rental from them alone of £760[32]. Albion Buildings as a whole, therefore, must have yielded rents well in excess of £1,000 a year.

The properties in Dale Street and Spear Street became vacant at New Year 1828 and work on them proceeded immediately – and jointly, because some of the premises fronted onto both streets. A yard for storing building and other materials was acquired on a six-month lease and by mid-February three old warehouses had been demolished and foundations for new ones were being laid. At the time of Thomas's death building there was well advanced; and another warehouse – at 54, High Street – had just had its roof repaired[33].

So, to the very end of his life, there was no let-up. Moreover, besides the new projects, there had been steady business with the tenants of other properties. Particularly when premises changed hands but also at other times, it was customary to accede to reasonable requests from tenants as to how they wished their offices and showrooms to be set up - with desks, counters and so on. It was William Buckley's job to ascertain particular needs and to inform Marchanton, who then transmitted requests to Warwick Hall. They were invariably accepted, with the result that the total amount of work involved at any juncture was very considerable. During the entire process money was made available, as required, from Jones & Lloyd, Thomas's bank in Manchester. In addition to submitting periodic summary accounts with their respective vouchers (which are referred to in the correspondence but none of which has survived for this period), Marchanton also provided a weekly summary of current needs. Thomas settled most of the larger bills from suppliers and sub-contractors, while Marchanton dealt with the less substantial ones and with wages. If in any week rental income and petty receipts threatened to prevent him from doing so, he informed Thomas (as far in advance as possible), who sent him bank notes or a cheque on Jones & Lloyd[34]. Significantly, throughout these years not a single remittance to Warwick Hall is recorded, and the evidence suggests that there was none.

Scale and quality were the key characteristics of Thomas Parker's urban development programme in Manchester. Uninterested in replacing like

---

31   Pkr A, 3/10/6, 14, 16, 18, 30, 3/17/11 & 47, JM to TP, 1 Sept. 11 & 30 Oct. 7, 14 & 20 Dec. 1827, & 15 Mar. 1828; 3/10/2, J. Patterson to TP, 4 Oct. 1827; 3/10/17, J. Burton to TP, 10 Nov. 1827; 1/20/4, T. Howard to TP, n.d. but 1827.

32   Pkr A, 3/10/23, T. Langstrom to TP, 5 Dec. 1827.

33   Pkr A, 3/17/16, 19, 28, 30, 32, JM to TP, 10, 22 & 26 Jan., 20 & 29 Feb. 1828; 3/17/7-8, 11, JM to WP, 15, 26 & 31 Mar. 1828.

34   See e.g. Pkr A, 3/17/34, 41, 45, 54, 58, 60, JM to TP, 31 July, 2 & 14 Aug. 6, 15 & 29 Sept. 1827; 3/17/53, G. Heald to TP, 18 Aug. 1827.

Figure 13. Architect's impression of the warehouse in Birchin Lane.

with like, his buildings were on a large scale and finished to high standards. The contemporary description of them as warehouses is potentially misleading (Figure 13). All the new buildings would appear to have been four storeys high with cellars in addition. An architect's impression of one of them has survived – the warehouse in Birchin Lane, which was never embarked on because the deal with the would-be vendor fell through. This shows a majestic urban building, much less like a warehouse than a business headquarters[35]. And this is precisely what these new buildings were. Many of the premises were shared between various businesses but, for virtually all the entrepreneurs involved, apart from those who needed storage space only in one of the cellars, they showcased their endeavours. This was the key point at which they dealt with customers in their counting houses (many with baywood counters[36]) and displayed their wares in custom-built showrooms. Those in Albion Buildings would appear to have been the grandest of all, but many of the others were built to a similar scale. The warehouse in Mosley Street, built for Cardwell & Longworth in 1825-26, was described as a property 'of....magnitude'; like Albion Buildings, it was insured for £5,000. After his partnership was dissolved in 1827, Longworth converted the property into a silk mill with 400 hands, much to the consternation of Thomas's insurance broker, Mr. Langstrom, since the insurance on it had not been upgraded[37]. The complex

35   Pkr A, 1/16/15, 'Plan of Warehouse…in Birchin Lane', n.d. but 1821 (see Figure 13). Pkr A, 3/11/24, n.d. but mid-1820s, is a sketch of the frontage of nos. 32-42, Mosley St. (see Figure 14). All the premises had four storeys plus basement cellars, and an accompanying floor-plan illustrated the cheek-by-jowl nature of multi-occupancy.

36   Pkr A, 3/10/30, JM to TP, 20 Dec. 1827.

37   Pkr A, 3/17/32, JM to TP, 10 Jan. 1828; 3/17/31, J. Taylor to TP, 14 Jan. 1828.

so laboriously wrested from Newton was ultimately one of five bays fronting on Stable Street; its masonry was specified to be 'of the best Huddersfield stone', the golden millstone grit common in that vicinity; and, as with one of his competitors, Thomas insisted that it have an inscription stone[38]. Indeed, during this spate of development competition was keen, not just among businesses wishing to lease prime sites in the town-centre, but also from other developers. Among those vied with were a Mr. Radcliffe, Mr. Bannermans, Mr. McFarlane, Mr. Christie (a vendor to Thomas Parker in 1825), and a Mr. Sandiford at Bridgewater Buildings[39].

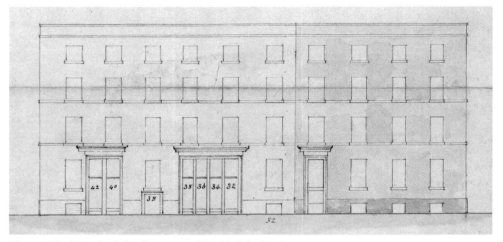

Figure 14. Sketch of the frontage of 32-42, Mosley Street.

The sources do not allow us to get close enough to Thomas Parker to unravel his motivation for building development. At one level he seems to have revelled in the cut and thrust of business, however complex and multi-faceted. He did not welcome crises – no-one would have done – but he relished the search for solutions, as he demonstrated with Stocks and Heaton Mersey. For years he withstood James Penny's endemic pessimism about the export trade and his own judgement eventually proved sound. If in his endeavours as an urban developer, he sought to leave lasting monuments to his uncle's efforts in the cotton trade, or simply to invest remuneratively, he also succeeded. In doing so he left his family with significant annual income from the rents of town-centre property in Manchester.

38   Pkr A, 1/3/26, 'Specification in Stable St.', n.d. but 1825-26; 3/17/66, J. Patterson to TP, 7 July 1827.
      'Above all in the northern cities...sound red brick and good stone were more readily obtainable
      than in London'. In later years Yorkshire stone was brought into Manchester by rail, but it was also
      keenly sought after during this earlier period. That from Huddersfield would have come by canal,
      the longest canal tunnel in Britain – under the Pennines at Standedge – having been opened in
      1811. – Hitchcock, 'Victorian Monuments of Commerce', 63-64.
39   Pkr A, 3/14/29 & 61, 3/17/ 19 & 54, JM to TP, 24 Feb. 2 June & 14 Aug. 1827, 20 Feb. 1828; 3/10/3,
      SS to TP, 4 Oct. 1827.

THE HALL, ESTATE AND VILLAGE AT WARWICK BRIDGE

Thomas Parker's fourth preoccupation during these years was with the development of his newly-acquired property at Warwick Bridge. In addition to his grant of arms, this was the public symbol of his rise from merchant to gentleman. He built a new hall at Warwick as a demonstration of his means and status and, as was fashionable, engaged in extensive tree-planting and landscaping there. As opportunities arose, he rationalised and expanded his holdings; and during the short period of his permanent residence he played an increasingly prominent role in local affairs. He made notable improvements to the village and also became an energetic promoter of the scheme to turnpike the road from Carlisle via Warwick Bridge to Brampton, which was (and still is) on a main route across the Pennines to Newcastle. In the last year of his life he was appointed high sheriff of Cumberland. Although a deep purse and a fine mansion were necessary prerequisites for nomination to this position, no-one could aspire to it who had not gained the confidence of leading members of the county community. Thomas certainly did so, as further testified by the more than conventional tribute paid to him after his untimely death.

In considering this aspect of his career, an irony emerges. While a few photographs of it have survived, the new Warwick Hall was totally destroyed by fire in 1930; only Thomas's pedimented stable block and his gatehouse have survived, so it is difficult to assess his major achievement there[40]. Otherwise, the evidence of his activities at Warwick is fragmentary: most of the surviving documents relate to his endeavours elsewhere and consist mainly of letters to rather than from him. Because they lived at a distance, with only a few of them visiting Warwick Hall and then only rarely, his correspondents had little to say about his life there, other than the warmth of his hospitality, because they knew so little about it. The surviving record, therefore, is slim and often difficult to interpret securely. Nevertheless, while not evidenced in as much detail as his other activities, his overall achievement at Warwick Hall and in its vicinity is not in doubt.

Thomas bought the estate from a Robert Warwick, originally not a Warwick at all, but a Robert Bonner who subsequently changed his surname to Warwick. The estate was named after the Warwick family, catholics who were fiercely committed to the Jacobite cause; who accommodated Bonnie Prince Charlie as he passed through the area in 1745; and who, having been headed by Francis Warwick who left very substantial debts, died out in the direct male line with his demise in 1772. The encumbered property descended to his only surviving sister, Ann Warwick, after whose death it passed to a Ralph Maddison of Gateshead, and then to his brother, John, both of whom

---

40   M. Hyde & N. Pevsner, *The Buildings of England: Cumbria: Cumberland, Westmorland and Furness* (New Haven & London, 2010), 662-663.

Figure 15. Portrait of Thomas Parker (1784-1828).

died without issue, the latter in 1784[41]. Meanwhile, Bonner Warwick's father, Thomas Bonner, who hailed from Callerton in Northumberland, had begun buying up the Warwicks' property and continued to do so. He left it to Robert, who was once described as 'a banker, dealer and chapman', the sort of multifarious entrepreneur with whom Thomas Parker was familiar. Among other things, Bonner Warwick owned shares in the old brewery in Carlisle, reached agreement with over 30 small proprietors on the enclosure of Warwick Common, and purchased property which was merged with the Warwick Hall estate. However, he himself got into serious financial difficulties and in 1798 began to mortgage his property heavily. Thereafter, he did not have his troubles to seek. In 1811 he parted from his wife, Mary, *nee* Atkinson, of Carlisle, with whom he had had four daughters; and in 1817 the Court of King's Bench gave judgement against him for his mortgages. Finally, in 1821 he was declared bankrupt and his properties in Cumberland,

---

41   Parsons & White, *History, Directory and Gazeteer*, 384.

Northumberland and Durham were sold to enable his creditors to recoup their capital[42]. It was this which enabled Thomas to clinch the deal.

The Warwick Hall estate then ran to some 962 acres, 63 of which consisted of tree plantations. Apart from the hall, park and three fields for horses, there were four farms and ten small crofts or cottage holdings. No contemporary rentals have survived, but some three or so decades later leased property brought in some £1,280 annually. Rents had moved forward in the interim, so in all probability the rental in 1822 amounted to less, perhaps significantly less, than £1,000 a year. Thus, despite negotiating the purchase during the post-war recession, at £45,000 Thomas paid a high price for it. It was auctioned in 13 lots and bidding for the larger lots must have been fiercely competitive. Particularly in view of its splendid position near the banks of the Eden, Warwick Hall was undoubtedly a highly desirable property. It is equally clear that Thomas (Figure 15) derived little income from it and that this was far exceeded by his outlay. At some point after his purchase, he vested part of the Warwick estate (though how much is unrecorded) in his wife, Mary, who enjoyed this for the rest of her life and was free to dispose of it as she wished[43].

On his return to Cumberland Thomas's reputed wealth created a stir in the region and, with James Penny being used as an intermediary, enquiries were made as to whether he wished to purchase additional property – firstly at Silloth on the Solway coast, and later at Hayton, where the would-be vendor thought Thomas might be attracted by the ruined castle on the property. Thomas was unimpressed by the rental income of both in relation to their guide prices and politely but firmly declined, though in the case of Silloth he asked to be kept informed of future developments; but that was the end of the matter. In November 1824, however, he did purchase, for just under £500, a small plot of land which abutted on the Warwick Hall estate. In March 1826 he reached agreement with a William Stordy of Warwick for an exchange of Stordy's Church Close and Cock Hill for Thomas's two fields, Cropands and Nort Acre, plus £250[44].

For the five years following his major purchase, much of Thomas Parker's time and many of his resources were devoted to developments at Warwick, especially his early decision to build a new home there (Figure 16). The old hall, though substantial, was in poor condition, not having been occupied

---

42 It seems, however, that two to three years earlier Thomas had reached agreement in principle with at least one of Bonner Warwick's creditors: for, in the proclamation of 12 July 1819 detailing the freight by H.M.S. *Warspite* (see above), he is described, albeit prematurely, as 'of Warwick Hall'.

43 CAS (C), DB/74/2/78/175, Auction Lot Map, Warwick Hall Estate, 1821; DB/74/2/78/51, Estate Rental, c. 1860.

44 Silloth & Hayton: Pkr A, 1/3/7, T. Howard to TP, n.d.; 3/11/8, JSP to TP, 14 Dec. 1824, which includes a copy of H. Vernon to JSP, of 11 Dec. 1824; 3/8/2, TP to T. Howard, 14 Dec. 1824; Purchase: 3/11/20, Account, Hodgson & Nanson, Solicitors, Nov. 1824; Exchange: 3/15/38, Terms, 25 Mar. 1826.

Figure 16. The Hall at Warwick built by Thomas Parker and destroyed by fire in 1930.

by a family for several, perhaps many, years. If he was to make his mark in the area, Thomas had to improve on this. Nowhere is there mention of an architect, and it seems likely that he not only built the new hall but designed it too. When completed, it had two floors and was broadly 'L'-shaped, with the servants' quarters and utilities in the smaller wing to the rear, and the main rooms along the front[45]. The work proceeded in two phases. A distinctive feature of the completed building was a set of curved windows installed in the main rooms at the front of the house, overlooking the Eden. These were ordered from Newcastle as late as July 1826, so it appears that the first phase, down to the early summer of 1825, was devoted to demolition and then to the erection of what later became the servants' wing[46]. Thomas and Mary spent much of this earlier period in the house at Ardwick Green, but they were almost certainly at Old Town House, their ancestral home, in May 1825; or at least it was to there that their mail was directed[47]. They moved into the lesser wing at Warwick Hall shortly afterwards. The house became fully habitable late in 1827, just as Thomas was about to take up the high shrievalty.

What is clear, and may explain his eventual recourse to it in Manchester, is that most of the work on the hall was done by direct labour. All surviving enquiries, specifications, further queries and invoices proceeded directly to,

---

45   While there is no contemporary room plan, a list of rooms features in an inventory of furniture compiled after Mary Parker's death in 1857; and still more valuable is a comprehensive room plan for both storeys, illustrating the installation of central-heating in the 1920s by the Liddells, who bought the property from the Parkers in 1901. – CAS (C), DB/74/1/6, Furniture Account, 1857; DB/74/P/85, Room Plan, 1920s.

46   Pkr A, 2/4/50, Richardson & Son to TP, 6 July 1826.

47   Pkr A, 2/11/7, JSP to TP, 28 May 1825.

and from, Thomas Parker. They demonstrate extremely close attention to detail. Required measurements, discounts offered and the quality of goods on arrival were pursued and scrutinised remorselessly, and on at least two occasions Thomas corrected an invoice in favour of a supplier[48]. It was a complex exercise in project management. Many supplies were obtained locally, but Penny organised numerous and varied shipments from Liverpool to Carlisle, and regular consignments of timber and glass were brought overland from Newcastle.

In March 1825 Thomas and Mary Parker left the house at Ardwick. Henceforward, when in Manchester they stayed either with the Healds at Parr's Wood or with friends in the town. They moved to Cumberland in May, 25 crates of their belongings following them in the smack *Carlisle* to Carlisle, and 22 by *Rosina* a few days later. There were further removals in June – a bookcase, four crates of books and one of window blinds. By the time another eight crates were shipped in July, Mary Parker's mother and a sister had joined them for an extended stay, helping them to organise matters in their new home[49]. Later shipments suggest a more advanced stage of settling into the one wing completed by then, as well as a persistent search for economy; 13 crates of empty bottles and a sack of corks in July; and in August no less than one-and-a-half hundredweights of the 'finest yellow soap'. At that stage they were all taking a break in a house at Skinburness, near Silloth, while work on the second, larger wing got underway. William Buckley, whose work in Manchester Thomas had come greatly to admire, supplied measurements and estimates of the timber required for 'the framework'; and Stocks, supported by Buckley, recommended that a Josh Walker, who worked at Heaton Mersey, should travel to Warwick to assist: 'he understands such things well and would not require much more than his meat for his work'[50].

The project proceeded steadily from that point though, noticeably, not as rapidly as current projects in Manchester. The new Warwick Hall was in all respects a much finer building and material supplies were not as readily available there as in Manchester; nor, crucially, was a large pool of craftsmen and labourers. Thomas strove for perfection, which took time. Nevertheless, by February 1826 the ground floor of the second wing was nearing completion when Thomas Lear, a favourite retainer, sent nine cases of organ parts from the house at Heaton Mersey. Later that month estimates were received from Carrick & Birrel of Rockliffe, near Carlisle, for internal timber of the 'best American Yellow Pine'....laid down at Warwick Hall'. 1,270 ft. of it were

48   Pkr A, 2/4/58, W. Armstrong to TP, 13 June 1826 and 3/17/44, E. Richardson & Son to TP, 11 Sept. 1827. For further examples of his attention to detail, see 2/5/75, TP to Messrs Davenport, 21 Feb. 1826 and CAS (C), DX/1089/40/1, J. Birrell to TP, 20 May 1826.

49   Pkr A, 2/11/5, W. Dowson to TP, 23 May 1825; 2/11/ 3, 13 & 18, JM to TP, 25 May, 23 June & 16 July 1825; 2/11/24, SS to TP, 23 July 1825.

50   Pkr A, 2/26, 38, JSP to TP, 26 July & 27 Aug. 1825; 2/11/39, SS to TP, 31 Aug. 1825; 2/11/40, T. Kirkpatrick to TP, 31 Aug. 1825.

ordered. In March James Penny shipped casks of paint and six bolts of sheet lead for the roof, the main timbers of which were of 'excellent Baltic' from Carrick & Birrel. The shell of the roof was completed in April. Further large consignments of timber came from Rockcliffe and 'Memel' wood for sash windows was sourced from Newcastle. In May Ralph Dodds, a plasterwork specialist in Newcastle, corresponded with Thomas about the design of the cornices and centrepieces of the ceilings on the ground floor, probably those of the dining and drawing rooms. By then too work had begun on Thomas's pedimented stable block. Twenty-six coping stones and six troughs were sent from Manchester, and Penny forwarded a large quantity of nails from Liverpool[51].

Figure 17. Part of the grounds at Warwick Hall in the early 1900s.

Thomas also embellished the parkland surrounding Warwick Hall (Figure 17). In November 1825, W. & T. Hutton, tree nurserymen of Carlisle, sent him their catalogue, which listed numerous species and their varieties. Some were priced per 100 and some per 1,000; and 'as we hold an extended stock at present, we are enabled to offer them as low, if not lower, than many in the trade'. In the new year Mary Parker sent bushes from the garden of the house at Heaton Mersey; and in February Stocks confirmed that the gardeners there 'will attend to your [other] orders and get them off'[52].

---

51   Pkr A, 2/4/14, JM to TP, 6 Feb. 1826; 2/4/5 & 3/15/30, Carrick & Birrel to TP, 21 Feb. & 3 Apr. 1826; CAS (C), DX/1089/40/1, J. Birrel to TP, 20 May 1826; Pkr A, 2/4/6 & 3/15/3, 9, 22, JSP to TP, 20 Feb. 23 Mar. 12 & 26 May 1826; 3/15/21, G. Oliver to TP, 20 Apr. 1826; 3/11/22, R. Dodds to TP, 5 May 1826; 3/15/12, Endorsement to J. Burton to TP, 4 May 1826.

52   Pkr A, 3/19/1, W. & T. Hutton to TP, 30 Nov. 1825; 2/4/14, JM to TP, 6 Feb. 1826; 2/4/7, SS to TP, 18 Feb. 1826.

Richardson & Son of Newcastle supplied glass: 800m feet of plain glass in July 1826; and later 'ground or obscure glass', and bent glass for the windows at the front. When specifications of the latter were forwarded, 'there must be wooden moulds of the bend sent at the same time to enable us to get the exact sweep'[53]. It may have been this unusual feature which persuaded James Losh of nearby Wreay, in his diary for that day, to note 'a large Gentleman's House, not built with much Taste' as he passed through Warwick Bridge on 19 October 1826[54]. Following the receipt of additional sheets of lead from Liverpool, the roof was finally completed in January 1827. Thereafter, the emphasis switched to the interior. There was much meticulous correspondence about china and other accoutrements and in August Thomas struck a deal with Gilles & Shepherd, coach & harness makers of Manchester, for delivery of a coach 'of the very best materials and workmanship' for a sum of £205. Characteristically, he ensured delivery by the middle of January 1828 by requiring a forfeit of £100 if this deadline was not met. Equally predictably, the bill was paid promptly on 31 March, only a week or so before his death. In a summary published shortly afterwards, the hall was described as 'a neat and pleasant mansion, shielded on the west and north with thriving plantations, and commanding an open, beautiful, and extensive prospect [towards] the Eden'[55].

Meanwhile, Thomas had become a leading supporter with some of his neighbours of a plan to turnpike the road from Carlisle to Brampton which, at about its mid-point, passed the entrance to the Warwick Hall estate. On 20 April 1826, just less than a year after he had finally moved north, a meeting was held 'at the house of Margaret Scott of Warwick....of the owners and occupiers of lands and tenements of the parishes of Wetheral, Warwick and the neighbourhood'. The 15 attendees agreed to proceed. Along with two others, Thomas made the leading subscription of £50 to defray initial expenses and was elected to the project's steering committee. A week later it was agreed that 'the great and increasing weight of carriage' on the road from Carlisle to Brampton (and onwards to Newcastle) merited concerted action. It was resolved to solicit the Duke of Devonshire, the area's leading landowner, and Carlisle Corporation for support to apply to parliament 'for an act to make' the route 'a turnpike road, and such branches as are thought expedient'. Thomas contributed a further £200 to the fund then established to promote the project. In July the scheme was announced in the local press. Much to his dismay, progress was slow. While a plan of the route was well

---

53   Pkr A, 2/4/50, Richardson & Son to TP, 6 July 1826.
54   Carlisle Library, Local Studies Collection, B 320, Diaries of James Losh, Volume covering the period 28 Sept. – 22 Oct. 1826. I owe this reference to Adrian Allen.
55   Pkr A, 3/10/74 & 3/14/54-55, JSP to TP, 19 Dec. 1826, 27 Apr. & 10 May 1827; 3/14/39, Davenport, Tinney & Co. to TP, 17 Mar. 1827; 3/14/51, JM to TP, 12 Apr. 1827; 3/12/14-15, Giles & Shepherd to TP, 31 Aug. 1827; Parsons & White, *History, Directory & Gazetteer*, 385.

advanced by November 1827, it had yet to be submitted. Matters moved forward more briskly thereafter but progress was threatened by an overall subscription which fell short of what was required. By January 1828 £2,800 had been raised which, even when the estimated cost was reduced to £3,201, remained insufficient. Somehow the gap was closed and one correspondent's commiseration that Thomas had 'so much trouble about the Turnpike Bill' perhaps implied that Thomas had played a part in closing it. The enabling legislation was passed shortly after his death[56].

Another project harked back to earlier years, when his uncle, Robert, had built a Sunday school for the youthful workforce at Heaton Mersey and been closely involved with its massive neighbour, Stockport Sunday School. Firmly convinced of what he might best do for the young people of any community, Thomas proceeded to build a Sunday school for the village of Warwick shortly after his arrival there. It was (and remains) a substantial, imposing building of two storeys and fine, cut stone, with an auditorium upstairs and with cottages on either side for superintendents. The school was sited on rising ground to the rear of Warwick Hall, near the planned line of the new road from Carlisle to Brampton. Thomas left £1,500 in his will for its additional furbishment, and required his executors to use this legacy 'to fulfil my wishes and intentions as if I had lived to carry them into execution myself'. He also built two day schools in Warwick Bridge, one for boys and the other for girls. Overall, he 'made considerable improvements in the village' and was 'a liberal benefactor' to its poor[57]. In a short space of time his impact in the locality was considerable.

Finally, during the course of 1827, conscious of his growing standing among the local gentry and of his duties as a leading J.P. which took him there, Thomas decided to build a town house in Carlisle. He negotiated successfully to acquire a 200-year lease of a plot of land opposite the Brick Inn in English Street which, until then, had formed part of the garden of the Duke of Devonshire's house in the city. He arranged for a road to be 'staked out' to separate his prospective property from that of his noble neighbour and at the time of his death everything was finalised except the building clauses in the proposed lease[58]. Thomas's executors decided not to proceed with the matter but, along with the evidence of his other activities during his last year, this project confirms that his illness was unexpected and came on

56 Pkr A, 3/11/23, Memorandum, 20 Apr. 1826; 3/12/3, Draft Memorandum, 28 Apr. 1826; 3/10/19, W. Nanson to TP, 26 Nov. 1827; 3/17/18, 22, 24 & 29, G.G. Mounsey to TP, 26 Jan. 11 Feb. & two of n.d. but Feb. 1828; 3/17/20, T.H. Graham to TP, 15 Feb. 1828; *Carlisle Journal*, 22 July 1826.

57 Hyde & Pevsner, *Cumbria*, 662; Parsons & White, *History, Directory and Gazetteer*, 384; P.J. Mannix & W. Whellan, *History, Gazeteer and Directory of Cumberland* (Whitehaven, 1847, re-published Whitehaven, 1974), 211-212; Pkr B, 28, Thomas Parker's Will, 28 Mar. 1828.

58 Pkr A, 1/13/13, R. & G.G. Mounsey to Messrs. Hodgson & Nanson, 13 May 1828; 1/13/14, W. Nanson to WP & the Mounseys, 14 May 1828; 1/13/24, Mounseys to WP, 30 June 1828; 1/13/25, W. Nanson to WP, 18 July 1828; 1/13/27, Mounseys to WP, 21 July 1828.

suddenly – so suddenly that he was unable to discharge many, if any, of his duties as high sheriff for 1828.

A VERDICT

Other than that his illness was 'complicated', we do not know what caused Thomas's death. Early in January 1828 he was reported to be suffering from a 'severe indisposition'. William Parker came north from Skirwith Abbey to join him, and to help him conduct his most pressing business, of which, as we have seen, there was a great deal. By mid-February, following treatment from a Dr Headlam, Thomas was thought to be 'getting well', but his improvement did not last. He deteriorated steadily thereafter; Samuel Stocks rushed north to see him at the end of March, and he died at Warwick Hall on 9 April[59].

As with his uncle before him, his will of 28 March 1828 – executed just over a week before his death – paid eloquent testimony to the extent of his wealth. He left legacies amounting to over £32,000, and earlier in a separate transaction had given £1,000 as the founding donation for the establishment of Carlisle Infirmary. Without requiring any money lent to others to be called in, the sums he bequeathed were to be free of legacy duty and had to be paid (like his uncle's) within a year of his death. The will was exceedingly generous to Thomas's wife, Mary, who was already in personal possession of part of the Warwick estate. Besides everything in the hall and other premises at Warwick (together with £3,000 for their continuing enhancement), she received £15,000 (plus £200 immediately) in addition to the life annuity of £1,000 which she already enjoyed. Thomas's cousin, Christopher Parker of Petteril Green, was left the handsome sum of £10,000. There were smaller bequests to other cousins, relatives and servants, including one to his favourite old retainer at Heaton Mersey, Thomas Lear; £1,500 to Warwick Sunday School; and £500 to each of the British & Foreign Bible Society, the Church Missionary Society, the Wesleyan Missionary Society, Manchester Infirmary, and Stockport Dispensary. While (except for Mary Parker's landed property) his brother, William, was to inherit all the estate at Warwick, Old Town, Manchester, Stockport and elsewhere, subject to Robert's life interest in some elements, Thomas made two things clear. But for Robert's incapacity he would have made substantial provision for him; as it was, he required Robert to be looked after faithfully for the rest of his life. Finally, should William, who was unmarried, fail to have lawful issue (which seemed likely),

---

59   *Carlisle Journal*, 12 April 1828; Pkr A, 3/17/28, SS to TP, 26 Jan. 1828; 3/17/20, T.H. Graham to TP, 15 Feb. 1828; G.G. Mounsey to TP, n.d. but Feb. 1828; 3/17/11, JM to WP, 15 Mar. 1828; 1/13/5, J.E. Headlam's Bill, 23 Apr. 1828. Dr. Thomas Emerson Headlam (1777-1864) received his medical education at Edinburgh University and then practised briefly in Durham; and later for many years in Newcastle, where he was among the town's most prominent personalities. 'In his day he was one of the most eminent of English provincial physicians'. – *The Lancet*, 5 March 1864, 286-287. I am grateful to Mr. Adrian Allen for this reference.

the property was to devolve on the male heirs in succession of Christopher Parker of Petteril Green[60].

Obituaries in local newspapers tended then (as now) to err, sometimes substantially, on the side of generosity to the deceased. However, in the light of the evidence here, that for Thomas Parker in the *Carlisle Journal* of 12 April 1828 delivered a singularly apt verdict. He was:

> a character deservedly esteemed…His judgement was remarkably sound and practical, rendering him strikingly qualified for the projection of advantageous plans and, combined as it was with unwearied perseverance, directing their execution to a prosperous issue. [Notable are] the improvements already introduced by him to the village and neighbourhood of Warwick, and particularly the provision he has there made for the religious instruction of the rising generation[61].

The author was undoubtedly referring to Thomas's few years of activity in the locality, but his judgement also rings true of all his subject's endeavours. In what were always testing and, at times, severely difficult circumstances, Thomas Parker had managed a diverse, complex and expanding portfolio with acute judgement, considerable flair and consummate skill. Virtually everything he touched turned to good account and the legacy of his success lasted for many years. Aged 43, he had not expected to die so soon. Nor had his great-great-grandfather, Christopher, who built Old Town House. Unlike so many other members of their family, both were cut off in their prime.

---

60   Pkr B, 28, Thomas Parker's Will, 28 Mar. 1828.
61   *Carlisle Journal*, 12 April 1828.

Chapter 6:

A Landed Proprietor, 1828-56: Manufacturing and Urban Development

A CHANGE OF REGIME

William Parker was a very different man. After returning to Cumberland in 1822, he had occasionally visited his brother at Warwick Hall, which was 20 miles from Skirwith Abbey over rudimentary roads and rough country. After Thomas's death, William was obliged to visit Warwick regularly and for extended periods; but he was always reluctant to be away from his own home for long, and ensured that his visits, not only to Warwick but also to Carlisle, and even Penrith, were as brief as practically possible. He had always been frail and became more so as the years passed. Nonetheless, like many delicate people who are often reported to be unwell and who, therefore, take great care of themselves, he survived for far longer than either he or anyone else would have predicted, dying at the age of 67 in 1856.

Indifferent health may have heightened other characteristics. Widely regarded as an unduly anxious man, he pored over bills, vouchers and accounts, cross-checking one against the other, picking up the tiniest arithmetical errors and making an issue of them. Probably unwittingly, in satisfying himself he sometimes created the impression of distrusting others. Thus, when Marchanton gave Stocks some timber left over from a city-centre building project, knowing he would put it to good use at Heaton Mersey, William queried this too[1]. Thomas Parker would not have given it a moment's thought. A fundamental difference in the attitude of the two brothers was soon brought to bear on family affairs. Whereas Thomas had put his wealth to work to create more wealth, William was self-confessedly averse 'to laying out money where I can avoid it'[2]. Presiding over business matters meticulously and laboriously, he found relaxation in art. According to family testimony, he was a more than competent water-colourist[3]; and he steadily purchased what became a fine collection of prints and paintings. His temperament and predilections, however, did not prevent him from imposing his own stamp on family affairs. Though utterly risk-averse, and in this respect so very different from Thomas Parker, his was a changed regime in

---

1   See e.g. Pkr A, 1/13/34 & 3/17/4, Jones, Lloyd & Co. to WP, 15 Apr. & 1 Aug. 1828; 1/13/71 & 1/14/43, J. Burton to WP, 28 Aug. 1828 & 4 Apr. 1829; 1/13/39, 79, 3/18/28, 68, JM to WP, 15 Aug. 1828, 4 Feb. 1829, 4 Nov. 1837 & 7 Mar. 1840.
2   Pkr A, 1/8/1, WP to Capt. Wanchope, 1 Jan. 1833.
3   Pkr B, 24, '[Ms] Outline of a Family', 15.

other ways too, with sharply altered priorities and more modest but distinct achievements.

Although William had been a silent partner in some of Thomas's commercial activities, he set his face firmly against further exporting. In April 1828 there was better news from Buenos Aires of a resolution of its differences with Brazil. Simultaneously, the bullion, so riskily sent overland from Mexico City to Vera Cruz by the Penny brothers and then shipped to England, arrived safely; the consignment of gold and silver dollars yielded £508[4]. Yet both developments left William cold. There was residual business, particularly the pursuit of meagre dividends from bankrupt clients, at least one of which went back to 1811 in Robert senior's day. Several other customers had failed more recently and soon after Thomas's death his client in Lisbon, William Studart, went bankrupt. However, while there were fleeting references to him, James Stubington Penny ceased to play a part in Parker business affairs; as did James Burt and other cloth suppliers[5]. The family's long-standing involvement in overseas trade came to an abrupt end. In this respect above all Thomas Parker's death marked the end of an era.

This had significant consequences for Samuel Stocks at Heaton Mersey. Thomas Parker had heeded his last-minute plea against a rent increase but, if Stocks anticipated that other arrangements would also proceed as before, he was sorely mistaken. Having produced a batch of quiltings which he hoped William would snap up for export, Stocks was obliged to sell them on the home market for a poor out-of-season price[6]. No longer even an informal partner, he became merely a lessee and had to fend for himself. He provided advice about warehouse lettings, but invariably through James Marchanton, rarely dealing directly with his landlord, and then only in emergencies. There was no resumption of the detailed reportage and candid correspondence so characteristic of his relations with Thomas Parker.

Beyond Cumbria William's pre-occupation was with the warehouses in Manchester. Much work remained to be done to round off Thomas's projects: and, in the face of difficulties in the cotton industry and fierce competition from other developers, some years passed before the return on investment there became both assured and substantial. In contrast to his predecessor William relied very heavily on two men in particular. The regularity of his correspondence was not complemented by prompt or sure decision-making, and James Marchanton's powers of persuasion towards what he, the Healds and others regarded as appropriate policies were sorely taxed; but Marchanton soldiered on long and faithfully, for an annual salary of £30, rising to £40 from

---

4   Pkr A, 3/17/1, Wilson, Hardisty & Co. to TP, 17 Apr. 1828; 3/17/2, Jones, Lloyd & Co. to WP, 24 April 1828.

5   Pkr A, 1/8/2, 2/5/ 60, 64-65, 3/18/66, JM to WP, 5 Apr. 31 May, 21 June & 11 Aug. 1830, 21 Oct. 1837; 1/8/24, WN to WP, 18 Jan. 1830.

6   Pkr A, 1/13/1, 11, SS to WP, 22 Apr. & 7 May 1828; 1/13/35, W. Grant & Bros. to WP, 7 May 1828; 1/13/48, JM to WP, 29 Aug. 1828.

the mid-1830s[7]. William's other close, professional confidant was William Nanson, a solicitor in the practice of Messrs. Hodgson of Carlisle who had been employed by Thomas following his move to Warwick Hall (Figure 18). Between 1818 and 1847, alongside his work for the practice, he was town clerk of Carlisle, and was eventually succeeded in both capacities by his son, John[8]. Nanson's services were invaluable, not only in terms of legal advice, but in a host of practical, everyday matters as he strove to ease the concerns of his anxious client.

Figure 18. Portrait of William Nanson, solicitor to the Parkers (1820s-1850s).

Although a joint executor with Christopher Parker and James and George Heald of Thomas's will, William took the lead. Probate was readily obtained

---

7   Pkr A, 3/18/54, JM to WP, 3 Feb. 1837. Marchanton's salary was sometimes in arrears (see 1/8/57, JM to WP, 2 Apr. 1829), suggesting that he had other employment/income.
8   The multifarious activities in and around Carlisle of William and John Nanson are evidenced in the records of Messrs. Hodgson, Solicitors and Clerks of the Peace at CAS (C), D/Hod.

and Nanson assured him that other matters would be straightforward since William was the 'sole residuary legatee'. The bulk, if not all, of Thomas's charitable legacies were paid by the end of May 1828, evoking grateful responses, not least from the Wesleyan Missionary Society who received their £500 in mid-April, and whose administrator confessed that the society was 'now borrowing large sums…to carry on'. As an executor William was generally untroubled by dubious claims for debts owed by the deceased, in contrast to the experience of his brothers and cousin following Robert senior's death in 1815. However, Mary Carter, a Piccadilly fishmonger, maintained that she was owed £3.16s. 7d. for deliveries of lobster and salmon between April and August 1822; her bill had not been delivered previously 'on account of my not knowing where to apply for it'. Marchanton thought it *very probable* that no such account is owing from yourself or [your] brother'[9].

William's characteristic determination to discharge his duties punctiliously led to one major new departure which significantly altered the context of operations. The Court of Chancery had jurisdiction over the affairs of individuals of unsound mind, or at least of those formally brought to its attention. Thomas Parker had never involved the Court in Robert Parker's affairs, assuming personal responsibility for safeguarding his interests. William judged this to be inadequate and possibly dangerous; perhaps encouraged and certainly guided by Nanson, he entered into formal proceedings with the Court. In return for safeguarding William's position vis-a-vis his handicapped brother, the Court had to be fully informed of the details, especially the financial details, of the provision made for Robert, and of the management of his assets. To this end, Robert's finances were accounted for separately from William's, though the latter was awarded an annual sum to cover Robert's maintenance. Heaton Mersey and Tithe Barn Hill, which Robert had been allocated under the settlement of 1822, remained his, as did a share of the profits of the partnership, T. & R. Parker & Co., still trading when Thomas died. Other than agreed maintenance, William had no access to these earnings, and it was no consolation to him that Thomas and Robert had agreed a 70%/30% split of the responsibility for the payment of Sarah Parker's annuity, leaving William to discharge the larger sum. At least it had become possible by this time for routine business to be conducted via an extraordinary master in Chancery in regional centres such as Carlisle and Penrith, so that Nanson was spared regular trips to London; but there were some. All major matters were presided over by the Lord Chancellor and his officials in the capital. This procedural decision insured William against any accusation that he derived personal benefit from his oversight of Robert. On the other hand it reduced the income at his disposal and, in doing so, increased his anxiety

---

9   Pkr A, 1/13/10, WN to WP, 30 Apr. 1828; 1/13/2, J. James to J. Heald, 22 Apr. 1828; 3/19/2, W. Dixon to WP, 19 May 1828; 1/8/41, JM to WP, 10 Oct. 1829. There was one abject begging letter from a Stockport man, claiming that he had worked for the Parkers for 30 years and that 'frequent donations' from Thomas Parker had hitherto saved him 'from the dreaded alternative of the workhouse'. There is no record of a response. – Pkr A, 1/13/23, J. Cook to WP, 18 May 1828.

about money matters, which was at its height in the years immediately after his succession to Thomas's estate. Like everyone else involved with the Court, he was severely frustrated by what he described as the 'proverbial slowness' of its proceedings[10].

Although Nanson approached Chancery shortly after Thomas's death, it took a year for William to be formally recognised as responsible for 'the person and estate of your brother'. One of the masters in Chancery then investigated the nature of Robert's mental incapacity in order, among other things, to determine the level of maintenance to be awarded. An affidavit of Robert's property also had to be submitted, together with attested details of the operations of T. & R. Parker & Co.; and of the legal basis and subsequent discharge of Sarah Parker's annuity. The Court required further information, including inventories, of Robert's personal possessions. And £5,000 had to be lodged with the Bank of England as security for his real and personal estate[11]. Years earlier Robert's furniture, books and plate had been removed from Tithe Barn Hill and stored at Heaton Mersey. William had them listed and valued, and planned to sell them In June 1830, however, Chancery ruled against their sale on the grounds that Robert 'might be restored to health and would probably regret the loss of such articles' – only, subsequently, to relent in regard to the furniture. Everything was transported by canal to Kendal and then overland to Skirwith Abbey, and the furniture was sold at auction in Carlisle in June 1831[12]. Meanwhile, the responsible master in Chancery had taken exception to the manner in which various accounts had been set out and insisted on 're-modelling' them. Subsequent versions were finally approved in July 1831[13]. Inevitably, the earliest dealings with Chancery were long drawn-out and tedious, but later business was somewhat less irksome. Nevertheless, many of the endeavours of William's regime were subject to Chancery's firm legal constraints. In addition, his personal approach to these and other matters was characterised by caution. In sharp contrast to what had gone before, there was a lack of flair.

HEATON MERSEY: REFURBISHMENT AND RATIONALISATION

Chancery proceedings were singularly ill-suited to managing a complex manufacturing concern such as Heaton Mersey, where crisp decision-making was required if production were not to be disrupted and profits lost. Here,

---

10   Pkr A, 1/13/36, 2/5/8, WN to WP, 8 Aug. 1828, 21 July 1831. For an example of the use of an extraordinary master in Chancery, in Penrith, see Pkr A, 2/5/32, WN to WP, 3 Nov. 1830. William's views about the tardiness of the Court's proceedings were expressed to a fellow sceptic, Samuel Stocks. – Pkr A, 3/9/6, 18 Feb. 1842. Their judgement was widely shared, the classic, near-contemporary, fictional account being in *Bleak House* by Charles Dickens, first published in 1853.

11   Pkr A, 1/13/36, WN to WP, 8 Aug. 1828; 1/8/18, 43, 73-75, Same to Same, 31 Mar. 20 & 22 Apr. 19 Sept. 1829 & 20 Feb. 1830.

12   Pkr A, 1/3/24, JM to WP, 29 Oct. 1829; 1/8/23 & 2/5/11, 20, 64, 66-68, WN to WP, 9 & 24 June, 13 & 26 July 1830, 4 June & 5 July 1831.

13   Pkr A, 2/5/11, 13, 18 & 35, WN to WP, 17 Dec. 1830 & 15 Mar. 11 May, 5 July 1831.

there was also a delicate issue of man-management: of all people, Samuel Stocks was unlikely to remain phlegmatic in the face of protracted delays. He was largely left to his own devices, but this was not always possible; and from the outset he was reminded not only of William's limited room for manoeuvre, but of his own too. In May 1829, in the face of an urgent need to install a new engine for the waterwheel, Nanson baldly summarised the position to William. 'Mr. Stocks has to satisfy not *you* but the *Officers of the Court of Chancery* as to the propriety of *every*thing he requires'; and his forthright advice was that Stocks should involve his own solicitor[14]. While the petition to Chancery to embark on this work was successful, it was perhaps Stocks's frustration at having to endure such proceedings which persuaded William to renew the lease of Heaton Mersey for an unimproved rent in February 1830. Yet despite this, and given Stocks's aversion to lawyers, his patience could not be relied upon[15]. When another problem – this time with the weir – arose in the following year, a tricky scenario ensued. A petition to Chancery was submitted on 16 July 1831 but within a week, long before any response could be expected, Stocks had completed the remedial work, so that permission had to be obtained retrospectively. Nanson regarded this as extremely dangerous, whereas to Stocks it was mere commonsense. While permission was granted, the solicitor's wrath appears to have had a lasting effect. Routinely, there were many subsequent engagements with Chancery, and some unanticipated ones – in 1837, for example, when a boiler burst – but ruefully Stocks endured them without further risk or mishap[16].

One fresh development at Heaton under William was the purchase of additional property near the works in 1832. Although this had some premises on it, most of it was farmland, and freehold at that. It was likely to have been regarded as a sound investment because of the increasing demand for housebuilding sites on the outskirts of Stockport and Manchester. With Stocks as a key intermediary, William acquired the property from a Mr. Goulden and a Mr. Egerton. Egerton at least stayed on in the area and William was able to purchase further property there from him in 1851 and 1853. These later acquisitions were not freehold but held under leases for lives renewable forever, an arrangement often used as a basis for building development and suggesting that the holdings had already been subject to it[17].

In 1833 Stocks's eldest son, another Samuel, attained his majority (and was henceforward known as Samuel junior), and a few years later he was taken into partnership by his father. While this was a natural progression for a family steeped in manufacturing, it was also welcome to Stocks senior in

---

14   Pkr A, 1/8/71, WN to WP, 9 May 1829.
15   Pkr A, 1/8/7, WN to WP, 9 Feb. 1830. See above,
16   Pkr A, 2/5/7-10, WN to WP, 8, 16, 21 & 22 July 1831; Pkr B, 20.
17   Pkr B, 31, Will of W. Parker, esp. Codicil of 18 June 1842. In 1838, following the first purchase, the property at Heaton Mersey ran to just short of 100 acres. – Stockport Local Heritage Library, Higham Notes, Map & Survey of Heaton Mersey.

the light of Chancery's regular calls for authorised accounts and other papers. Before long it was Samuel junior who dealt with routine business at the works, and not long after that before he was in correspondence with William. He was often joined at work by his cousin, Benjamin, son of Bernard Stocks, though whether Benjamin was formally engaged in the partnership is doubtful[18]. A series of wholly unexpected developments disturbed the equilibrium of the partnership between father and son, and of William Parker too.

In January 1839 an extremely violent gale wreaked havoc across the British Isles, not least in the north of England. Happily, Marchanton was able to report that 'very little damage [was] done' to the properties in Manchester. Heaton Mersey was less fortunate. In one of his rare direct communications with William Parker, Stocks senior reported that:

> The storm has done very little harm at the Works. The chimney is standing and as firm as ever. Slates in abundance were blown off the roofs and glass broken, but all the cost will not be large. The [Sunday] School did not fare so well. A stack of chimneys fell and went through the roof but was stopped at the first floor. Trees blown up in all directions[19].

The damage was soon repaired. Shortly afterwards, however, the school was at the centre of a sectarian dispute which rumbled on for years, and which, in view of the pride which they took in the facility, caused acute distress to William Parker and the Healds, and to the Stocks family as well.

Under his will of 1815 Robert senior had endowed the school with £500; once invested, the proceeds were to be devoted by the churchwardens of Didsbury to defray the cost of any repairs and to purchase clothing and footwear for the pupils; and, as we have seen, the 'bounty' (as it was described) was used to good effect. Difficulties arose only following the appointment of a new, High Church incumbent to the parish of Didsbury, the Rev. W.J. Kidd. A zealous and active pastor, he conducted a parish survey which confirmed his suspicion that nonconformist denominations, especially the methodists (who, led locally and strongly supported financially by James Heald, had recently opened a new training establishment in Didsbury) had won over many of the local populace. His response was to use every means in his power to win them back, including an insistence that his churchwardens take greater control of the distribution of the Parker endowment. William and the Stocks were Low Church anglicans (as was William Nanson), ecumenical for their day, and correspondingly relaxed about nonconformity. Thomas Parker's widow, Mary, was a strong supporter of Methodism and, at some point during these years, allowed Warwick Sunday School to be used as a

---

18   Pkr A, 3/18/ 53-54, 57, 59, JM to WP, 21 Jan. 3 Feb. 27 Apr. & 8 June 1837.
19   Pkr A, 3/18/44, JM & SS to WP, 19 Jan. 1839. Reckoned to have been of tornado force in many areas, the storm caused massive damage in Britain and Ireland. See L. Shields & D. Fitzgerald, 'The "Night of the Big Wind" in Ireland, 6-7 January 1839', *Irish Geography*, xxii, Issue 1 (1989), 31-43. I am grateful to Trevor Parkhill for this reference.

methodist chapel. While wishing to avoid controversy, all were firmly opposed to any interference with the established arrangements for the management of the endowment, particularly the tradition that the teachers at the school chose the recipients and personally handed over the bounty. For years they had allowed methodists the use of a room for preaching. It was this and similarly ecumenical elements in the school's curriculum which underlay Kidd's opposition; he also made great play with the fact that Stocks senior, who had regular contact with the school, had once been a methodist. Above all, the wealthy James Heald, so close to Parker and Stocks, was the leader of the local methodist community[20].

During the winter of 1840-41 there was a vigorous exchange of correspondence between the parties, which Kidd threatened to publish in the newspapers. This provoked an anguished letter from William, who stressed his

> dislike of obtruding on the public any little matters in which I am concerned, and which I have always hitherto had the happiness to escape. I may say also that it would be more especially objectionable to me as it regards the feelings of my brother Robert who, though from his state of mental affliction is not alive to every passing event, would be very much so on any controversy in which he would be so closely connected coming under his notice in the newspapers...which constitute his almost only reading[21].

No publication ensued, though the threat lingered in the background. Before long most people in the locality were aware of the dispute.

It had long been customary for the schoolchildren to attend Didsbury church on the first Sunday of each month. This was discontinued, which did nothing to cool tempers. Though personable in various face-to-face meetings, Kidd was a doughty opponent – intellectually agile and articulate – and was able to convince many waverers that he had the best interests of the local community at heart. In December 1841, for example, in the face of widespread distress following a severe downturn in the trade cycle, he established and widely promulgated a Heaton Mersey relief fund to alleviate local poverty. William did not subscribe, having already sent £20 for distribution among the workers at Heaton Mersey[22]. The legal position of the Parkers appeared to be very strong: the churchwardens 'had no power but to receive and appropriate the money as directed'[23], and henceforward they were required to account for their handling of one tranche of money before receiving another. However, in a major act of retaliation, Kidd instituted legal proceedings 'to stop the

---

20   Pkr A, 1/14/1, SS jnr to WN, 30 Mar. 1842; 3/16/1, Printed Circular 'to the Inhabitants of the Parochial Chapelry of Didsbury' from Rev. W.J. Kidd, March 1841; Hyde & Pevsner, *Cumbria*, 662; Million, *Didsbury*, 111, 123.
21   Pkr A, 1/14/5, WP to Kidd, 1 Feb. 1841.
22   Pkr A, 2/14/206, SS jnr. To WP, 20 Nov. 1841.
23   Pkr A, 1/14/6, Relief Fund, 2 Dec. 1841; 1/14/2, J. Heald to WP, 17 Dec. 1841.

payment of the interest accruing from the legacy', pending a root-and-branch re-consideration of the entire arrangement; and he was successful.   Even when he moved to another post, there was no end to the matter.   The teachers eventually secured the intervention of Stockport Sunday School, to which that at Heaton Mersey was affiliated, but this also failed to produce a solution. Ultimately, in 1857, a year after William's death, the matter came before the County Court of Lancashire, which replaced the churchwardens with a new board of trustees, four in number, of whom James Heald was one; and who were free to distribute the money as originally intended[24].   Until 1840 the Sunday School at Heaton Mersey was an achievement which was totally unalloyed.   If in a prolonged and roundabout way the Parkers won their case, it was by then a soured victory, a rare and largely negative return for their philanthropic endeavours; and a cruel one too, for there was little from which they derived more satisfaction than Heaton Mersey Sunday School.

During the earliest stages of these distressing developments the economy once again plunged into recession.   This time the downturn was prolonged and widespread – in December 1840, for example, all dealings were halted at a bank in Penrith[25].   The cotton industry was particularly badly affected by the changed economic circumstances.   In March 1842, Samuel junior told Nanson that 'at present a very poor prospect presents itself for the cotton trade – the market yesterday, according to the Guardian Newspaper, being at lower rates than were ever before known'[26].   Precisely what happened at Heaton Mersey from this point onwards is difficult to establish with certainty, for the previously near-continuous record becomes patchy and then steadily diminishes.   What is clear is that, in the midst of generally very difficult economic conditions, serious incidents occurred which called for crisis management; and that the nature of the business changed from manufacturing across the spectrum to specialisation in bleaching and dyeing.

In July 1840 the works had suffered a 'dreadful calamity' – a very serious fire which, at an initially estimated cost of £16,000, totally destroyed the seven-storey building where spinning operations were conducted.   Both the Parkers and the Stocks always insured their properties appropriately and updated their policies as required, so the financial impact as far as fixed capital was concerned was probably limited.   On the other hand, together with the loss of finished goods, the subsequent disruption of production schedules forced Samuel senior into bankruptcy with his side of the business although, in collaboration with a Mr. M.L. Tait, he continued to operate successfully in marketing from his Manchester warehouse, sending valuable orders to the reduced capacity at Heaton Mersey.   Samuel junior continued there with an undertenant, Mr. Jackson.   The incident obliged him to engage in further

24   CAS (C), DX/1089/41/10-11, 14, WN to WP, 13 & 18 Nov. 1843, 3 Dec. 1844; Heginbotham, *Stockport: Ancient and Modern*, ii, 294.
25   Pkr A, 3/18/18, JM to WP, 5 Dec. 1840.
26   Pkr A, 1/14/1, SS jnr to WN, 30 Mar. 1842.

complex business in Chancery, with delay on this occasion stemming from the need to disentangle the details of the previously joint operations of father and son. Then, in February 1842, there was a second fire, this time in the calendaring and finishing department which, while not damaging machinery, destroyed goods to the value of £3,000[27]. One consequence of the second catastrophe was that Samuel junior decided to emigrate to Australia. Arriving in Adelaide in December 1842, he went on to make a name for himself, and a considerable fortune, in the South Australian copper-mining industry[28].

Convinced of the potential of the works, reluctant to see much of his life's work dissipated, and never relinquishing hope of a possible return, Stocks senior endeavoured to secure a viable future for Heaton Mersey. He resumed regular correspondence with William Parker and strongly recommended that he attempt a sale to the Cookes, a very wealthy business family. William tried to strike a deal with them, only for the Cookes to opt out[29]. By mid-1842, having taken over his son's interest, Stocks himself was back in business at Heaton with Jackson. After a few months, however, both had judged that spinning and weaving were now out of the question. Stocks also concluded that bleaching and dyeing alone would not support two people. He decided to withdraw and set off to visit his son in Australia[30]. Jackson was keen to carry on alone but needed William Parker to finance his takeover from Stocks. Travelling to Skirwith Abbey in an attempt to negotiate this, he found that William (in what appears to have been a diplomatic manouevre) was too ill to see him, and he returned to Manchester a disappointed man[31]. Two years later, having returned from Australia, Stocks senior was somehow once again back in business at Heaton Mersey, this time with M.L. Tait, his erstwhile partner at the Manchester warehouse. For some months in late 1844 their relationship did not run smoothly. Stocks successfully pressed hard for investment in new buildings and machinery without first seeking his landlord's permission: but Nanson reported that 'what is done has been generally well done'. William and Nanson found a third-party intermediary who successfully arbitrated differences and got things back on track. In December Nanson visited Heaton Mersey and found that the bleaching and dyeing business was 'fully employed' and operating very satisfactorily. He reported what many others knew already from long experience: 'dealing in very plain and decided terms with Mr. Stocks is the best way of managing him and [what was perhaps surprising] he submits more easily than might be expected'[32]. While the detailed record ends there, over £1,000 worth of

---

27   *Stockport Chronicle*, 31 July 1840 & 4 Feb. 1842; *Stockport Advertiser*, 31 July 1840; Pkr A, 3/18/20, JM to WP, 22 Aug. 1840; CAS (C), DX/1089/41/ 3-6, WN to WP, 27 Dec. 1841, 14 & 27 Jan. & 9 Feb. 1842.

28   Pkr A, 3/9/9, SS to WP, 10 Feb. 1842; Wikipedia, 'Samuel Stocks (c.1786 – 1863)'.

29   Pkr A, 3/9/6, SS to WP, 18 Feb. 1842; 1/14/1, SS jnr to WN, 30 Mar. 1842

30   CAS (C), DX/1089/41/7, J. Jackson to WN, 13 June 1842.

31   Pkr A, 3/9/7, J. Jackson to WP, 21-22 June 1842; 3/9/8, SS to WP, 22 June 1842.

32   CAS (C), DX/1089/41/14, WN to WP, 3 Dec. 1844.

new buildings were erected in 1845-46 and Stocks was still in partnership with Tait in 1847. The widespread commercial crisis and financial panic of that year finally brought him down[33]. He failed to win election as M.P. for Stockport and with his wife, Barbara, he emigrated permanently to Australia, arriving in Adelaide in May 1848.

There was a sad, painful but nonetheless honourable sequel to the long tenure and service of Samuel Stocks at Heaton Mersey. Samuel junior had prospered through mining copper at Barra, north of Adelaide. The South Australian Mining Corporation with which he was involved had made a successful bid for the Wheal Grey part of the proposed mining area, which, unlike other parts, had turned out to be immensely rich in copper. Samuel junior got on to the board of the corporation. He subsequently became its chairman, and then site manager of Section 1283, which he promptly christened 'Stockport', and made a fortune. Later, however, he took to drink, squandered his fortune and died, aged 37, in 1850. His obituary in the *South Australian Register*, while lauding his earlier achievements, was candid about his later dissolution. Following a petition calling for the editor's dismissal, a counter-petition won much heavier support including, notably and sensationally, that of Stocks senior, whose letter of support for the editor was published. The younger son, Thomas Parker Stocks, died of consumption in 1853. After Barbara's death Stocks married again in 1858. He was a member of the Anglican Diocesan Synod, was appointed to the South Australian Destitute Board and, almost predictably, was secretary of Christchurch Sunday School in Adelaide. To the end, as the newspaper episode demonstrated, Samuel Stocks was his own man. He died in Adelaide in 1863[34].

Meanwhile, Nanson had been deeply impressed by Stocks's partner, M.L. Tait. He was 'invaluable', 'most desirable for the works', and 'fully' understanding his 'liabilities as tenant'. When economic recovery came beyond 1847 it proceeded apace, and Tait continued as sole lessee for many years. In 1862, six years after William's death, he was paying £2,400 a year in rent for Heaton Mersey, only marginally more than Stocks had paid decades earlier[35], although by then the scope of its operations was much reduced. Thus, for most of the period from the early 1820s to the mid-1850s William's net income from Heaton Mersey yielded slightly more than the cost of Sarah Parker's life annuity of £1,000; and it is doubtful if it did as much as that during the troubled 1840s. In financial as well as in many other ways Robert junior's incapacity was costly indeed.

Unlike Thomas, William enjoyed a somewhat formal but nonetheless cordial relationship with Sarah Parker. He had yet to attain his majority at the

---

33   CAS (C), DX/1089/41/19, WN to WP, 11 Feb. 1846; Ward-Perkins, 'The Commercial Crisis of 1847', 263-276.

34   Wikipedia, 'Samuel Stocks (c.1786 –1863)'.

35   CAS (C), DX/1089/41/14, WN to WP, 3 Dec. 1844; Pkr A, 4/1/4, WP to M.L. Tait, Lease of Heaton Mersey for 21 years, 1862.

time of her marriage to his uncle in 1808 and may have been more indulged by her than was then possible with his older brothers, leaving him to feel more warmly than they towards her. They corresponded intermittently, regularly exchanged good wishes through intermediaries such as Marchanton, and there were occasional gifts for Sarah of game from Skirwith. More significantly, in 1837 they jointly and successfully promoted an application for Margaret Dodgson, a girl from Appleby (not far from Skirwith), to gain admission to the Manchester Deaf and Dumb School; and by his will, 'as a remembrance', William left Sarah £50 worth of mourning jewellery. Knowing how sensitive his employer was to financial considerations, Marchanton often forwarded detailed and tantalising reports of Sarah's health, which on several occasions, sometimes for months, was poor[36]. She too, however, lived until 1856, having received £1,000 a year from the estate for over 40 years. By then the works at Heaton Mersey housed a business very different from that left by Robert senior in 1815. Nevertheless, it constituted a valuable element of what William left to his successors.

The Property Portfolio in Manchester

Following the end of exporting activity which left Stocks largely to shift for himself at Heaton Mersey, William Parker's major concern beyond Skirwith Abbey and Warwick Hall was the management of his substantial portfolio of town-centre property in Manchester. For several years matters there did not go well. The cotton industry experienced almost a decade of poor years from the mid-1820s[37] which, together with stiff competition from other developers, made it extremely difficult to attract fresh tenants and to deal successfully with existing ones. Some of Thomas Parker's development projects – in Dale St. and Spear St. for example – had still to be completed and, while externally the complex at Albion Buildings was finished, much internal work remained. William had little or no experience of this area of business. More seriously, his initial approach to managing this aspect of his affairs differed substantially from that advocated by his advisers.

Work still outstanding on the various premises was finally completed only in May 1830, some two years or so after Thomas Parker's death. The final stages were protracted partly because of previously unforeseen difficulties – with drains, sewers and the requirements of highway surveyors, for example; partly because, to secure tenants, their particular wishes regarding room layout and fitments had to be negotiated; but also because William dithered, anxious above all to control costs. There were several additional factors. By

---

36   Pkr A, 1/13/75-76, JM to WP, 19 Dec. 1828 & 23 Jan. 1829; 2/5/62, Same to Same, 30 July 1830; 2/18/38, 43, 53, 59-61, 67, 72 & 76, Same to Same, 21 Jan, 8, 17 & 26 June, 23 July 1837, 9 Mar. & 11 Aug. 1838, 1 Feb. & 20 July 1839.

37   Pkr A, 1/8/12, 61-62, 66 & 1/13/11, 15, 20, 59, 72, JM to WP, 6 & 19 May, 27 June & 20 Nov. 1828, 30 Jan. 19 Mar. 7 & 22 May 1829, 29 Jan. 1830.

the close of the 1820s everyone was striving to survive further bad times in Manchester and, with many new warehouses becoming available in the town centre, would-be tenants bargained tenaciously, while some existing ones claimed to have obtained Thomas's agreement to certain changes which, by then, were difficult to verify.   Throughout 1829 Marchanton was often obliged to report a complete absence of enquiries about possible lettings; and some of the few that arrived were dismissed because Stocks's knowledge of the personalities involved in the cotton trade led him to urge their rejection. This in turn produced complaints from estate agents about the influence he exerted.   Moreover, many of those with whom it was decided to deal were interested in letting only cellars, though the policy was to let whole warehouses if possible.   Restricting their accommodation to bare essentials, merchants wanted space to hold their goods but awaited better times before bidding for larger premises.   There was also a frequently unresolved tension between their requests for longer-term leases, and William's wish for shorter ones as a means of creating more frequent opportunities for rent increases[38].

Though routinely in correspondence with Marchanton, William was largely out of touch with the reality of the Manchester property market, having rarely visited the town during the previous six years. At the outset, he adopted a slide-rule approach to setting the rents of the new premises at Albion Buildings and in Dale St. and Tib St. He got Marchanton to measure the precise square yardage of all parts of the properties, and then to divide this into their calculated total cost, to arrive at what William regarded as economic rents for each warehouse. Thus, it was reckoned that the cost of Albion Buildings, when completed, would amount to £12,000: this was divided by the ten separate units according to their size; and 10% of the resulting sums (more than twice the standard rate of interest) was demanded as rent[39].   Thereby, William priced himself out of the prevailing market; and, as some existing tenants elsewhere moved out, a growing number of warehouses became vacant. He was cutting off his nose to spite his face but, partly because his advisers dealt with him tentatively, it took some time to persuade him of this.

Marchanton first sounded the alarm about this rigid approach in September 1828, though he was soon joined by others. 'Such warehouses as yours will let, but their value may be underrated at first. And I think if they were set at low rents at first they might afterwards, if found of more value, rise to it'. A month later John Burton joined the debate. Owning premises surplus to his own requirements, though in a less central location, he found 'no difficulty in readily letting' them, but felt that 'the pile of warehouses built and building' in the centre of Manchester 'will reduce the value of neighbouring warehouses'.

---

38   Pkr A, 1/8/16, 48, 60-61 & 1/13/1, 6, 22, 29, 38, 40, 53, 62, 73 & 81, JM to WP, 22 & 25 Apr. 14 & 18 July, 13 & 22 Aug. 31 Oct. & 26 Dec. 1828, 9 Jan. 25 Feb. 7 May, 5 June & 22 Aug. 1829, 17 Feb. 1830.

39   Pkr A, 1/8/65, JM to WP, 27 Mar. 1829; 1/13/ 30 & 78, Same to Same, 25 July 1828 & 13 Feb. 1829.

He had 'seen Jas. Marchanton several times about the warehouses and, as they are now certainly too numerous, so many having been lately built, I advise very moderate rents'. The Healds agreed with these judgements[40]. By mid-1829 the situation had deteriorated markedly. For months there had been very few enquiries about Parker premises and when one applicant was told the terms on offer 'his answer was [that] he had met with more room for a third of the money'. When one low offer was received for a cellar in Pall Mall, Marchanton thought it 'better to take that or even less than have the premises unoccupied [for] half a year or a year'. William, on the other hand, believed 'that the present unfavourable state of things may perhaps stop in some degree the speculation in warehouse building'. Marchanton politely disabused him: fresh development was continuing apace and 'we may still expect [that] the supply will for some time continue to be greater than the demand'. Later, according to Marchanton, while Burton 'thought it not well to let off a part, [he] finally said it might perhaps be best to do so as it would the sooner bring business into the neighbourhood'. When one offer was received in September 1829 'it was too little to pay you proper interest for the cost of the premises, but the question is now that better is not likely to be got'[41]. At that point, just as there were some signs of economic recovery, William began to relent. Gradually, all but the lowest offers, even for parts of warehouses, were grudgingly accepted – generally on three-year leases, instead of the one year hoped for by William or the seven years looked for by most tenants[42]. It was against the background of this reluctant switch of policy by William that Thomas Parker's spate of development was finally completed during the early summer of 1830.

Marchanton's accounts from February 1828 to January 1834[43] cast further light on William's approach to this aspect of business. Under Thomas Parker the flow of income for investment was towards Manchester; money raised elsewhere had been relentlessly devoted to developments there. Under William this pattern was sharply reversed. He insisted that Marchanton minimise expenditure and retain very limited working reserves. During 1828, when urban development in central Manchester remained hectic, Marchanton remitted a mere £141.10s.0d., much to William's dismay. Thereafter, despite the difficulties alluded to above, remittances northwards assumed a strong upward trend – £1,104 in 1829, and £1,865, £2,010, £2,304 and £2,754 respectively in the following four years. Thus, William quickly became a mere rentier, and did so ever more successfully once he had begun to heed sound advice. He had few liquidity problems: in February 1830 his account at Forster's Bank in Carlisle was in substantial credit; and down to April in that year Burton repaid over £6,000 of a previously even

---

40   Pkr A, 1/13/47 & 59, JM to WP, 19 Sept. & 20 Nov. 1828; 1/13/60, J. Burton to WP, 29 Nov. 1828.
41   Pkr A, 1/8/ 46, 48, 53, 55 & 60, JM to WP, 5 June, 13 & 21 July, 22 Aug. & 5 Sept. 1829.
42   Pkr A, 1/8/44 & 2/5/ 6, 56, JM to WP, 9 Sept. 1829, 21 May 1830 & 29 July 1831.
43   Pkr A, 1/12/1-2, 5-9, 11-26, JM to WP, Feb. 1828 – Jan. 1834.

larger debt to Thomas, though prior to the latter's death he had been under no pressure to do so[44]. Nonetheless, during these early years, particularly of engagement with Chancery, William was acutely anxious about cash flow.

As trade recovered and remittances increased, William became somewhat less fretful. Always keeping his employer fully informed, Marchanton was gradually left to act on his own initiative and increasingly did so. Externally, the properties were re-painted once every four or five years and internal arrangements came to be dealt with more systematically. Most tenants met the initial costs of interior refurbishment and then negotiated adjustments to their rents, which were steadily raised as three-year leases came up for renewal. At one point in 1840, having briefly summarised his dealings with one tenant, Marchanton told his employer that 'it does not appear necessary to trouble you further', a remark which would have been regarded by both parties as inadmissible only a few years earlier, but which by then went unchallenged. From this point onwards Marchanton's letters often apologised for bothering him 'with uninteresting details' beyond what might have been regarded as strictly necessary[45]. As he relaxed, however, William became more determinedly reclusive, which was how in his later years he was generally regarded. By the late 1830s he began to receive offers to purchase individual properties, but was firmly disinclined to sell other than 'on very good terms'[46]. He retained his holdings, keenly aware of how valuable they had and were likely to become.

Another welcome development concerned the fine house and gardens at Tithe Barn Hill in Heaton Norris, developed by Robert senior, relinquished by his widow after his death, and occupied by Robert junior until he fell ill. For several years the property had been let to a businessman, Thomas Salter, who lost heavily in overseas trading ventures, was persistently in arrears with his rent, and distinctly nervous as to his tenurial prospects when William took over. In 1837, after almost a decade of further arrears, the property was let much more successfully to a Mr. Dyer, a solid citizen who owned a cotton mill in Stone Street, Manchester. He had built a fine house nearby, wanted to enhance it by buying Tithe Barn Hill and adding its gardens to his own, but could not do so under the arrangements with Chancery. He took a lease of the property instead, further improved it (though not without queries from William), and enjoyed both premises for many years. His own house later became the palace of the bishops of Manchester[47].

As we have seen in connection with Heaton Mersey, the economy, and particularly the cotton industry, encountered severe difficulties during the

---

44   Pkr A, 1/8/22, T. Forster & Co. to WP, 20 Feb. 1830; 1/8/3, J. Burton to WP, 5 Apr. 1830.
45   Pkr A, 3/18/23 & 24, JM to WP, 16 & 24 Apr. 1840.
46   Pkr A, 3/9/4, JM to WP, 12 Aug. and reply of 17 Aug. 1842. For earlier offers, see 3/18/33, 35 & 68, JM to WP, 4 Nov. 1837, 26 Oct. & 21 Dec. 1839.
47   Pkr A, 1/13/7, T. Salter to WP, 28 Apr. 1828; 2/5/5 , 41, JM to WP, 3 Dec. 1830 & 7 Sept. 1831; 3/18/ 56, 58 & 61, Same to Same, 7 Apr. 13 May & 26 June 1837; 4/1/2, Statement, n.d. but c.1860.

1840s. The effect on Parker properties, however, was less serious than in earlier years. In attempting to have their rents reduced, their premises let for longer terms or to gain some other advantage, some tenants threatened to quit, but few of them did so. By this stage many Parker holdings were regarded as almost ideally located and among the finest in the town, and tenants contrived to hold on to them if possible. There was one problem. In addition to William's periodic bouts of ill-health, James Marchanton fell seriously ill during the autumn of 1840, and again in February 1842. He recovered but was never again quite his old self. A few years later he began working on a part-time basis, and was frequently consulted by his successor, who Marchanton dealt with 'like a father'. He was again 'very unwell' during the winter of 1850-51 but in March 1851 (the last we hear of him) was 'a great deal better'[48]. He had assiduously guided the family's endeavours in the centre of Manchester for over a quarter of a century.

From the mid-1840s this key role was discharged by Henry Bridge, who lived in Didsbury, not far from Parr's Wood and Heaton Mersey. He had previously worked for the Healds, and had dealings with William which were carefully guided by them. Bridge undoubtedly brought fresh energy to bear on warehouse management and during the later 1840s oversaw the first wholesale repair and refurbishment programme since the properties had been built. The programme was costly but, according to Bridge, 'we have improved all of them beyond the outlay'[49]. This time there were few grumbles from William, even though around the turn of the new decade, perhaps on account of further rent increases, an uncomfortably large number of premises were vacant. Recovery from this position was swift. No less than £1,300 a year came in from only seven lettings in Mosley St. and York St. in 1850 and by September only one warehouse was untenanted. In the following March the entire portfolio had merely one rent arrear, of £15 from a single tenant. Candidly confident, Bridge hoped 'by and by to have nothing to do but receive the rents and put the money in the bank'[50]. By 1851 precisely what William had always hoped for was finally achieved. Largely as a result of Thomas Parker's foresight, income from properties in Manchester town centre was substantial, and was to constitute the single most valuable element in William's own legacy.

---

48   Pkr A, 3/18/8 & 3/9/15, JM to WP, 5 Dec. 1840 & 1 Mar. 1849; 3/9/6, SS senr to WP, 18 Feb. 1842; 3/9/1 & 17, H. Bridge to WP, 4 May 1849 & 24 Mar. 1851.
49   Pkr A, 3/9/1 & 17, H. Bridge to WP, 4 May 1849 & 24 Aug. 1850.
50   Pkr A, 3/9/1, 12, 14, 16-17, 20-21, H. Bridge to WP, 4 May & 17 Nov. 1849, 28 Feb. 22 May, 24 Aug. 6 Sept. & 26 Nov. 1850

Chapter 7:

A Landed Proprietor, 1828-56:
Estate Development and Dispositions

The Properties in Cumberland

According to long-established family custom, Thomas Parker had been buried near Old Town, in the graveyard at St. Mary's Church in High Hesket. To consolidate this tradition, as well as to acknowledge his brother's considerable achievements, William decided to erect a mausoleum over the new grave. He had seen vaults in Didsbury churchyard which he admired and sketches of these, and of two others there which 'Burton thought worth notice', were supplied by Marchanton. The mausoleum was completed just before Christmas 1828; and it was there that many other deceased Parkers, including William himself, were buried in later years (Figure 19)[1].

Apart from his duties as lead executor and those associated with the Court of Chancery, William devoted much attention immediately after Thomas's death to the situation of his widow, Mary. Possessing her own property at Warwick and with the use of the Hall for life, she determined to stay where she was, and did so until just before her own death in 1857, though she frequently visited her own family at Parr's Wood, and her mother, brothers and sisters were regular guests at Warwick Hall. Although the Hall had been completed a few months before her husband's death, it was not fully furnished and there was still much work to be done in the grounds. As we have seen, Thomas left £3,000 in his will to further embellish the interior; outside a barn was built to hold fodder for the horses. Shortly after his brother's death William advertised for tenders to make 'a cutting through Warwick Hill', a major undertaking, to improve the new road's route past the estate. Iron railings were erected around the demesne and further batches of trees were planted. In January 1829, ahead of that year's growing season, a gardener from Heaton Mersey came north for three years with the aim of raising the gardens at Warwick Hall 'to their proper splendour'. Later that year, as the new turnpike road was progressing beyond the demesne, a new carriageway was constructed between the main entrance and the hall. The

---

1   Pkr A, 1/13/51, 53-54, JM to WP, 2 & 31 Oct. & 5 Nov. 1828; Hyde & Pevsner, *Cumbria*, 409. A monochrome, sepia sketch of the mausoleum (see Fig. 19) was completed in 1842 by Sam Bough, then only 20 years old, and is among the earliest known works of this celebrated artist – Carlisle Library, Local Studies Collection, BOU/2/4. I am grateful to Denis Perriam for this reference and to Stephen White for making it available.

Carlisle/Brampton turnpike came into full use in 1830[2].

Figure 19. The Parker mausoleum in High Hesket churchyard by Sam Bough.

Compared with his brothers and his cousin, Christopher Parker of Petteril Green, William seems to have been less enamoured of business and commercial life; unlike them, for instance, Robert senior had not appointed him as an executor of his will. Nor did William later behave like a typical member of the Cumberland gentry, as they did. He was not an active justice of the peace. In 1830, as with Thomas before him, Christopher Parker was appointed high sheriff of the county: but there was never any question of William following them, and he was grateful when Nanson advised him that his presence at this or that meeting of the justices was unnecessary. When Nanson thought it advisable for William to put in an appearance, he tended to soften the blow by offering him dinner and a bed for the night[3]. His attendance was minimal – designed to show his face and keep loosely in touch with local affairs, but no more. On the other hand, he appears to have taken more relish in matters at Warwick Hall and Skirwith Abbey than he did in those further south, exhibiting some of the enthusiasm for estate and agrarian matters which was notably absent from other aspects of his affairs. Beyond doing his duty to the family, his chief ambition was to lead a quiet life, but he enjoyed being a rural landowner.

2   Pkr A, 3/11/5, 'Particulars', 17 Oct. 1828; 3/19/3, W. & T. Hutton to WP, 23 Oct. 1828; 1/13/67, SS to WP, 15 Jan. 1829; 1/8/35, P. Clark to WP, 26 Nov. 1829; D. Perriam, 'Troubled Bridge over Warwick', *The Cumberland News*, 21 April 2012, 34.

3   Pkr A, 1/8/18, 69, 1/13/ 37, 56, 58, WN to WP, 13 Aug. 3 & 7 Nov. 1828, 11 May 1829, 20 Feb. 1830.

Most owners in Cumberland held properties of only modest value and, even when Skirwith Abbey and most of the Warwick estate were combined under his proprietorship, William was no exception. Much land (as true of William, as it had been of Thomas) was held under customary tenures and yielded uneconomic rents which were ameliorated from time to time by the receipt of fines of one kind or another. Ownership was commonly much less remunerative than it was elsewhere in Britain. When one of his few substantial tenants, in arrears with his rent, failed at Holmegate in the winter of 1829-30, William raised £1,114 from the sale of his stock, crop and implements[4]. Another significant holding was Moorhouse Hall, near Warwick. In September 1828, shortly after William took over, the current occupant relinquished her tenancy and proposed to live more cheaply on the Isle of Man. It took three years to find a successor, a Captain Wanchope, who was related to the locally powerful Howard family. No rent accrued during that period and, when Wanchope asked for improvements, including a water closet, William approved, but only on condition that Wanchope paid for them[5]. At Warwick William was occasionally targeted as a potential purchaser by those keen to sell up and move on. He purchased a few closes at nearby Wetheral in 1838, and later acquired land even nearer to the heart of the estate from relatives of the original owners, the Warwicks[6].

Most tenants at Warwick, together letting only a small proportion of the estate, were much less substantial – cottagers who derived most of their wherewithal from by-employments such as spinning, weaving and leatherwork and were correspondingly vulnerable. This was evident in 1831 when the River Eden overflowed and caused severe damage to the holdings of those like Thomas Hall, who lived by the riverbank. Under his lease Hall was responsible for keeping the bank in good order but, at £70, the cost of the repairs necessary after the flood was beyond him. With the work having to be done quickly William agreed to pay half and, ultimately, probably paid more[7]. On another occasion his endemic anxiety about costs led him into a serious misjudgement. Initially, he employed Patrick Clark as steward at Warwick. When a sum of £100 could not be accounted for he sacked Clark and replaced him with Thomas Sowerby. Later Clark was found to be innocent, and the £100 to be safe, but he was not reinstated. Sowerby was kept on a very tight leash regarding expenditure and was irritated by this, and in November 1831 he tweaked William's conscience by revealing that, in

4   Beckett, 'Landownership in Cumbria', 140-145; Pkr A, 1/8/19 & 2/5/53, WN to WP, 22 Jan. & 27 Sept. 1830.
5   Pkr A, 1/13/45-46, L.B. Hamlin to WP, 3 & 6 Sept. 1828; 2/5/16-17, WN to WP, 19 Mar. & 4 Apr. 1831; 1/8/1 & 2/5/3, 12, Wanchope to WP, 25 Mar. 1831, 17 Oct. & 31 Dec. 1832.
6   Pkr B, 31, William Parker's Will, Codicils of 7 Sept. 1838 and 2 Nov. 1853.
7   Pkr A, 2/5/21-22, 36, T. Sowerby to WP, 10 Feb. 30 Mar. & 21 Apr. 1831; 2/5/15, WN ton WP, 12 Mar. 1831.

order to meet running costs, he had been borrowing from Thomas's widow, Mary Parker[8].

The situation at Skirwith was very different from that at Warwick (Figure 20). More remote and on higher ground, much of the land there was near the margin of cultivation. The main crops were oats, bigg and hay, and animal husbandry was largely devoted to sheep. The key objective for owners was not merely to help in sustaining sound tenants, but to attract them in the first place. When William moved there Skirwith was a hamlet rather than a village and over the years he did much to improve the place – building and letting the Sun Inn and a number of cottages, and providing financial support for the erection of a school there, and for the maintenance of a schoolmaster. Towards the end of his life, as his income spiralled, he made two purchases of land in the same parish, of Kirkland, as Skirwith Abbey: first of all at Staingills, and then in Langwathby. He remained in the market for property and finally acquired additional farms at Culgaith, near Skirwith. Shortly before his death he negotiated with the Church Commissioners to build a church and parsonage to serve the village of Skirwith. He provided the land and he left money to cover building costs and to endow the living, which were 'said to have cost him £9,000'[9].

Figure 20. Skirwith Abbey and the high Pennines.

Earlier, with limited income from rents William was keenly interested in farming on his own account and he encouraged useful economies of scale

8   Pkr A, 2/5/14, 19, WN to WP, 16 & 30 Mar. 1831; 2/5/1, T. Sowerby to WP, 17 Nov. 1831.
9   Pkr B, 21, Material relating to Skirwith; 24, '[MS] Outline of a Family', 15; 31, William Parker's Will, Codicil of 2 Nov. 1853.

between his two main properties. Across the summer, the horses at Skirwith were brought down to Warwick in relays to feed off its richer pasture, and additional grazing was let to those locals seeking it. Fodder crops for both properties were bought from various outlets according to price, and both were supplied with seeds via annual orders from merchants in Manchester[10]. William took a particular interest in sheep rearing. Having been commissioned by other local owners to travel to St. Ninian's Fair in Northumberland to purchase ewes, Patrick Clark was able to replenish William's flocks at little additional cost; and the fine tups he managed served several different flocks at Warwick and Skirwith. Successive trials – of carrots, turnips, cabbages and mangolds – sought to identify the optimal winter feed for sheep; and Thomas Salter, the tenant of Tithe Barn Hill in Heaton Norris who was persistently in arrears with his rent, was asked to supply William with a sketch of his 'most approved method for constructing a cover for hay'[11]. On at least one occasion, ever keen to boost income, William echoed the activities of his forbears by arranging for his sheep to be driven to market in Manchester. For decades past butchers had been a prime source of information about the practicalities of droving. On 12 February 1830 Patrick Clark, having consulted 'several of the Carlisle butchers', reported that:

> the whole of them says that for the Manchester market the sheep ought to be off on Sunday [the] first. Thomas Dalton sends some off the week after next and says that he would deliver ours at Manchester for 1s.3d. each. About 12 or 13 miles a day is as much as they ought to go. If we had meat sufficient I would think Dalton's proposition not out of the way: but as there is not sufficient keep for that time you must just act as you think best[12].

William found some means of sending them off immediately. How many were driven and how much he got for them are unrecorded. They were sold for him by Samuel Burton, John's brother, on 24 February, who returned a certificate from the purchasers to the effect that the deal had been struck 'at the full market price of this day'[13].

It is from this period that we again get a glimpse of Old Town House which, because it had been held by Thomas Parker and was closer to it than to Skirwith, was administered from the Warwick Hall estate. In addition to Old Town, the surrounding property included the Salutation Inn in High Hesket, and several cottages, gardens and orchards in and around the village, all of which were let. Apart from the short period during the 1820s when Thomas

---

10   Pkr A, 1/8/34, P. Clark to WP, 21 Sept. 1829; 1/8/10 & 3/18/13, JM to WP, 14 Apr. 1830 & 6 Mar. 1841; 2/5/36, T. Sowerby to WP, 10 Feb. 1831.
11   Pkr A, 1/8/9, 34 & 37, P. Clark to WP, 21 Sept. & 26 Oct. 1829, 15 Mar. 1830; 2/5/36, T. Sowerby to WP, 10 Feb. 1831; 3/14/45 & 3/18/19, JM to WP, 9 Jan. 1836 & 10 Oct. 1840.
12   Pkr A, 1/8/5, PC to WP, 12 Feb. 1830.
13   Pkr A, 2/3/30, Certificate, 24 Feb. 1830; 1/8/21, JM to WP, 27 Feb. 1830.

may have lived there during the building of the new Warwick Hall, the house had been let for many years, though at no stage was there any question of selling it. In October 1829, under a power of attorney so that he had no need personally to attend the manorial court at Hesket, William gained admission to Thomas's customary holdings   Unspecified improvement work was going on there soon afterwards, whose purpose was probably to turn the property into a conventional farm as distinct from a service point at the junction of the adjacent drove roads, for with the coming of coastal steam shipping and the railways the cattle-droving trade was in decline[14].

The house and its adjoining outbuildings were at the centre of 177 acres of arable and meadow land straddling the turnpike road from Penrith to Carlisle. The tenancy was renewed in 1846 for 14 years at an annual rent of £157.10s. 0d., and included clauses about the timetable for payments of rent and taxes; a requirement that the tenant live there and keep it in good repair; and others regarding rotation, arbitration in the event of disputes, and so on. While all these stipulations were standard by the mid-nineteenth century, one clause was not. The tenant was 'to supply to the landlord in each year not less than 20 quarts of cranberries, if so many are produced'[15]. This unusual requirement reveals an interesting feature of the Old Town property. A short distance from the house, north of the road to Armathwaite, lay Tarn Wadling (which, incidentally, bred 'some of the finest carp in the kingdom')[16]. In the boggy ground to the west of the tarn, on part of which the Old Town property abutted, grew copious cranberry bushes whose fruit, according to contemporaries, could not 'be equalled in quality and flavour'. William ensured that a good quantity of the fruit was collected and reserved for his use[17].

Among William's contributions to High Hesket and its hinterland was the provision he made for a new school there, as Thomas had done at Warwick Bridge and he himself had done at Skirwith. A school had been built on the north side of St. Mary's churchyard in the mid-eighteenth century and Robert senior had provided money for its upkeep. By the 1850s the building was in poor condition. William also worried that it was 'not in a very favourable situation as, being so near a burial ground, [it] gives the idea at least of unhealthiness, and I presume there is no access to it but through the

14   Pkr A, 1/8/ 38-40, WN to WP, 10 & 17 Oct. and JM to WP, 15 Oct. 1829.
15   CAS (C), DB/74/8, Tenancy Agreement, 14 August 1846.
16   Parsons & White, *History, Directory & Gazetteer*, 482.
17   I owe this quotation from an advertisement in the *Carlisle Journal* of September 1853 to Sheila Fletcher of Lazonby and Denis Perriam. Cranberries grew well on the poor, acidic soils of parts of the north and then, as now, were prized for making sharp sauces to go with the game which flourished on William's property. In north-east Cumbria they featured prominently at the market in Longtown, from where barrels of them were sent to London. The tradition has died out in England; most of the cranberries which we now enjoy, in one form or another, come from North America. – G.L. Routledge, *Longtown*, (Carlisle, 2000), 5; A. Davidson, (ed.), *The Oxford Companion to Food* (Oxford, 1999), 223.

churchyard, which is very unseemly'. A search began for a suitable alternative site. In 1853, when such could not be found, William donated a plot from the Old Town property: this lay on the south-west side of the village, next to the turnpike road. He then provided £145, almost half the sum required, to build (handsomely in the local red sandstone) both the school and a residence for the master. The establishment flourishes to this day. In William's time, in further pursuit of his family's long-standing convictions, it was also used as a Sunday school[18].

The evidence relating to William's performance as a landed proprietor is scattered and uneven: there is little material, for example, about his home at Skirwith Abbey beyond the fact that he installed plate-glass windows in the drawing and dining rooms in 1841 (no doubt to improve their insulation); that he established tree plantations around the house to ameliorate its exposed situation; and that, predictably, he employed a number of servants, including both a butler and a housekeeper. There was also regular employment for a joiner, and for day-labourers on the estate as it was gradually expanded[19]. If he can be said to have revelled in anything, it was in his role as a rural landowner. As in everything else, his chief aim was carefully to husband his resources; but towards the end of his life, as his wealth grew, he exhibited commendable concern for the local communities over which he presided. Ironically, he was able to do so only by deploying income from his urban properties in Manchester, where his heart was much less engaged.

A QUIET LIFE

William customarily endorsed each incoming letter with the date of its receipt and of his reply. A slave to anxiety, during his early years in charge he must often have dreaded the arrival of the mail with its regular reports of difficulties with warehouse lettings in Manchester, which he had to regard as his chief source of income. Yet, living over 20 miles from Carlisle and with Marchanton permanently at his beck and call, there were benefits from his close contact with one of Britain's fastest-growing towns. Goods forwarded from Manchester contributed significantly to the comfort of his quiet, uneventful life at Skirwith Abbey. He bombarded Marchanton and the Healds with orders for items which were unavailable in Cumberland; which locally, at least in his view, were of inferior quality; or which it was simply more convenient to acquire through them. In 1828 the wagons deployed northwards by Hargreaves took three days to reach Penrith, from whence a further half-day was required to carry goods to Skirwith. Two years later Marchanton informed him that, while Hargreaves charged 3s.

18   CAS (C), PR/35/ 82-84, 86 & 116; *Carlisle Journal*, 20 May 1853; Records relating to St. Mary's Church, High Hesket, collated by the late Rita Blake and now in the author's possession.
19   Pkr B, 21; 31, William Parker's Will.

6d. per hundredweight, the steam packet from Liverpool to Carlisle cost a shilling less for the same weight[20]. This would normally have been a clinching argument, except that the difference was largely, if not wholly, taken up by the cost of transit from Manchester to Liverpool, and from Carlisle to Warwick or Skirwith. Most of the goods which William obtained, therefore, came by mail coach or wagon from Manchester to Skirwith via Penrith.

Manchester was the obvious source of textile goods, so there was traffic in blankets, tablecloths and other covers, handkerchieves, buttons, mourning clothes and even tarpaulins. William bought his soap in Manchester and also got umbrellas, steel pens, watches, gold pins and a silver teapot from there, together with ginger lozenges, 'rouge plate powder' and snuff, to all of which he was partial. More specialised, high-quality metal goods, such as a safe, locks, and crests (embossed with the Parker arms) for carriage harnesses, were also easier to obtain in a major centre. Large consignments of cheese were sent frequently, not only to William but also to his friends in London and elsewhere. Cumberland had plenty of beef cattle but there was little commercial cheese making, whereas Manchester, and Heaton Mersey especially, were close to the Cheshire dairy industry. There was nothing quite as exotic as the turtle sent to Thomas Parker in 1827, but on one occasion William took delivery of a large quantity of 'American apples'. He also acquired a 'hydraulic machine' from Manchester. This was 'capable of throwing a full body of water' against a building from a distance of some ten yards, and was probably used to clear the walls of Skirwith Abbey of the lichen which accumulated in its cold, wet climate. There were also regular deliveries of the reports of the various charities which the family supported, such as Stockport Sunday School; and of the Manchester and Stockport newspapers which both he and Robert devoured, and to which William referred in his letter to the Rev. Kidd[21]. Apart from correspondence, southbound traffic was negligible, except for an occasional salmon from the Eden, game pies and, later, boxes of game[22].

Manchester was also the chief source of the information and services which enabled William to pursue his keen interest in art. There is no evidence of the origin of this interest. However, with money in his pocket from an early age, his activities as a collector seem to have been well established by the time he took over from Thomas Parker. By 1828 William already had an account with Olivants, Zanetti & Agnew in Manchester. This was a wide-ranging business, selling carvings, gildings and looking-glasses; and

20   Pkr A, 1/13/62, 2/5/61, JM to WP, 26 Dec. 1828 & 9 June 1830.

21   Pkr A, 1/8/32 & 1/13/62, JM to WP, 26 Aug. 1828 & 12 Nov. 1829; 2/5/27, 58-59, 61, 65, Same to Same, 22 Apr. 7, 9 & 21 June, 4 Nov. 1830 & 15 Mar. 1831; 3/18/19-20, 30, 49-52, 55, 59-60, 79, Same to Same, 1 Sept. 1 & 20 Oct. 30 Dec. 1836, 1 Mar. 8 & 17 June 1837, 18 Aug. 1838, 1 Feb. 22 Aug. & 10 Oct. 1840; 2/14,15, 70 & 210, Newspaper Bills, 1837, 1838 & 1842.

22   Pkr A, 2/11/35, JSP to TP, 18 Dec. 1825; 3/18/43, JM to WP, 1 Feb. 1839; 3/18/32, SS to WP, 28 Dec. 1839.

barometers, thermometers and hydrometers, as well as jewellery, cut-glass, lamps, imported china, bronzes, medals, coins and 'curiosities of every description'. It also framed pictures and prints, and dealt in 'ancient and modern paintings'[23]. Through them in December 1828 William pursued art works which had recently caught his fancy. Two months later he was anticipating delivery of two portraits, one commissioned earlier by Thomas and the other by himself. These were probably among the 'family portraits' later hung at Skirwith Abbey, which included studies of Christopher Parker of Petteril Green and his parents. There was much discussion with Marchanton about the safest means of transporting them to Skirwith; once framed, they were dispatched in specially constructed boxes, with the paintings firmly screwed down inside. Other works were purchased following scrutiny of the catalogues of exhibitions in Manchester and Liverpool regularly supplied by Marchanton. With William unwilling to leave Skirwith, the problem with this mode of purchase was that he did not see the works until their arrival there; and in October 1829, having forwarded 'two cases of pictures', Marchanton was 'glad' that William was 'not much disappointed....upon the whole as to their quality', though some were 'declined'[24].

As his anxiety about finance eased, William became more ambitious. In 1834 he bought a Rembrandt of 1651 – 'The Descent from the Cross' – from Viscountess Hampden; and in the following year a work of 1828 – 'East Cowes Castle' – by Turner. He also acquired a Titian, landscapes by Gainsborough and Morland, and works by Harding, Sir Francis Bourgeois, Cuyp – 'A Town on a River' – and 'after Wouvermans'. He had several of them refurbished by his dealers in Manchester, and sometimes, through them, in London. He remained active in the market for many years and ultimately owned a fine collection whose value steadily accumulated as the years passed. In November 1853, by a codicil to his will, he required his collection to 'be considered as heirlooms', and to stay at Skirwith Abbey for 'as long as the law will permit'. Simultaneously, he similarly designated his plate, linen, chinaware, books and furniture, suggesting not only that he wished to perpetuate his achievements, but also that by then he had purchased a wide variety of other goods of high quality[25].

Appropriately, art collecting was a soothing rather than a stressful pastime,

23   At some point this partnership dissolved, with Agnew (in Exchange St.) and Zanetti (at 100, King St.) continuing independently. William dealt through both. – Pkr A, 2/14/202 & 213, Bills of 30 Sept. & 20 Oct. 1841.

24   Pkr A, 1/8/41, 44, 46, 65-66; 1/13/70, 75, 78; 3/18/18, 50, 65, 81, JM to WP, 19 Dec. 1828; 13 Feb. 13, 19, 27 Mar. 5 & 9 Sept. 10 Oct. 1829; 1 Oct. 1836, 22 Sept. 1837, 10 Oct. 1838 & 5 Dec. 1840. For details of the paintings hung at Skirwith in the 1870s, see 4/20/9, Clutterbuck, Trevenor & Steele to E.W. Parker, 2 Feb. 1916.

25   Pkr B, 31, Will of William Parker, Codicil of 2 Nov. 1853; Pkr A, 2/14/202 & 213, Bills of 30 Sept. & 20 Oct. 1841. Details of the purchases are drawn from reports of researches prior to the paintings being auctioned. – Pkr A, 4/18/6 & 8, Christie to E.W. Parker, 9 & 19 June 1909.

because as he grew older William became increasingly unwell. He was ill for much of 1838 with some affliction of the throat. Then in June 1842 he was reported to be 'much indisposed'. In 1849 his health was initially 'not good' and later 'precarious', although by November he was 'so much better'. While there was no ultimate crisis as yet, during the early 1850s correspondents repeatedly expressed the hope that he was 'improving'[26].

Given this record, it was surprising to many that William was the last to die of the quartet who had succeeded Robert senior in 1815. After Thomas in 1828, the next to go was his cousin, Christopher Parker of Petteril Green, who was nine years older than him. His first wife, Mary (with whom he had four children), had died in 1814. In the following year Christopher had married Margaret Jefferson of Stoneraise; they had eight children before Margaret died in 1828. In 1833 Christopher took as his third wife, Mary, widow of Robert Sanderson Milbourne of Armathwaite Castle – just a couple of miles from Petteril Green – who produced a single child, a daughter, who died young. By then a very senior member of the local gentry, having served both as high sheriff and as deputy lieutenant, Christopher himself died, aged 63, in 1838[27].

Meanwhile, the second of the three brothers, Robert junior, had moved from Warwick Hall to Skirwith Abbey to live under William's care. Family members were resolutely discreet about his condition. Although he never regained mental stability, he occasionally ventured forth. He appears to have attended the funerals of Christopher's second wife and of Christopher himself in 1828 and 1838 respectively, for formal mourning clothes were purchased for him. And in June 1839 he travelled to Manchester, visiting Samuel Stocks at his warehouse there. Although he must have been accompanied, it was not by William; unfortunately, Marchanton missed seeing him. Robert lingered on in his twilight world for many years and, after donating £1,000 to the Cumberland Infirmary, he died intestate in 1850, with William administering his estate[28]. Stockport Sunday School had not forgotten Robert's endeavours on behalf of it and its affiliate at Heaton Mersey. They sent William a resolution, engrossed on vellum, recording their appreciation of Robert's early work. William responded with a further donation of £250, which finally discharged the debt on the massive building opened in Stockport in 1806. The school held a memorial service for Robert in August 1850 and in November a memorial tablet to the Parker family was erected in the great

26   Pkr A, 3/18/72, 76 & 78, JM to WP, 9 Mar. 2 June & 11 Aug. 1838; 3/9/7, J. Jackson to WP, 21 June 1842; 3/9/26, H.W. Taylor to WP, 26 Mar. 1849; 3/9/1, 14 & 22, H. Bridge to WP, 14 May & 17 Nov. 1849, 14 Jan. 1851.
27   See Pkr B, 5, Annotated Pedigrees of the 2nd and 3rd branches of the family; 24, '[Ms] Outline of a Family', 26, 30 & Appendix C, 3-4.
28   Pkr A, 1/13/51 & 3/18/ 40 & 72, JM to WP, 2 Oct. 1828, 9 Mar. 1838 & 4 June 1839.

hall[29]. William appears to have acted as auditor for Stockport Sunday School in the same capacity as had his uncle before him, for the accounts which he received were not only carefully scrutinised, but returned with his signature[30].

William himself lived on for another six years. He died at Skirwith Abbey on 26 January 1856, aged 67.

A Divided and Encumbered Inheritance

In 1828 William and many others had been shocked by the sudden onset of Thomas Parker's illness and his death three months later. Unlike them, however, William was unmarried and childless (which he remained), and left alone with a brother who was mentally incapacitated, and for whom he had not previously had to care. Riddled with anxiety about finance and the strategic decisions confronting him, he was acutely aware that he was now solely responsible for the management, and ultimately the disposal, of his family's assets.

Nothing is more revealing of his state of mind at that juncture than the will he made on 11 September, only five months after Thomas's death. By the time of his own death nearly 30 years later a host of developments had necessitated changes to the will – purchases of additional property, for example, and his decisions to finance a school at High Hesket and both a school and a church at Skirwith – as did the incapacity of one original trustee, James Stubington Penny, and the death of another, John Railton, both of whom were replaced. His solicitor, William Nanson, who survived all of them, drafted the will and the numerous subsequent alterations to it. It was a mighty labour, certainly in comparison with Thomas's will, over which Nanson had also presided, which ran to only a few pages. William insisted on catering for every conceivable eventuality and all possible attempts to circumvent or overturn the will. Each significant element was festooned with legal safeguards, requiring substantial qualifications and endless repetition. Here was a man who, for whatever combination of reasons, was deeply conscious of human frailty where property and money were concerned, and who was determined, if at all possible, to make his dispositions stick. Although at intervals several codicils were revoked, seven of them survived. The document ran to 116 pages[31].

Thomas had indicated in his will that, but for his brother's affliction, Robert would have been a major beneficiary. William did likewise, and also catered for the possibility that Robert might recover, marry and have children.

---

29   CAS (C), DX/1089/40/2, Report of 'A Special Meeting of the Trustees, Committee & Visitors of the Stockport Sunday School', 8 Sept. 1850; Heginbotham, *Stockport: Ancient & Modern*, ii, 389.

30   Stockport Museums, RD 17752, WP to J. Mayer, 30 Sept. 1837. I am grateful to Bronwen Simpson of Stockport Heritage Services for drawing my attention to this correspondence.

31   It is so bulky that it lies in a separate file at Pkr B, 31.

In the event Robert did none of these things and predeceased him. Thomas had also indicated that, if William died unmarried, he wished his property to descend to the male heirs in succession of Christopher Parker of Petteril Green[32]. William was faithful to this wish too, with one crucial difference: instead of devolving on a single heir the property over which William presided (which following Robert's death included everything, except Mary Parker's part of the Warwick Hall estate) was eventually divided between three male heirs. Christopher Parker died in 1838, as did the eldest surviving son of his first marriage, Robert Holme Parker, in 1847. The Warwick Hall and Old Town properties passed to this Robert's only surviving son, Thomas Holme Parker, who was a minor at the time of William's death. The properties in Manchester, much the most valuable part of the inheritance, together with the Skirwith Abbey estate, passed to the eldest son of Christopher's second marriage, another Christopher. An Anglican priest, he had been rector of Caldbeck 1834-54, then of Ormside 1854-56, and subsequently became the first incumbent of the new church at Skirwith as well as the local landowner[33]. Finally, having originally been earmarked for the Rev. Christopher Parker, the properties near Stockport purchased by William were left to another William Parker, the Rev. Christopher's younger brother and a further surviving son of his father's second marriage. Although we do not know whether Thomas Parker was privy to his brother's original intention to divide the main properties into two, this was catered for in William's will of September 1828. The third division, on the other hand, came very late indeed, in 1853.

The younger William Parker, aged 39, who lived at The Grotto, Yanwath, near Penrith, was then courting a minor: Mary, daughter of Edward William Hasell of Dalemain, a fine neo-Palladian house, some four miles west of Penrith on the road to Ullswater. The Hasells had been established at Dalemain since the seventeenth century and owned a sizeable estate in the northern Lake District, though it was much larger in acreage than in rental income. Not over impressed by what his young daughter's suitor had to offer her, nor perhaps by his age in relation to hers, Edward Hasell went to see William Parker at Skirwith Abbey and enquired whether he was prepared to augment his younger cousin's wherewithal. He was. By yet another codicil, the younger William was left Tithe Barn Hill, the works at Heaton Mersey, and the land bought from Goulden and Egerton in 1832 and later. The prospect of a marriage alliance with such a long-established family was warmly welcomed by William Parker. The couple married in 1854 and there is no doubt that this third division clinched the match. It came at a cost, however, with £10,000 of the value of the Stockport properties, plus a £300 annuity on the life of William Parker senior, being settled to the uses of the

---

32 See above, 103-104.
33 See Pkr B, 5, Annotated Pedigree of the 2nd branch of the family.

marriage. Edward Hasell also weighed in with £9,000 worth of insurance policies, the proceeds of which were also settled on the couple[34].

Bequests to individuals, most of which were granted by a codicil of 1838, were numerous and cumulatively substantial. Four of the younger children of Christopher Parker of Petteril Green each received £500. A total of £3,900 was left to three cousins and £50 each to three other, more distant relations. Members of the Calvert family, who were among William's few close friends, were granted a life annuity of £100 and a legacy of £2,000. Each of the final three trustees of the will, together with James Stubington Penny, who earlier had retired from the position, received £250 for their trouble. The sum of £500 was to be devoted to 'certain small periodical payments which I have been in the habit of making'– to support two widows, one in Heaton Mersey and the other in Stockport; and for the education of two minors, each of whom was to receive a further £250 on attaining a majority. And £50 went to a godson. However, by the time William died, an uncertain number of these bequests had been rendered redundant by the demise of the proposed recipients, so it is impossible to ascertain the full extent of his benevolence. William's bequests to charitable institutions, not subject to this constraint, rivalled those of his uncle and his elder brother. A sum of £500 went to each of the British & Foreign Bible Society, the Church Missionary Society, the Wesleyan Missionary Society and the infirmaries in Manchester and Carlisle. Stockport Infirmary was left £250 and Stockport Sunday School a further £100. The schools at Skirwith, Warwick and High Hesket received £500, £250 and £200 respectively. Finally, William was uncommonly generous to his employees, granting a life annuity of £35 to his housekeeper, £200 to each of two servants and £100 to a third, and £30 to his joiner. All the other servants in his employ in 1856 got £15 and 'a full suit of suitable and serviceable mourning'. Remarkably, similar suits were also provided for 'each of the tenants of my farms….in the parishes of Warwick, Hesket and Kirkland', for 'each of the weekly labourers….at Skirwith….usually employed by me', and for 'each of the respective wives of such tenants and labourers'. William was determined to be remembered by the residents of the communities over which he presided for so long.

Thus, in one way or another, William's property was heavily encumbered. Still more significantly, as had happened in the eighteenth century before the family's venture into industry, Parker property was divided when the prevailing tendency was to consolidate[35]. This time, with no such further venture in prospect, the outcome was uncertain. Young William Parker was able to clinch the match with Mary Hasell of Dalemain. The will's

---

34   Pkr B, 24, '[Ms] Outline of a Family', 40; CAS (C), D/Hod/5/77, Marriage Settlement, 27 Sept. 1854.
35   See above, 20.

Figure 21. Pedigree of William Parker's successors.

CHRISTOPHER (1775-1838) of Orton and Gilse, Westmorland, and of Petteril Green

A. married firstly, 1806, Mary (1786-1814) d. of John Chadwick of Manchester, and had issue:

    JOHN (1807-1814)

    MARY JANE (1809-1843)

    SARAH (1810-1859)

    ROBERT HOLME (1812-1847) of Petteril Green m. Elizabeth d. of Capt. John Richardson of Nunwick Hall (d. 1860), and had issue:

    JOHN RICHARDSON b. 1841 and d. 1841

    THOMAS HOLME of whom presently

    ANNIE (1843-1929)

THOMAS HOLME (1842-1901) of Old Town and Warwick Hall, m. 1864 Amy Emma Mary (1840-1895), d. of Rev. J. Butler of Burnley, and had issue:

    PERCY THOMAS HOLME (1865-1873)

    MAURICE HOLME b. 1866 and d. 1866

    CYRIL ROBERT HOLME (1869-1936)

    AGNES AMY MARY (1874-1939)

    CUTHBERT JAMES VERE HOLME (1880-1966)

B. married secondly, 1815, Margaret (d. 1828), d. of Robert Jefferson of Stoneraise, and had issue:

    CHRISTOPHER of whom presently

    THOMAS JEFFERSON (1818-1842)

    WILLIAM (1819-1892) of whom presently at C. below

    MARGARET (1820-1893)

    ALICE ELIZABETH (1823-1846)

    FRANCIS (1824-1901)

    NELSON (1827-1859)

    OCTAVIUS JEFFERSON b. 1829 and d. 1829

CHRISTOPHER (1816-1865) of Skirwith Abbey, successively Curate of Caldbeck, Rector of Ormside, and Rector of Skirwith, m. 1842 Sarah, d. of Edward Railton of Unthank (d. 1875), and had issue:

    CHRISTOPHER (1843-1869) of Skirwith Abbey

    EDWARD JOHN b. 1845 and d. 1845

    SARAH FRANCES (1846-?)

    ALICE MARY (1848-1855)

    WILLIAM (1850-1876) of Skirwith Abbey

    MARGARET (1852-1913)

    EDWARD WILSON of whom presently

    JOHN KNUBLREY (1853-1908)

    ALICE MARY (1856-1885)

    ELEANOR (1857-1858)

EDWARD WILSON (1853-1932) of Skirwith Abbey, m. 1880 Ada May Adelaide (1860-1940), d. of Frederick Cowper of Carleton Hall, and had issue:

> MARY VIOLET (1881-1884)
>
> KATHLEEN AMY 1882-1886)
>
> EDWARD CARLETON (1884-1900)
>
> FREDERICK CYRIL FRANCIS of whom presently
>
> THOMAS COWPER (1890-1917)

FREDERICK CYRIL FRANCIS (1888-1970) of Petteril Bank, Skirwith Abbey, Cracrop, Allegarth, Newbiggin Hall and Beaumont, Penrith, m. 1920 Phyllis (1901-1967) d. of Edward Buckton Cargill of Hessle, Yorkshire, and had issue:

> PAMELA MARY ELIZABETH (1922-1966)
>
> BRIDGET MARIOTA (1928-1983)

C. WILLIAM (1819-1892) of the Grotto and the Laithes, Penrith, and Carleton Hill, m. 1854 Mary (1834-1911), d. of Edward William Hasell of Dalemain, and had issue:

> WILLIAM HASELL (1855-1935), Vicar of Cockermouth
>
> MARY DOROTHEA (1857-1911)
>
> CHRISTOPHER JOHN of whom presently
>
> ALICE MARGARET (1860-1932)
>
> EDWARD THOMAS (1862-1942)
>
> CICELY (1865-1918)
>
> MABEL (1868-1923)
>
> AMY (1870-1955)
>
> SYBIL (1873-?)

CHRISTOPHER JOHN (1859-1932) of the Laithes, Penrith, m. 1882 Alice Mary (d. 1924), d. of Samuel Radcliffe of Oldham, and had issue:

> CHRISTOPHER MILES (1886-1959), m. firstly, 1911 Mary Ella Margery Carleton, d. of Frederick Carleton Cowper of Carleton Hall, and had issue:
>
> ANN, NANCY and JOAN, of whom nothing is known, and m. secondly, 1930 Gladys (1908-1983), d. of Lancelot Walker of Skelton, and had issue:
>
> GLADYS MARY (1932-1941)
>
> RUTH (1936- ?)
>
> CHRISTOPHER PETER (1942-?)

major beneficiary, his older brother, the Rev. Christopher Parker, came into a valuable inheritance, not least because the trustees were instructed to purchase additional property in order to augment the Skirwith Abbey estate. In his will a sum of £25,000 had originally been set aside for this purpose. Later William deleted the precise figure and encouraged the trustees to go further if suitable landed property appeared on the market. It remained to be seen how young Thomas Holme Parker would fare with his inheritance of Warwick Hall and the ancestral property at Old Town (Figure 21).

Chapter 8:

The Aftermath

It is scarcely surprising that, in the wake of these dispositions, the fortunes of the three beneficiaries differed markedly, though there were common features. To varying degrees, members of the family continued to exert influence among the county community, though not beyond it. As a result of the division of Parker property, their income was much less than that of their predecessor; and, albeit at a differing pace, their means were gradually eroded by factors beyond their control – deteriorating agricultural conditions and a poorer land market in the later nineteenth century, and in the twentieth century heavier taxation of larger incomes and the introduction of death duties[1].

In the case of William and Mary Parker of The Grotto, Yanwath, demographic factors once more played a part. The sums settled on the pair in 1854 became available only following the deaths of their respective benefactors. William Parker of Skirwith Abbey died within two years of the marriage, but Edward William Hasell lived on for a further 16 years, dying in 1872. Moreover, market conditions in the cotton industry steadily reduced the value of Heaton Mersey. Probably sickened by the failure to resolve the sectarian dispute at the Sunday school, William had latterly contemplated selling the works at Heaton Mersey. Within a month or so of William's death, Nanson advised the younger William to sell for the best price he could get. Not only did this prove impossible, at least at an acceptable price, but net income from the premises declined sharply. Although the property was let for £2,400 per annum in 1864, in order to secure these terms William had to covenant to pay £500 per annum for a decade to finance new buildings on the site. By 1873 the annual rent had been reduced to £1,800, and it was further reduced to £1,200 in 1891. The works were eventually sold, for an unknown sum, to the Bleachers' Association, in 1900[2].

Although William was a J.P. and deputy lieutenant for both Cumberland and Westmorland, master of the Ullswater foxhounds, and joint master of the Eamont harriers, he could not afford the leisured lifestyle of his benefactor. He farmed at Yanwath and lived at The Grotto for a few years before moving to nearby Carleton Hill. His major remunerative activity was as a land agent, and he was employed in this capacity – at the Warwick Hall estate and elsewhere – for the rest of his life. With property in the vicinity of Stockport

1   F.M.L. Thompson, *English Landed Society in the 19th Century* (London, 1963), 269-345.
2   Pkr A, 4/1/2, WN to W. Parker, 27 Feb. 1856; 4/2/1, Rentals from 1856; 4/1/4, 'Agreement: Conditions for a Lease', 30 Jan. 1862. For the sale of Heaton Mersey, see Pkr B, 20.

and Manchester much in demand for villa development, Tithe Barn Hill was sold for £10,000 in 1873. By then William and Mary had produced three sons and six daughters. The eldest son, William Hasell Parker, was vicar of Cockermouth for over 50 years from 1881. A third son, Edward, followed his father into land agency. Such property as the family owned was inherited by the second son, Christopher, following his father's death in 1892; and his eldest son, yet another Christopher, continued in farming and latterly became a noted local breeder of foxhounds[3].

The affairs of William's main beneficiary, the Rev. Christopher Parker, who inherited the Skirwith Abbey estate, proceeded much more promisingly. Nine months after William Parker's death, his uncle's widow, Sarah Parker, finally succumbed, having reached the ripe old age of 81. Thereby, the income of the main branch improved by £1,000 a year. Following his cousin's instructions and utilising his ample bequest, Rev. Christopher oversaw the erection of a fine church at Skirwith and a parsonage and school nearby[4]. He also managed to purchase additional property in the vicinity. Then, in 1860, he completed the major acquisition of the Cracrop estate. While there is no record of what he paid for it, it was 1,162 acres in extent, 'all lying within a ring fence', let for £784 annually and constituting a substantial addition to existing holdings. At that stage, following this and other purchases since 1828, the entire Skirwith estate was some 2,000 acres in extent. As far as Cracrop was concerned the single, but major, drawback was the property's location – many miles north of Skirwith, about halfway between Brampton and Longtown, and 14 miles from Carlisle[5].

Other problems were more personal. Like his cousin before him, Christopher did not enjoy good health. Together with his wife, Sarah, he embarked on a European tour in the early 1860s, only to return utterly exhausted. Some time later, out grouse shooting on Cross Fell, he suffered an acute attack of lumbago, and had to be carried off the fell. His eldest son, Christopher, was also sickly, suffering from kidney trouble from childhood. The father died, aged 49, in 1865; and the son followed him four years later, aged 25 and unmarried. A hiatus followed. A second son had died young so, under the line of succession established by the will of 1856, the estate

---

3   Pkr B, 24, '[Ms] Outline of a Family', 43-44, 47; CAS (C), DX/1089/41, W. Parker, Yanwath, in account with W. Parker of Skirwith Abbey, 1855-56. For the sale of Tithe Barn Hill, see Pkr A, 4/2/1, Rentals from, 1856 & Pkr B, 20; and for Edward's career in estate agency, DX/1089/40/5, Accounts, 1887-1922.

4   The church and parsonage were provided for in the final codicil (10 October 1855) of William's Will. As the design and fittings reveal, Rev. Christopher's religious inclinations were very different from those of his predecessors and the edifice, a 'fully developed High Church building', was possibly 'deeply shocking to the natives when new'. Moreover, the Parsonage was 'over-sized… with its own stable block'. – Hyde & Pevsner, *Cumbria*, 625-626.

5   Pkr A, 4/2/1, Rentals from 1856; CAS (C), DX/1089/40/4, Sale Particulars of the Cracrop Estyate, 14 Feb. 1860; Pkr B, 21 and CAS (C), DB/74/1/6, 'Surveys & Valuations, including…Skirwith Abbey', 1855-59.

was inherited by the third son, William, who meanwhile had emigrated, first of all to the United States and then to Australia; and who died unmarried in Melbourne in 1876. The next in line, the fourth son, Edward, had also left for Australia. On his return to Cumberland, apparently some years after 1876, he presided at Skirwith for over half a century, dying in 1932[6].

Even though his regime lasted for so long, remarkably few of Edward Parker's papers have survived and we know little about him. After returning from Australia to claim his inheritance, he lived permanently at Skirwith Abbey, serving as a J.P. for both Cumberland and Westmorland. Locally, he was known affectionately as 'Squire Parker' and, far from standing on his dignity and at a time when the sport was only becoming firmly established, he was an 'almost ever present' and leading member of the Skirwith village cricket club during the 1880s and 1890s; and in 1884 he helped to launch the first Cumberland county club. He was also a very keen golfer, a foundation member of Penrith Golf Club and the first president of the Cumberland and Westmorland Golf Union[7]. However, there were early signs of financial difficulty. The Skirwith estate was administered by William Parker of Carleton Hill, and then by his third son, Edward. They had problems in successfully letting farms on the estate: for example, one of them – Pea Top Farm in Culgaith – was let for £240 a year in 1887, £220 in 1894, £200 in 1898, and £180 in 1903, a fall of 25% in less than two decades. A few years later, in 1909, some of the paintings, so lovingly collected by William Parker and which he had striven to maintain permanently at Skirwith Abbey, were disposed of in London salesrooms; and there were further sales in 1916[8]. We do not know the fate of the properties in Manchester, but it seems likely that they were sold during this period, or shortly after the Great War when the fortunes of the cotton industry went into sharp decline.

Edward Parker's longevity posed considerable problems for his surviving son. Edward's first three children – a son and two daughters – died young, a reminder that the upper classes were not immune from levels of infant mortality which, by modern standards, were still shockingly high. As happened to so many other families during the Great War, another son was killed in action, in 1917. The survivor, Major Frederick Cyril Francis Parker, also served in the war and, marrying in 1920 a persistently extravagant lady, Phyllis Ford, had a position to maintain without income from the Skirwith estate. Indeed, not only did his father live until 1932 but his mother survived until 1940. Long before then Major Parker experienced severe financial

6   Pkr B, 5, Annotated Pedigree of the 3rd branch of the family; 24, '[Ms] Outline of a Family', 32-34, 38-40.
7   Pkr B, 24, '[Ms] Outline of a Family', 34, 40.
8   For Pea Top Farm, see CAS (C), DX/1089/40/5/ 2-4, 8 & 11, Letting Agreements, 1887-1903; and for sales of paintings, Pkr A, 4/18/6, 8, 10-13, 15-16, Christie to E.W. Parker, 9, 19, 22, 25-26, 28 June & 1-2 July 1909; 4/20/9, Clutterbuck, Trevenon & Steele to E.W. Parker, 2 Feb. 1916.

difficulties[9]. In 1923 he bought Petteril Bank House on the outskirts of Carlisle, which by the time of his father's death was heavily mortgaged. His solicitor's advice was to sell either Petteril Bank or Skirwith Abbey. He sold Petteril Bank and also part of the Skirwith estate in 1935 (when his mortgage portfolio had grown even larger), sold further paintings from Skirwith a year later, and by 1937 had persuaded his mother to move to another house on the estate so that he and his wife could live at Skirwith. They stayed there until 1956 when he bought Newbiggin Hall, near Temple Sowerby, where much of the evidence used in this study was found years later[10]. In 1969, two years after his wife's death, he moved to Beaumont House in Penrith, largely, it seems, to improve conditions for his second daughter, Bridget Mariota, who had developed multiple sclerosis, and who continued to live there very independently till her death in 1983. Major Parker died in 1970. He had no sons. However, a first daughter, Pamela, married a Victor Dunn, and it was their eldest son, Christopher Frederick Dunn, who inherited the remnants of the Skirwith estate, after having first adopted the surname Parker instead of Dunn – as we have seen with the Aglionbys[11], a common, if only nominal, preservative device adopted by the landed classes down the ages. He was still in possession in the 1990s, though by then the Skirwith estate had long been let[12].

In comparison with this experience, the decline and demise of the Warwick Hall and Old Town branch were relatively swift. At the time of William Parker's death in 1856, Thomas Holme Parker was a pupil at Radley School, from where he progressed to The Queen's College, Oxford, traditionally the college for Cumbrians. Until he attained his majority his affairs were overseen by three guardians whose management was monitored by the Court of Chancery. A leading Penrith estate agent, William Heskett, who lived at Plumpton, just south of Old Town, was appointed receiver of rents etc. during the minority and continued to manage Thomas's estate after he came of age in 1863[13]. Already by then, however, one particular development had curtailed his future prospects as the owner of Warwick Hall and Old Town.

Mary, Thomas Parker's childless widow since 1828, had continued to live at Warwick Hall, although she appears to have spent her last years with her Heald relatives at Parr's Wood, near Stockport. Having made a will in

---

9   Pkr A, 5/6/35, 'Proposed Mortgage...not carried on with', 1933. This document, which listed a prior series of mortgages for some £20,000, and which catered for a further mortgage, was his solicitor's response to a long-unpaid bill for £195.17s. 2d.   Not executed, it was nevertheless a remarkably candid reminder to his client of the debt. According to the current incumbent of Skirwith Abbey, many of the tree plantations established earlier by William Parker were felled in order to pay for death duties.

10   The voluminous Newwbiggin Hall Collection (cited here as Pkr A) was discovered in an attic and deposited with the Cumbria Archives Service in February 1982. It was brought to the attention of Robert Parker of Morecambe in 1990, and to mine in 2009.

11   See above, 53.

12   Pkr B, 24, '[Ms] Outline of a Family', 35-37, 40-41.

13   Pkr B, 24, '[Ms] Outline of a Family', 24; CAS (C), DB/74/55-56, 117.

April 1848, exactly two decades after Thomas's death, she died in 1857, a year or so after William. She was entitled to dispose of her property in any way she wished. For a widow of nearly 30 years standing, who had been left £15,000 by her husband, her will was unilaterally generous to her own family. Firstly, the land at Warwick which Thomas had vested in her, together with some there which she had purchased in the interim, was left to her brother, James. Three life annuities, left to two nephews and a niece and totalling £60 annually, were to be provided from her personal estate, which meant that money had to be invested to finance them. There were then seven bequests, mainly to methodist institutions and amounting to £1,500. Finally, she left over £15,000 to various members of the extended Heald family, including £10,000 to her brother, George. Similarly, any residue was to be divided between various Heald relatives[14]. There is no way of knowing whether William Parker was aware of his sister-in-law's dispositions; whether he was denied an opportunity of reacting to them; or whether he was content to let matters lie. The implications for Thomas Holme Parker were disappointing: not only was there nothing in the will for him personally, but part of the Warwick estate as it existed at William's death would not be his either.

Shortly after attaining his majority and with his future father-in-law presiding, Thomas married Amy, daughter of the Rev. J. Butler of Burnley in Lancashire. For several years after his succession he comported himself as one might expect of a local proprietor with a grand house at Warwick Hall. He served as a justice of the peace and as deputy lieutenant, and in 1871 was high sheriff of Cumberland. He was a major and later honorary lieutenant-colonel of the Westmorland & Cumberland Yeomanry Cavalry and, for a while, master of the Cumberland foxhounds. His main base, however, was only briefly in Cumberland. He had spent much of his youth in the south of England and perhaps never grew accustomed to life in the far north. As early as 1871 his chief address was in Cheltenham, and later he lived in Windsor and then in Reading[15].

One element of family testimony has delivered a largely negative verdict. According to his cousin, Major F.C.F. Parker, 'he certainly lived beyond his means....He may have been inept at financial matters and he was probably a spendthrift and extravagant, but he was unlucky to inherit so much wealth at such an early age, no doubt without competent advisers'[16]. This view was certainly motivated by the eventual loss of Old Town House. There is nevertheless a deep irony in it. Of all members of the family, none exhibited less capacity to manage his finances effectively than Major Parker; what enabled him to persist in steadily reducing circumstances was that he had

14   Pkr B, 28, Will of Mary Parker of Warwick Hall, 7 Apr. 1848.
15   Pkr B, 24, '[Ms] Outline of a Family', 24.
16   Pkr B, 24, '[Ms] Outline of a Family', 27.

considerably more to mismanage. While there may be some truth in this verdict, the evidence does not permit a sure judgement and it is probably nearer the mark to say that Thomas's means did not allow him to cut the figure expected in those days of the owner of Warwick Hall. A key factor, perhaps alluded to by Major Parker, was that, unlike William Parker of Yanwath, Thomas Holme Parker, inheriting so young, did not secure a means of income in addition to his inheritance; nonetheless he did not come into 'so much wealth'. Like a growing number of landowners during the later nineteenth century, he may have come to regard the stock market and similar financial avenues as providing a better return than land; for some, 'the social advantages of landownership had so diminished as to be no longer worth paying for'[17]

In 1855 the Warwick and Old Town properties had together brought in some £1,857. However, £344 of this came from temporary grazing and sales of wood, both of which were liable to sharp downward fluctuations. Leaving aside further sundries, the rental amounted to only £1,352 a year, and there was little prospect of this core income being significantly increased, especially during the agriculturally depressed years of the later nineteenth century[18]. Thomas and his wife produced five children; two of these died young but the rest had to be reared and educated and, to retain their value, Warwick Hall and its grounds had to be maintained. Before long Heskett's primary task was the management of a growing number of mortgages, of which there was a long sequence by the 1880s. Heskett's accounts also reveal further sales of wood as attempts were made to boost income. While the precise reasons for this indebtedness are unknown, the search for a final solution to his financial difficulties began as early as 1867 when Thomas arranged to break the entail on his property, thereby leaving himself free, if it became necessary, to sell it at some future date. In the early 1890s, as he approached his 50th birthday, he finally decided to sell all his land in Cumberland. No doubt with a view to maximising the return from any sale, the Old Town properties, valued at just over £8,000, were put up for auction in six lots although, significantly, for a decade efforts to sell them were unsuccessful. Most were bought by a Kendal businessman at the turn of the century. Having been predeceased by Amy in 1895 and then sold Old Town, Thomas Holme Parker died in the south of England in 1901. The sale of the Warwick Hall estate to the Liddell family followed later that year[19].

---

17   Thompson, *English Landed Society in the 19th Century* , 326.
18   CAS (C), DX/1089/41; DB/74/2/78/51.
19   CAS (C), DB/1, 104, 106; Abstracts of Title of T.H. Parker to the Old Town Estate, 1867 & 1889 (in the author's possession, courtesy of Mr. & Mrs. R. Ferguson of High Hesket); Pkr B, 28, Will of T.H. Parker, 14 Aug. 1896 and Certificate of Valuation, 29 July 1902; Robinson, *Guide to the Country Houses of the North-West*, 140-141.

Conclusion

In recent years there has been a lively debate about the fortunes of Cumbrian yeomen-farmers during the later eighteenth and early nineteenth centuries[1]. Against this background, it is clear that the experience of the Parkers as yeoman farmers, far from being typical, was extraordinarily successful. It was not, however, unique. From somewhat further south, in Lancashire, the family of Prime Minister Robert Peel rose to even greater success as leading cotton manufacturers from an even more 'modest' background[2]. It was not just their brave venture in the cotton industry which brought the Parkers to some prominence. Unlike others of their station, the seeds of their prosperity were sown well over a century earlier in their engagement with the cattle-droving trade.

There are few features of British agrarian history that have been as neglected as cattle-droving from Scotland (and Ireland) through England. For entirely understandable reasons, it has proved to be a peculiarly elusive feature of an economy which was for long dominated by agriculture. Because there were opportunities for smuggling, because in any case customs records before the Union have survived only partially, because duties were abolished by the Union and, perhaps above all, simply because cattle walked to market in a stage-by-stage movement which did not lend itself to record keeping, detailed evidence of the trade is slight and randomly distributed. Other than the routes which were used, it is difficult to get close to the flow of the droving trade – to get a grip on it – and so analysis of it, and still more of its economic consequences, has inevitably been sparse. Yet by piecing together the results of scattered research conducted over the past half-century or so, a chronological pattern emerges. We now know what an earlier generation of historians were unsure of: that within a decade of his succession James I brought peace to the Borders, which was only sporadically disturbed in succeeding decades and which, therefore, allowed an age-old activity to become more viable, to be encouraged and to develop further. By the late 1630s the trade was significant, and by the early 1660s substantial; and it was conducted mainly via the western routes through Cumberland. It grew thereafter, despite periodic fluctuations as a result of changes in government policy. It expanded vigorously after the Act of Union - although disrupted by

---

1   Three contributions provide a guide to the copious literature: D. Uttley, 'The Decline of the Cumbrian Yeoman', 121-133 and 'The Decline of the Cumbrian Yeoman Revisited', *CW3*, viii, 127-146; A.J.L. Winchester, 'Regional Identity in the Lake District: Land Tenure and the Cumbrian Landscape', *Northern History*, xlii (2005), 29-48.

2   S.D. Chapman, 'The Peels in the Early English Cotton Industry', *Business History*, ii, no. 2 (1969), 61. I owe this point to my colleague, S.J.S. Ickringill.

the cattle plague of the late 1740s and early 1750s – so that by the 1760s tens of thousands of cattle annually moved from north to south; and it continued to grow until the arrival in the early nineteenth century of more efficient means of transport for cattle in the form of coastal steam shipping and the railways.

The Cumberland village of Wreay, where the Parkers are first identified, was on one of the earliest known routes for droving from Dumfries to Penrith. Later, Carleton, where Christopher Parker first became independently located, lay next to one of the most popular drove roads, and Old Town House, which he built further south, was at its junction with another significant route, from the north-east. It was by seizing the opportunity to service this trade, and also, perhaps, by participating in it themselves, that the Parkers rose to prominence. Indeed, this was why Old Town House was built in the first place. Significantly, Thomas Parker's substantial extensions to the house and his erection of the huge, adjacent barn commenced within two decades of the Union. By 1760, as his brief inventory indicates, he was, for a yeoman-farmer, wealthy, able to supply money to his neighbours, thereby further enhancing his own income and oiling the wheels of the local economy.

For the Parkers there was another key factor. It has been said of Joseph Nicolson, the early historian of Cumberland, brother of Mary Nicolson who as a pregnant 16-year-old married Thomas Parker in 1696, that he 'was characteristic of an important section of north Cumberland society in the eighteenth century who, although they enjoyed only a modest income from landed property, were as deeply conscious of their family origins and connections as were the true landed gentry'[3]. This rings true of the Parkers too. For them such consciousness went back to the post-Restoration period, when they had been resident in the area for at least a century. In 1686, a decade before the Parker/Nicolson marriage, in an unusually formal and elaborate will, Christopher Parker charged his brothers as executors with responsibility for maintaining the family's 'quality and degree' – a strong, self-confident injunction from a man then on his death-bed. Shot-gun it may have been, but the marriage of 1696 achieved this objective. Parkers were regarded as good catches and the family continued to marry well during the eighteenth century, increasing their social status and in at least one instance, the marriage of Thomas's son, Christopher, augmenting their landholdings. Thereby they grew confident enough to buck the prevailing trend by dividing their property among various male heirs. They could not have done so without combining successful marriages with growing income from the droving trade. Unavailable to many of their kind, this was a powerful and winning combination. Without it they might never have reached the point where they

---

3   B.C. Jones, 'Introduction' to Nicolson & Burn (E.P. Publishing edn. Wakefield, 1976), i, vi.

could contemplate a radical new departure. Thus, while in comparison with later decades there is relatively little direct evidence from this earlier period, it points unswervingly in one direction – to their continuing success.

Deep loyalty to their geographic origins and connections persisted. All four of Robert senior's nephews were young when they moved to south Lancashire, and three of them were very young indeed. Yet this did not prevent them from returning to Cumbria at the earliest feasible opportunity.

Moreover, their experience throws additional light on the reality of customary tenure in Cumberland, which was virtually equivalent to ownership in fee simple. In 1807, despite having been absent from the area for many years, Thomas Parker had no difficulty in succeeding to his father's customary holdings at Old Town, and the same was true of his brother, William, after Thomas's own death in 1828. The security derived from being, in effect, owners of land as distinct from mere tenants underpinned the determination with which the Parkers pursued their dynastic endeavours. While this key feature of customary tenures has long been appreciated, a comparative aspect has perhaps been neglected. Similar, though not identical, systems emerged in other areas – parts of Ireland, for example – where land was poor, economic circumstances were uncertain, and solid tenants were hard to come by[4]. Whereas in long-settled and more prosperous regions the relationship between owners and tenants became thoroughly commercial, in Cumberland and elsewhere negotiating power between the two was balanced differently, and much less to the benefit of the ultimate owner, as the Parkers themselves experienced after purchasing Warwick Hall and Skirwith Abbey in 1822. Earlier, once established and consolidated, the customary system provided a solid basis on which families such as the Parkers could prosper, and it was a factor fundamental to their success. The mortgage on Old Town, for instance, used to 'start' Robert Parker, would have been exceedingly difficult, and probably impossible, under a different tenurial system.

They left Cumbria to pursue a fresh opportunity in the cotton industry in Lancashire. Robert senior was clearly a thoroughly able and charismatic individual – few of his contemporaries, one imagines, would have corresponded with Samuel Oldknow in the self-confident, candid but supportive terms that he did – but as a landless youngest son he had little option but to seek his fortune outside Cumberland. This, however, was not true of the others. Perhaps the most startling feature of this family's history is that Robert was eventually joined at Heaton Mersey and in Manchester not just by his eldest brother but also by four of his nephews, at a time when three of the latter were very young; and when the droving trade, far

---

4   See P. Roebuck, 'The Making of an Ulster Great Estate: the Chichesters, Barons of Belfast and Viscounts of Carrickfergus, 1599-1648', *Proceedings of the Royal Irish Academy*, 79, Section C (Jan. 1979), 1-25 and 'Rent Movement, Proprietorial Incomes and Agricultural Development, 1730-1830' in P. Roebuck, (ed.), *Plantation to Partition: Essays in Ulster History* (Belfast, 1981), 81-101.

from slackening, was approaching its height. Business in the cotton trade was so hectic and multi-faceted that there was more than enough for them and their associates to do, although for many years the newcomers must have been hugely dependent on Robert senior's previous cotton-trading experience. A collective approach to their intrinsically risky endeavours made good sense, providing some safety in numbers; but it was remarkable nonetheless. Moreover, in measuring their achievements we should recognise that prolonged success in the cotton trade was unusual: the success of most families engaged in manufacturing cotton 'did not last a generation'[5].

One key to their success was the fact that, to a far greater extent than most families, the Parkers hunted as a pack. The earlier division of their property had demonstrated this, as did the willingness of Robert senior's eldest brother, Thomas, to leave the final disposition of the fruits of their success to him; and the same instinct was evident later, not least in Robert's handsome bequests to his five nieces, and the manner in which the interests of the mentally-ill younger Robert were scrupulously safeguarded over many years by his two brothers. The single blemish on this record came from 1808, with the family's unease at Robert's late marriage to the very much younger Sarah Pollitt though, apparently, even this disquiet was stifled and eventually overcome in the interests of solidarity.

Their experience in cotton manufacturing and marketing graphically illustrates the size and scope of the opportunities and the threats which emerged during the course of Britain's first industrial revolution. The general economic trend was upwards, particularly in the cotton industry, and the wealth which could be created there dwarfed most other possibilities. Periodically, however, particularly during the three decades or so after Waterloo, there were downward fluctuations, sometimes so sharp as to extinguish hope of personal retrieval, as in the case of no fewer than three generations of the Stocks family.

For two generations the Parkers not only survived but prospered before, under William, their withdrawal began. In the light of their judgement of trading conditions, they expanded and contracted both the scale and the nature of their production, discontinuing calico-printing and then resuming it, acquiring additional spinning capacity and then relinquishing it, and buying a coalmine before selling it some years later when it proved uneconomic. Notably, however, they were under Thomas Parker in the vanguard of the introduction of power looms during the early 1820s; and it was he who seized the opportunity to invest in warehouse development. Later, having for long been engaged across the spectrum of cotton manufacturing, Heaton Mersey specialised in the bleaching and dyeing to which the works, on its semi-rural site next to the Mersey, had always been well suited. They also proved adaptable

---

5   Chapman, *Cotton Industry in the Industrial Revolution*, 42.

as marketeers, ultimately concentrating on those far-flung markets where the prospects (though not the promise) of greater returns seemed brighter. Significantly, in evaluating their performance, it is important to recognise that most cotton manufacturers produced for the domestic market. Only a minority, including some foreign immigrants to Lancashire, were involved in exporting cotton cloth, and the Parkers were among them[6]. They were powerfully assisted by what grew into an impressive network of contacts in the trade, by one of the best country banks of their era, by effective arrangements for insurance, and by fiercely competitive providers of transport. Overland carriage was much slower and more expensive than was water transport. Internally, canal development eased this problem considerably, although the performance of heavy wagons and of mail coaches in particular (even as early as the 1780s in their dealings with Samuel Oldknow) was strikingly impressive. However, the single most crucial element in their success as manufacturers and marketeers was external. After establishing themselves, and even during the war years, the Parkers were able to ship their wares all over the world, an aspect of their business which brought prolonged success.

In the longer term it was the canny, resourceful and quick-witted who survived and prospered. Robert senior and his nephew, Thomas Parker, steering their activities adroitly, had these qualities in abundance. Robert junior may also have had them until he fell ill; his close family evidently believed so. William Parker did not possess them. One characteristic which he may have shared with his two brothers was weak health, and the possibility arises from this evidence of all three having been adversely affected by the poor physical conditions in which they spent much of their early lives.

One attribute which they all shared was an unwavering commitment across this long period to Anglicanism. A significant number of them became ordained ministers of the Church of England and/or had spouses whose fathers were such. Their loyalty to St. Mary's Church in High Hesket intensified as the years went by and was amply demonstrated long before the erection of the family mausoleum there in 1828. One of the reasons why, despite the rawness of his candour, they valued Samuel Stocks was that he too was a man of strong religious convictions, who shared, even latterly in Australia, their long-standing commitment to the Sunday school movement. Nor was their religious persuasion of an exclusivist kind, for they were explicitly sympathetic to Methodism and their other substantial charitable donations also favoured institutions of an evangelical hue. In a very conventional sense they were principled people: nobody's fools when it came to money, but conscious of a need to share their good fortune with those amongst whom they lived, and who materially helped to generate their wealth. Robert senior's activities on behalf of the labouring poor went far

---

6   Smith, 'Manchester as a Centre for Manufacturing and Merchanting Cotton Goods', 64-65.

beyond the norm for his day and were publicly acknowledged as doing so. His nephews followed his example, both in the institutions they founded or favoured and in their treatment of individuals. Thomas Lear and the two widows who benefited from William Parker's 'periodical' payments and by his will, were not the only old retainers to be supported for the rest of their lives, and family members were uniformly generous to others who had served them personally. They could afford to be, of course, but their behaviour in this respect went much further than that of most of their contemporaries.

With the exception of William Parker, the last of the direct line, their collective spirit did not persuade them to be risk averse: far from it. Christopher Parker, who built the first phase of Old Town House, seized his main chance by exploiting the location of his holdings vis-a-vis the droving trade whose future, in the face of successive shifts of government policy, was far from certain; and the rise to considerable prosperity of his long-lived son, Thomas, was similarly based, though the Act of Union and its impact on the trade, while immense, were likewise not entirely predictable. The subsequent entry to the cotton industry, however, was of a different order of magnitude. The Parkers bought the works at Heaton Mersey from Samuel Oldknow whose career dramatically illustrated the dangers inherent in the cotton business. Great fortunes were both made and lost and, with so many of their activities dependent on the vagaries of technological development and the uncertainties of overseas trade, particularly during the Revolutionary and Napoleonic wars – to name but two of the many variables – family members displayed considerable nerve and judgement. In the wake of the mental breakdown of Robert junior, the decision to rationalize their business interests in the early 1820s was sound; but opposing temptations to persist, or to withdraw completely, were there nonetheless, as is clear from the actions of William and his cousin, Christopher Parker, under the agreement for the partition of Robert senior's assets. That Thomas Parker, even after the mental collapse of Robert junior, chose a middle course – to lease production to Stocks but personally to continue in overseas marketing and sales – can be put down to sheer business acumen. That was impressive, but his embarkation on property development in Manchester, and the energy and skill with which he pursued his objectives in that regard, were perhaps even more so.

During a short but remarkable career Thomas's achievements rivalled those of his uncle: it may not be too much to say that they exceeded them. Fewer than six years separated the agreement with his brothers and cousin, and his death – by which time he had brought all his endeavours to good account. In all probability very few, if any, of his contemporaries were aware of the full gamut of his activities. William knew of some of them, Samuel Stocks of more, and perhaps Marchanton and James Stubington Penny of even more; but probably none of them would have comprehended the whole. His wife, Mary, and other members of the Heald family, particularly James, may have done so, but for most of the time the Healds were, in Parr's Wood, at a considerable geographical remove from him. Essentially and practically, following Robert junior's breakdown, Thomas was on his own, by his choice, and solely responsible for judgement calls on a whole range of issues. At considerable expense, he rescued Stocks and provided a viable future for Heaton Mersey. At great risk and amidst a myriad difficulties, but nonetheless very profitably, he procured and exported cotton goods all over the world. With keen foresight he acquired and developed inner-city properties in Manchester to the point where they promised to provide, and eventually succeeded in providing, his family's major single income stream. In addition he built a new hall at Warwick, refurbished the estate, and made significant contributions to the life and fabric of the community in Warwick Bridge. In such a short period his achievements were huge but, apparently, as far as the public record was concerned, only his obituarist in the *Carlisle Journal* glimpsed the breadth of his capabilities. Had he lived for as long as most members of his family, his success would very probably have been even greater, and public recognition of it more commensurate with its worth.

William Parker was fundamentally uninterested in manufacturing and marketing. Perhaps this stemmed from his early formative experience. Four years old when his uncle bought Heaton Mersey, he may always have resented the move from rural Cumberland to the wholly different and thoroughly unattractive industrial environment further south, for Manchester and Stockport and their environs were among the most blighted of English landscapes during the first industrial revolution. From 1822, having returned to circumstances which he found more congenial, William did not expect to succeed his brother so soon or, indeed, at all. Initially engulfed by the shock of his unexpected bereavement, he was alarmed by the responsibilities which succession brought with it. As his brother had done, he could have assumed personal responsibility for Robert junior and continued without recourse to Chancery, but he decided instead to play for safety. Causing persistent difficulty and considerable delay, this nevertheless achieved his personal objective. However, it also ran counter to his other instinct, which was to maximise income wherever possible. For some time William resisted the advice offered by his subordinates and friends as to how to handle the Manchester properties. Losing a good deal of income in the meantime, he eventually bowed to their recommendations, but with deep reluctance. He found other decisions easier, abandoning Thomas's plan for a town house in Carlisle and, above all, abruptly ending the family's long involvement in the export of cotton cloth. This latter decision left his operation much more risk free, although its income stream also declined markedly. Henceforward, he relied mainly on his rents from Manchester and, with relatively modest personal and no family needs, he was able to do so comfortably, whilst at the same time investing, as opportunities arose, in purchases of property both at Heaton and near Skirwith, as well as in his art collection. Towards the end of his life he had much more income than even this required and he had no difficulty in further expanding the Skirwith estate. His key inclination, first rehearsed within a few months of Thomas's death but returned to frequently for the rest of his days, was to execute an extraordinarily generous will. Being a reluctant and not very capable businessman, perhaps he always felt unworthy of the wealth that his family's endeavours brought his way. The final version of his will divided his property and left it heavily encumbered. A year or so later, under the will of Mary Parker, Thomas's widow – who may have been permanently embittered by her husband's early death – dispositions were further disseminated by her decision to leave all her property, together with the bulk of yet another batch of substantial legacies, to her own family, the Healds.

All this demonstrates that there were two things against which no family could effectively insure itself: the personal behaviour and decisions of successive incumbents, and their demography. Ultimately, in the case of the Parkers, these factors coalesced during the late 1850s in the form of wills. Males of the previous generation either died unmarried or failed to reproduce. The deepest irony of this family's history is that when they were making their way moderately but steadily they experienced no difficulty, to put it mildly, in producing direct heirs; but when they had made their fortune, they were barren or remained unmarried. There is no doubt that this powerfully influenced the final dispositions of successive incumbents. Robert senior made it abundantly clear in his will of 1815 that, if he had had a son or sons with Sarah, all his real estate would have devolved on them. Then, even though in 1828 Thomas Parker left his property to a cousin and his male heirs in succession, he had earlier disposed part of it to his wife, who later proceeded to leave it to her brother. Hoping against hope, however, both he and William indicated that if Robert junior produced lawfully begotten issue, that issue would be the major beneficiary. In the event Robert never recovered and never married. Not even having a nephew, William initially left all his property to the half-brother of Thomas's beneficiary; and finally hived off part of it to yet another such younger relative to clinch the latter's marriage. Having failed to reproduce themselves, incumbents tended to disperse their hard-won gains, with significant implications for those who came after them.

Following his marriage to Mary Hasell, William Parker lived a more comfortable life than for many years he could have expected. His inheritance facilitated this, but little more. For some years the Rev. Christopher Parker and his descendants did much better. Through the powers vested in his cousin's trustees, the estate was substantially expanded, but mainly at Cracrop, some considerable distance from its main base at Skirwith. His successors had to grapple with the welter of factors which brought the landed classes as a whole into decline before, during and beyond the Great War. Their achievement, assisted by a strategic change of surname, was to cling on to a contracting estate during the twentieth century. At Warwick Hall and Old Town Thomas Holme Parker seemed, initially, to offer the possibility of maintaining some position for the family, and was not only himself long lived, but one of his sons survived until 1966. It was not to be, either because Thomas's landed income was too meagre from the start, because he was a poor manager of money, because from his upbringing and education his heart was never in rural life in the north-west, or from some combination of all three factors. Long before the turn of the nineteenth century, his affairs were in difficulty and he decided to cease being a landowner.

One consequence of demographic failure, especially when coupled with economic decline, is that successes recede into the past and are often forgotten. This book has served to resurrect the considerable achievements of the Parker family and the vibrant role they played in the economic development of the north-west. Much physical evidence of their endeavours remains. The Sunday school at Heaton Mersey was demolished in 1967 and its massive neighbour in Stockport met the same fate three years later[7]. However, Skirwith Abbey, the church, parsonage and school, what was once the Sun Inn, and other of William Parker's developments there remain for all to see. The Liddells built a new hall at Warwick following the fire which destroyed that erected by Thomas Parker, and on the same site, with its commanding view of the Eden. Yet Thomas's pedimented stables and gatehouse survive, as does the building nearby which housed the Sunday school with which he provided the village[8]. At High Hesket the school and what was once the schoolmaster's house remain, and not far away is the ancestral home – Old Town House. Externally it is not much different from when it was finally extended in the eighteenth century. The hub of the family's activities for over a century, it was subsequently the initial and vital means whereby their great industrial venture got underway. In mute testimony both to their origins and to their eventual success, it still stands.

---

7   Their demise was duly noted in one issue of the Parker Family History Newsletter (no. 35, Sept. 1991 in the possession of Cathie Parker of Maughold, Isle of Man), a series regularly produced by Robert Parker of Morecambe before his death in 1994..

8   Hyde & Pevsner, *Cumbria*, 625-626, 662-663.

Bibliography

I PRIMARY SOURCES (MANUSCRIPT)

Cumbria Archives Service, Carlisle

WDX/Pkr/1/1-7 The Newbiggin Hall collection: 7 boxes of files, containing correspondence and other papers from the late 18th to the 20th centuries (referred to above as Pkr A)

WDX/Pkr/2/1-50 50 volumes/files of copy documents and other papers, collected by the late Robert Parker of Morecambe (referred to above as Pkr B)

DB/1, 74, 104, 106 Miscellaneous estate papers, north-east Cumbria

D/Hod Records of Messrs. Hodgson, solicitors and clerks of the peace, Carlisle

D/MBS Records of Mounsey, Bowman & Sutcliffe, solicitors, Carlisle

D/Ric Records of the Rickerby Estate, and of the Brunstock House Estate

D/Van Accounts & rentals, Hutton-in-the-Forest Estate

DX/1089/40 & 41 Records of the Parker family of Skirwith Abbey

PR/35 Records of the parish of Hesket-in-the-Forest

Carlisle Library, Local Studies Collection

B 320 Diaries of James Losh

BOU/2/4 Materials relating to the artist Sam Bough

The John Rylands University Library, Manchester

SO Oldknow papers (edited transcripts available on the internet via ELGAR)

Stockport Central Library, Local Heritage Library

Higham notes

Typescript: S.M. Cobbing, 'Portrait of a Victorian Village: Heaton Mersey 1851-1881'

Stockport Museums

RD 17752 Correspondence of William Parker with Stockport Sunday School, 1837

II PRIMARY SOURCES (PRINTED)

Calendar of State Papers, Domestic Series

Carlisle Journal

Manchester Mercury

Stockport Advertiser

Stockport Chronicle

The Exchange Herald: Aston's Manchester Commercial Advertiser

The Cumberland News

The Gentleman's Magazine

The Monthly Magazine or British Register

III INTERNET

www.legarthm@levin.pl.net   Transportation of a convict to Australia

www.'Old Family Names of Manchester and the North-West', *Papillon Graphics' Virtual Encyclopaedia of Greater Manchester*

www.Wikipedia, 'Samuel Stocks (*c.*1786-1863)

IV SECONDARY SOURCES

Allen, H. *Donaghadee: An Illustrated History* (Dundonald, 2006)

Anon. 'Dr. Thomas Emerson Headlam (1777-1864)', *The Lancet*, 5. March 1864.

Appleby, A.B. *Famine in Tudor and Stuart England* (Liverpool, 1978)

Beckett, J.V. 'Landownership in Cumbria c.1680–c. 1750', unpublished D.Phil. Thesis, Lancaster University, 1975.

Belchem, J. (ed.) *Liverpool 800: Culture, Character and History* (Liverpool, 2006)

Bonser, K.J. *The Drovers* (London, 1970)

Boumphrey, R.S. See Hudleston, C.R.

Brock, A.A. (ed.) *Irregular Marriages, Portpatrick, Wigtownshire 1759-1826* (Dumfries, 1997)

Burn, R. See Nicolson, J.

Campbell, R.H. *Scotland since 1707: The Rise of Industrial Society* (Oxford, 1965)

Campbell-Smith, D. *Masters of the Post: the Authorised History of the Royal Mail* (London, 2012)

Carus-Wilson, E.M. See Ward-Perkins, C.N.

Chadwick, E. *Report on the Sanitary Condition of the Labouring Population* (London, 1842)

Chaloner, W.H. 'Manchester in the Latter Half of the Eighteenth Century', *Bulletin of the John Rylands Library,* 42 (1959-60), 40-60

Chapman, S.D. 'The Peels in the Early English Cotton Industry', *Business History,* ii, no. 2 (1969), 61-89

"   "   *The Cotton Industry in the Industrial Revolution* (London, 1987)

Cullen, L.M. *Anglo-Irish Trade 1660-1800* (Manchester, 1969)

Davidson, A. (ed.) *The Oxford Companion to Food* (Oxford, 1999).

Davis, R.   'English Foreign Trade, 1660-1700', *Economic History Review,* 2nd Series, vii, 2 (1954), 150-166

"   "   'English Foreign Trade, 1700-1774', *Economic History Review,* 2nd Series, xv, 2 (1962), 285-303

"   "   *The Industrial Revolution and British Overseas Trade* (Leicester, 1979)

Deane, P. *The First Industrial Nation* (Cambridge, 1979)

Dick, M. 'Urban Growth and the Social Role of the Stockport Sunday School' in J. Ferguson, (ed.), *Christianity, Society and Education: Robert Raikes, Past, Present and Future* (London, 1981), 53-58

Dictionary of National Biography

Edwards, M.M. *The Growth of the British Cotton Trade 1780-1815* (Manchester, 1969)

Engels, F. *The Condition of the Working Class in England* (London, 1892)

Ferguson, J. (ed.) See Dick, M.

Fitzgerald, D. See Shields, L.

Furness, W. *History of Penrith* (Penrith, 1894)

Gavin, J.B. 'The Bishop of Durham, the West March Border Negotiations, and the Treaty of Carlisle, 1597', *CW2,* lxxiii (1973), 120-142

Haldane, A.R.B. *The Drove Roads of Scotland* (Newton Abbot, 1973)

Hall, A.R. *Wreay* (Carlisle, 1929)

Hartwell, C. *Pevsner Architectural Guides: Manchester* (London, 2001)

Heginbotham, H. *Stockport: Ancient and Modern,* ii (London, 1892)

Hitchcock, H.R. 'Victorian Monuments of Commerce', *Architectural Review,* 105 (1949), 61-75

Houston, R.A. *The Population History of Britain and Ireland 1500-1750* (London, 1992)

Hudleston, C.R. & Boumphrey, R.S. *Cumberland Families and Heraldry* (Kendal, 1978)

Hutchinson, W. *The History of the County of Cumberland* (Carlisle, 1794)

Hyde, F.E. *Liverpool and the Mersey: An Economic History of a Port, 1700-1970* (Newton Abbot, 1971)

Hyde, M. & Pevsner, N. *The Buildings of England: Cumbria: Cumberland, Westmorland and Furness* (New Haven & London, 2010)

James, F.C. *North Country Bishop* (London, 1956)

Jones, B.C. 'Introduction' to Nicolson & Burn (Wakefield, 1976)

Jones, G.P. 'King James I and the Western Border', *CW2*, lxix (1969), 129-151

Kay, J. *Moral and Physical Conditions of the Working Classes* (London, 1832)

Laqueur, T. *Religion and Respectability: Sunday Schools and Working Class Culture* (London, 1976)

Lascelles, D. *The Story of Rathbones since 1742* (London, 2008)

Lewis, M.J. See Lloyd-Jones, R.

Lloyd-Jones, R. & Lewis, M.J. 'The Economic Structure of "Cottonopolis" in 1815', *Textile History*, xvii (i) (1986), 71-89

Lowther-Bouch, C.M. *Prelates and People of the Lake Counties: A History of the Diocese of Carlisle 1133-1933* (Kendal, 1948)

Macdonald Fraser, G. *The Steel Bonnets: the Story of the Anglo-Scottish Border Reivers* (London, 1971)

Machin, R. 'The Great Rebuilding: A Reassessment', *Past and Present*, no. 77, 1 (1977), 33-56

Mannix, P.J. & Whellan, W. *History, Gazeteer and Directory of Cumberland* (Whitehaven, 1847, re-published Whitehaven, 1974)

Marshall, J.D. 'Drovers, Fairs and Cattle Routes' in *Old Lakeland: Some Cumbrian Social History* (Newton Abbot, 1971), 76-96

" " *Portrait of Cumbria* (London, 1981)

McIntyre, W.T. 'The Fords of the Solway', *CW2*, xxxix (1939), 152-170

Million, I.R. *A History of Didsbury* (Didsbury, 1969)

Moffat, A. *The Borders* (Selkirk, 2002)

Nicolson, J. & Burn, R. *The History and Antiquities of the Counties of Westmorland and Cumberland*, 2 vols. (London, 1777)

Owen, E.R.J. *Cotton and the Egyptian Economy: A Study in Trade and Development* (Oxford, 1969)

Oxford Dictionary of National Biography

Parker, F.H.M. 'The Parkers of Old Town: with Some Notes on the Branthwaites of Carlingill and the Birkbecks of Orton Hall', *CW1*, xvi (1900), 104-116

Parsons, W. & White, W. *History, Directory and Gazeteer of the Counties of Cumberland and Westmorland* (Leeds, 1829)

Pevsner, N. See Hyde, M.

Pollard, S. 'The Factory Village in the Industrial Revolution', *English Historical Review*, lxxix, no. cccxii (July 1964), 513-531

Power, Sir D'Arcy *Plarr's Lives of the Fellows of the Royal College of Surgeons*, ii (London, 1930)

Pressnell, L.S. *Country Banking in the Industrial Revolution* (Oxford, 1956)

Prevost, W.A.J. 'A Journie to Carlyle and Penrith in 1731', *CW2*, lxi (1961), 202-237

,, ,, 'The Turnpike and Custom Post at Alisonbank', *CW2*, lxxiii (1973), 282-297

Redford, A. *Manchester Merchants and Foreign Trade*, i, *1794-1858* (Manchester, 1934)

Reid, T.D.W. (ed.) *Heaton Mersey, A Victorian Village 1851-1881* (Stockport, 1985)

Robinson, J.M. *A Guide to the Country Houses of the North-West* (London, 1991)

Robson, M.J.H. *Ride with the Moonlight: the Mosstroopers of the Border* (Newcastleton, 1987)

Roebuck, P. 'Post-Restoration Landownership: the Impact of the Abolition of Wardship', *Journal of British Studies*, xviii, 1 (Fall, 1978), 67-85

,, ,, 'The Making of an Ulster Great Estate: the Chichesters, Barons of Belfast and Viscounts of Carrickfergus 1599-1648', *Proceedings of the Royal Irish Academy*, 79, Section C (Jan. 1979), 1-25

,, ,, 'Rent Movement, Proprietorial Incomes and Agricultural Development, 1730-1830' in P. Roebuck (ed.) *Plantation to Partition: Essays in Ulster History* (Belfast, 1981), 81-101

,, ,, 'The Parkers of Old Town and District in Cumberland: Yeomen Farmers, Industrialists and Landed Proprietors, 1630-1900', *CW3*, x (2010), 177-196

,, ,, 'Cattle-droving through Cumbria after the Union: the Stances on the Musgrave Estate, 1707-12', *CW3*, xii (2012), 143-158

,, ,, 'Cattle-droving through Cumbria, 1707-12: New Evidence from the Musgrave Estate', *CW3*, xiii (2013), 256-260

Routledge, G.L. *Longtown* (Carlisle, 2000)

Schofield, R.S. See Wrigley, E.A.

Shields, L. & Fitzgerald, D. 'The "Night of the Big Storm" in Ireland, 6-7 January 1839', *Irish Geography,* xxii, Issue 1 (1989), 31-43

Slicher van Bath, B.H. *The Agrarian History of Western Europe A.D. 500-1850* (London, 1963)

Smith, R. 'Manchester as a Centre for Manufacturing and Merchanting Cotton Goods 1820-30', *University of Birmingham Historical Journal,* iv (1953-54), 47-65

Smout, T.C. *Scottish Trade on the Eve of the Union* (Edinburgh & London, 1963)

Stenton, M. (ed.) *Who's Who of British Members of Parliament* (Hassocks, 1976)

Summerson, H. *'An Ancient Squire's Family': the History of the Aglionbys* (Carlisle, 2007)

Thirsk, J. (ed.) *The Agrarian History of England and Wales,* v *1640-1750* (Cambridge, 1984)

Thompson, F.M.L. *English Landed Society in the Nineteenth Century* (London, 1963)

Thompson, W. 'Cattle Droving between Scotland and England', *Journal of the British Archaeological Association,* 37 (1932), 172-183

Towill, S. *Georgian and Victorian Carlisle* (Preston, 1996)

Tyson, B. 'Architecture of Lakeland Beekeeping', *Country Life,* clxxi (18 Feb. 1982), 408-409

"   "   'The Cattle Trading Activities of Sir Daniel Fleming of Rydal Hall, 1656-1700', *CW3,* ii (2002), 183-199

Unwin, G. *Samuel Oldknow and the Arkwrights: the Industrial Revolution at Stockport and Marple* (Manchester, 1924)

Uttley, D. 'The Decline of the Cumbrian Yeoman: Fact or Fiction', *CW3,* vii (2007), 121-133

"   "   'The Decline of the Cumbrian Yeoman Revisited', *CW3,* viii (2008), 127-146

Ward-Perkins, C.N. 'The Commercial Crisis of 1847' in E.M. Carus-Wilson, (ed.), *Essays in Economic History,* iii, (London, 1962), 263-279

Walker, J. *The History of Penrith* (Penrith, 1858)

Watson, G. *The Border Reivers* (Alnwick, 1988)

Whellan, W. See Mannix, P.J.

White, W. See Parsons, W.

Whyte, I.D. *Agriculture and Society in Seventeenth-Century Scotland* (Edinburgh, 1979)

Winchester, A.J.L. 'Regional Identity in the Lake District: Land Tenure and the Cumbrian Landscape', *Northern History*, xlii (2005), 29-48

Woodward, D. 'The Anglo-Irish Livestock Trade in the 17th Century', *Irish Historical Studies*, xviii (1973), 489-523

    "   "   'A Comparative Study of the Irish and Scottish Livestock Trades in the 17th Century' in L.M. Cullen & T.C. Smout, (eds.), *Comparative Aspects of Scottish and Irish Economic and Social History 1600-1900* (Edinburgh, 1977), 147-164

Wrigley, E.A. *Population and History* (London, 1969)

Wrigley, E.A. & Schofield, R.S. *The Population History of England 1541-1871: A Reconstruction* (London, 1981)

Index